There's an old East Tennessee saying—

*"Only three generations
from the plow handle
to the silk hat."*

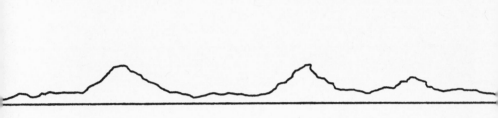

SECOND EDITION

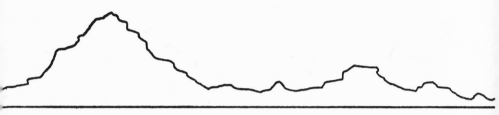

KNOXVILLE
Betsey Beeler Creekmore

THE UNIVERSITY OF TENNESSEE PRESS • KNOXVILLE

PRINTED IN THE UNITED STATES OF AMERICA

Preface

The author of this book, Mrs. Betsey Beeler Creekmore, was born and reared in Knoxville. In early childhood she became interested in the stories of Knoxville's
growth. This interest continued to grow until she decided
to write this book. Through extended search in published
histories and documents and through numerous interviews
with members of Knoxville's older families and with persons interested in the city's history, she gathered the materials for use in this book.

Special emphasis is given to the unpublished stories
gathered through these personal interviews. After all, it is
the people who make a community or a city. That spot of
ground which men call Athens does not embrace the immortal city. It bears up its masonry; but the ideas of the
great people who made her immortal will continue to live
in the minds of the well-informed throughout the relent-
less march of time.

Mrs. Creekmore has assembled the facts of her story
and without changing those facts with extravagant state-
ments she has adorned them with the charm of fiction.

JAMES D. HOSKINS

Fifteen Famous Firsts
Associated with Knoxville

First English fort in the Southwest (Fort Loudoun, 1756)

First military draft in America (John Sevier drafts men TO STAY HOME from the Battle of King's Mountain—Revolutionary War)

First planned city in the West (Knoxville, 1791)

First capital of the Territory South of the River Ohio (Knoxville, 1791)

First duly elected Territorial Legislature in America (Knoxville, 1794)

First non-sectarian college in the West, possibly the first in America (Blount College, now The University of Tennessee, chartered in 1794)

First capital of Tennessee (Knoxville, 1796)

First United States Senator to be tried for impeachment—and the only one (William Blount, 1797)

First co-eds (Blount College, 1804)

First man in history to perfect an entirely new alphabet or syllabary (Sequoyah invents a phonetic alphabet so that the Cherokee may have a written language, 1821)

First and principal stronghold of Union sympathy within the Confederacy itself (East Tennessee during the War Between the States)

First state readmitted to the Union after the Civil War (Tennessee, 1866).

First national park given by the people to the government (Great Smoky Mountains National Park)

First experiment in public power (Tennessee Valley Authority)

First atomic bomb built (Oak Ridge)

Contents

Illustrations

PHOTOGRAPHS   FACING PAGE

Photographic credits: University Photographic Center (*Indian Mound,
First Presbyterian Church, Sevier-Park House, Crescent Bend, School
for the Deaf, Bleak House, Fort Dickerson, Island Home, Craighead–
Jackson House, Hoskins Library, Mall Greenery, Humanities Com-
plex*); Thompsons Commercial Photographers (*Blount Mansion, Swan
Pond, Sevier Monuments, View of Smokies, Norris Dam, Dogwood*);
Mr. Jean Giesler (*Smokies' Bear*); U. S. Atomic Energy Commission
(*Oak Ridge*); Bill Tracy (*Coliseum, City Hall, Mall Market, Night
View, Aerial View*); Harley Ferguson (*View from Garden*).

Introduction

"Where shall I begin . . . ?

Why, begin at the beginning, . . . and go on till you come to the end; then stop."

Lewis Carroll was right: that is the best way to tell a story. The story of Knoxville, however, cannot be fitted into this admirable pattern, for it begins long before the actual beginning, and the end is nowhere in sight.

Although they are based on factual material, these chapters make no claim to be considered as history, except in the sense that history is no more and no less than the story of people and what happened to them. A *bona fide* "History of Knoxville" would run to several weighty tomes containing hundreds of incidents and thousands of names—the difficulty is not therefore a lack of material, but an over-abundance of it; the question not one of sources, but of choices.

It is really high time that a new day of approbation dawned for Knoxville, with a sundial set to "mark none but the sunny hours." Entirely too much has been said and written of late about the shortcomings of our great nation and her great men. It has been the fashion to criticize, to humanize—to reach the opposite extreme from what was called the "saccharine sentimentality" of the nineteenth century by being "realistic" (which has all too often meant "pessimistic"). A whole generation has grown up knowing little about George Washington except that he did *not* cut down his father's cherry tree with a hatchet. The South in the abstract, Tennessee in general, and Knoxville in particular have been favorite topics for the debunkers of history, and the blackest possible interpretation of events past has been the favored one. This kind of history is discouraging to read; historical writing has been in a sort of "dark of the moon." But even the inconstant moon goes through many phases, and when we are most attracted by her, she is insisting that we look on the bright side.

CHAPTER ONE

The Cherokee in Tennessee

Logically, the story of Knoxville begins with the first settlement of it, which, as everybody knows, occurred in 1786. Or did it?

The rich Valley of East Tennessee had been home to many different peoples before the first white man ever set eyes upon it. Archaeologists who sift the soil of Indian village sites and mounds read in successive layers the story of occupation and conquest of this area that perhaps dates back to 1,000 B.C. when the Woodland Indians roamed the forests. It was the climate that attracted these first "first settlers," for they had been driven southward from the region of the Great Lakes by climatic changes. These Early Woodland Indians were not large men, but they were fierce fighters—archaeologists have measured their skeletons and counted the number of arrowheads imbedded in their bones to reach these conclusions. They were hunters

1

and trappers in an area that abounded with deer, elk, and bear. They cooked their meat on rude fireplaces that were no more than a ring of flat stones. They did not go in for farming, but they did make pottery; thus, from its earliest beginnings, East Tennessee might be said to have leaned to industry rather than to agriculture.

After the Woodland Indians came another people, whom *their* successors called the Mound Builders. These were the Indians known to archaeologists as the Mississippian Indians, and they possessed a remarkable degree of what we are pleased to refer to as civilization. They were hunters, to be sure, but they also planted some crops. They were deeply religious, and they even dabbled in the arts, for on the steep rocky cliffs and the stone walls of caves they painted quite recognizable pictures with red ocher paint. These Mississippian Indian groups are known in historic times as the Creeks, the Choctaw, the Chickasaw, the Natchez, and others. They had a common language, known as Muskhogean, and anthropologists conjecture that at some long-forgotten time they may have moved north from Mexico to settle at last in the areas they inhabited when the white men came.

By the time that the first white settlers found their way to the Valley, East Tennessee was the home of Indians who were quite distinct from the Mississippian groups who were living in the rest of the South. These Indians called themselves "Ani-Yunwiya," which meant "Principal People." In 1540, when Hernando de Soto passed through a portion of their territory, the other Indians evolved a new name for the "Ani-Yunwiya." De Soto's interpreters told him that these Indians were called "Tciloki," which means "People of a Different Speech" in the Muskogee tongue. Henceforth, the Spanish called the area in which these people lived Chelaque Province. Not averse to a name which set them apart from their Indian neighbors, the Principal People soon began calling themselves the Chelaque or Cherokee.

Historians are careful to refer to the Cherokee as a nation, rather than a tribe, for they lived in towns that were banded together in a form of representative national government. Where did they come from? Nobody knows. But the fact is that they were closely related to the Iroquois, who had a similar form of government, and with whom they shared a common language. Authorities believe that the Cherokee language is an older form than that of the Iroquois. Whatever their origin, the Cherokee were among the most intelligent and advanced of all North American Indians, and the true story of what happened to them is far stranger than fiction.

What were they like, these people who were living in the Valley of East Tennessee when white men in the eighteenth century began to explore the lands west of the Great Smoky Mountains? The Cherokee nation at this time already had a culture that might have been envied by many of the more civilized people of the world—they were well fed, well clothed, well housed, and by their own standards, well governed, rejoicing in an elementary form of democracy that they liked extremely well. Not only that, they were able by reason of strength and cleverness to protect their way of life. Small wonder, then, that the Cherokee are often spoken of as a proud race.

When the first white settlers came across the Great Smoky Mountains, they found that the Cherokee had built for themselves in the foothills of these mountains a well-planned series of towns. Each of the towns was centered with a council house, seven-sided or circular in shape, in the middle of which a ceremonial fire was always kept burning. Here the chiefs and braves of the town gathered to make the decisions for the people. The most important of all the Cherokee towns was Chota, on the Little Tennessee River about thirty miles from present-day Knoxville. This was the Cherokee's sacred city, or city of refuge, which meant that anyone who could reach this town was safe from his enemies so long as he remained within it. Even a criminal might escape pursuit if he could only enter Chota, and often Indians from other tribes and, later, white men availed themselves of this custom and took sanctuary within the "beloved city." It was well understood that any refugee who ventured outside the town would instantly be killed by the very braves who would fight to protect him while he was inside it.

Within their towns, the Cherokee lived well, even by modern standards. Their houses were not the tepees of the nomadic tribes, but were rather elaborate structures whose size was determined by the number of members in the family. The houses were cleverly constructed of posts, driven upright into the ground at intervals, which were then interlaced with saplings and finally plastered with clay. They had a very effective type of central heating, for the fire kept constantly burning in the middle of each house kept them warm and comfortable in winter.

Cherokee braves wore shirts and trousers of fringed deerskin, sewn by the squaws with needles of bone and strong sinews for thread. The women of the nation wore similarly made dresses, and everybody had comfortable deerskin moccasins. From the skins of bears and foxes robes were made which served as winter overcoats or as blankets for the shelf-like beds within the houses.

In the matter of food, also, the Cherokee fared well. They were not entirely dependent upon their skill as hunters, although the braves were masters of the bow and arrow and excelled at fishing, trapping, and snaring birds. They supplemented this meat not only with the wild fruits and nuts in which their region abounded, but also with farming. Each Cherokee home had its garden, carefully tended by the squaws, where (although they had no tools except primitive stone and wooden ones) they regularly planted and cultivated corn, beans, pumpkins and squash. In addition, the town had fields that belonged to all its inhabitants, and both men and women were required to work at planting and harvesting the town garden. The Cherokee had no use for laziness, holding firmly to their tribal rule that "he who will not work shall not eat."

When the crops raised in their gardens were scanty, the canny Cherokee dug wild tubers which they roasted as we do potatoes. They were very fond of chestnuts, which they prepared in many different ways, and acorns (ground and mixed with cornmeal) were a staple of their diet. From black walnuts they extracted oil, which they used for the seasoning of foods, much as we use butter. They gathered too the small peas from the wild pea vines for use as a vegetable, and the plump wild grapes and abundant wild berries served as their ready-made desserts.

With so much available to cook, it is not surprising that the Cherokee squaws were skilled in the art of cooking. They gathered their vegetables and fruits in baskets woven of cane or white oak splits, and made cooking pots of clay for themselves. They had wooden bowls and plates,

and spoons made of carved clamshells, as well as sharp
knives of flint. With this equipment, they prepared stews
of meat and vegetables, while roots and ears of corn were
roasted in the hot ashes of the cookfire. They baked
bread, too, by placing coarsely ground cornmeal moistened
with bearfat on a platter in the hot ashes and covering it
with an inverted pottery bowl over which more ashes
were raked.

So the Cherokee in the eighteenth century enjoyed a
comfortable and well-regulated life comparable to the life
of the first white settlers in all save one respect. The
Cherokee were illiterate, for the very good reason that they
had no written language.

Although their homes were so comfortable, and by
Indian standards even luxurious, the Cherokee loved to
travel. They roamed their own lands and visited other
tribes. They went into the common hunting grounds of
Middle Tennessee and Kentucky on lengthy hunting trips.
They made war, for one reason or another, on tribes near
and far. When Indians traveled, they always went in single
file, so their "roads" needed to be only wide enough to accommodate one person at a time. However, they were
very clever at finding the best and easiest path to follow,
and their well-worn trails were added to from year to year.
The great North-South Indian Highway followed the
Valley of East Tennessee through the Cherokee country
and was used by all the tribes who wished to travel it.
There also was an East-West Highway, across the very
mountains themselves, crossing the Smokies at the spot we
still call Indian Gap.

It was the very excellence of these roads that brought
trouble to the Cherokee, for white men could follow them

as well as Indians and the first explorers who entered the
Tennessee country did just that. As early as 1673, the
Cherokee in the Tennessee country were visited by English
traders from Virginia. As time passed, trading with the
Cherokee became a profitable enterprise for colonists from
Virginia and South Carolina, who offered cloth and
blankets, knives and guns, and paint and trinkets in exchange for the fine furs that the Indians accumulated on
their winter hunts.

Adventurous explorers visited the Cherokee often,
finding them and their way of life fascinating. One of these
visitors, Sir Alexander Cuming, invited seven of the Cherokee chieftains to accompany him on a trip to England in
1730. This was the very sort of thing that appealed to the
Cherokee, for it was travel in the grand manner. As Poca-
hontas had been a hundred years earlier, the chieftains
were received in England with great kindness and courtesy,
although they were of course the objects of much curiosity.
Everywhere they were elaborately entertained, and the
climax of their visit was their presentation to the King
himself. The proud, ceremonious Cherokee were greatly
impressed by this visit, and thereafter regarded the English
as their special friends, referring to the British sovereign as
Great-King-Over-The-Water. The youngest of the chieftains who visited England in 1730 was Attakullakulla, or
Little Carpenter, and he fully repaid at a later date the
kindness thus shown him.

The dignified Cherokee, so fond of pomp and ceremony, were always willing to make treaties with the white
men, though the outcome of the treaties was often disastrous. In the French and Indian War, the Cherokee nation
signed a treaty of mutual aid with the English, who prom-

ised to build a fort on the Little Tennessee River and send a garrison of soldiers to protect the Indian towns. The Cherokee had chosen the English side of the quarrel because their traveling braves had noticed that the French did not hesitate to destroy the property of the various tribes in their path, while the English were more careful for the property rights of the Indians. To comply with the terms of this treaty, a force of British troops arrived from South Carolina in 1756, under the command of Captain Raymond Demere. Following the Indian trails from South Carolina to the Tennessee country was a far easier route than crossing the Smokies at Indian Gap.

A site was selected on the Little Tennessee River, not far from the sacred city of Chota, and construction of the promised fortification began. The fort was named in honor of John Campbell, the fourth Earl of Loudoun, who was Commander-in-Chief of all the British forces in North America at the time. Fort Loudoun was planned as a faithful copy of European fortifications of the day, and was more elaborate than frontier forts in other parts of the country. Diamond-shaped, it boasted a bastion projecting at each corner. It was of earthwork construction, with a huge dry moat or ditch around the outside and also a palisade barrier of sharpened logs. The digging of the moat was accomplished first, and the dirt removed from this ditch was then used to build a thick wall of earth around the enclosure. An extra defense measure was a hedge of thorny honey locust bushes, very effective against an attack by scantily clad Indians. The two largest of the corner bastions were named King Bastion and Queen Bastion, in honor of George II and his Queen Caroline. The two smaller bastions were called Prince of Wales and Duke of Cumberland.

The Cherokee watched fascinated as the palisades and bastions of the fort took shape, and admired the tools of the British soldiers and the skill with which they used them. The building of this first English fort in the area west of the Great Smoky Mountains (which was then called the Southwest) was no mean achievement, for it had to be constructed of materials available on the site, with whatever tools could be carried to the spot over the narrow Indian trail from South Carolina. The Cherokee were quite as proud of it as were the British who had built it.

The crowning achievement of the building of the fort was the arrival of its twelve guns. In order that the cannon might be brought across the mountains on the narrow trail, each was placed crosswise over a pack-saddle on a horse's back and lashed round the body of the horse with leather straps. Several times it happened that a cannon caught on a tree beside the path, throwing and breaking the back of the horse that carried it. Burdened thus, the horses could travel less than six miles a day. The Cherokee were delighted with these cannon, which were used chiefly to celebrate the King's birthday or a Cherokee victory; but the fort's commander felt that the very presence of the guns did much to prevent an attack on Fort Loudoun by the French and their Indian allies.

The scarlet-coated British troops themselves were greatly admired also by the Indians, who made many gestures of friendship to their allies. When the British gave several horses to the Cherokee, the princely gift was received with great rejoicing by the tribe.

Cherokee braves, mounted on their new steeds, promptly set forth to join the English in fighting against the French and the Indian tribes allied with them. They traveled the great North-South Indian Warpath through Tennessee and Virginia and proved themselves able fighters. At the close of the campaign, the Cherokee started the long trip south toward their homes. Some of the warriors had lost their horses during the campaign, and as they passed through southwestern Virginia they came upon a herd of horses grazing unprotected. Those braves whose horses had been lost selected for themselves replacements from among this herd. Probably they thought that the horses were wild; certainly they had no idea that anyone would object to the loss of a few of them. The Virginia settlers who owned the horses, however, took an entirely different view of the situation. This was horse-stealing! And horse-stealing was one of the most serious crimes of the frontier country. The settlers immediately followed the Cherokee, took back the missing horses, and killed several of the Indians who were found with stolen horses in their possession.

To the proud Cherokee, this was an act of war, and they proceeded to take matters into their own hands. Returning to Chota, the war party reported to the Cherokee chiefs and braves their loss of face at the hands of the English in Virginia. There had been other points of disagreement between the Cherokee and their British allies; for years, some of the chiefs had been urging that the nation disregard their treaty of mutual aid. Attakullakulla, however, now grown old and wise and revered, still liked and respected the power of the Great-King-Over-The-Water and had been able to persuade his people not to fight

against their friends the British. Tensions were steadily
mounting, and the incident of the horses made a powerful
impression. In the council house of every Cherokee village the story was repeated, and the braves donned their
war paint and their headdresses of turkey feathers, and
gathered at Chota ready for war with the British.

Of course, there were no British in the Tennessee
country except the small garrison of soldiers that had remained to man Fort Loudoun during the French and Indian War, so it was Fort Loudoun that the Cherokee attacked. The Indians were easily able to place the fort under
siege, for it was too far away from other British forces to
have received aid. Two expeditions, one from South Carolina and the other from Virginia, were sent to relieve the
fort, but neither was able to reach the Overhill Cherokee
country. After months of near starvation, the British soldiers
demanded of their officers that the fort be surrendered. A
messenger was sent to the great Cherokee chieftain, Oconostota, at Chota, with an offer of surrender if the Indians would promise to spare the lives of those within the
fort and treat them as prisoners of war to be exchanged
for Indian prisoners held by the British. To this the Cherokee agreed; so the English flag was hauled down from Fort
Loudoun's flagpole, and the red-coated soldiers marched
out of the fort to surrender to Oconostota.

A group of Indian guides were furnished to escort the
defenders of the fort back to South Carolina, and soldiers
and guides set forth together along the trail. However, at
the end of the first day's march, the guides disappeared one
by one into the gathering dusk. Captain Demere, realizing
that this meant great danger for his men, posted a heavy
guard around the camp. At daybreak, one of the guards

reported the approach of a large band of armed and painted Indians. Almost before the warning could be given, the Indians opened fire on the camp from all sides, killing Captain Demere and about thirty others. A few of the soldiers were able to escape, and managed to make their way back to South Carolina with the news of the fall of Fort Loudoun, but some of the British were taken prisoner and were borne off by their captors to various Cherokee towns.

The Cherokee were often inconsistent in the manner in which they treated their prisoners of war. Sometimes they made slaves of their conquered foes, while at other times they treated their prisoners as honored guests. On rare occasions, prisoners were adopted into the tribe, and even more rarely were elected chiefs. Captain John Stuart, one of the British officers at Fort Loudoun who was taken prisoner, had the good fortune to fall into the hands of one of his Indian friends when Chief Attakullakulla bought him from the braves who had actually captured him. He was taken to the home of the Chief, where he was treated as a member of the family. After some time had elapsed, the Chief announced that he was going on a hunting trip, and that he would take no one with him except his prisoner, the white captain. On the hunting trip, Attakullakulla permitted Captain Stuart to escape, after carefully pointing out to him the trail back to an English camp.

For a time the Cherokee themselves occupied Fort Loudoun, of which they had been so proud; but after they had examined it to their hearts' content, they tired of it, and burned it to the ground. Then the Indians returned to peaceful pursuits, happy with the fine herd of horses the English had left with them, and feeling that the insult they had received at the hands of the Virginia settlers had been suitably avenged. Although the British never returned to Fort Loudoun, the fort had served its purpose by keeping the Cherokee on the English side during the French and Indian War until it was too late for their desertion to influence the result of the conflict.

In 1761 another British expedition defeated the Cherokee and forced them to sue for peace. One of the English officers, Lieutenant Henry Timberlake, so impressed the Cherokee chieftains that, after the signing of this treaty, they invited him to pay them a visit in their various towns. Lieutenant Timberlake took careful note of all the things he found unusual and interesting during his visit, and later wrote a book about his experiences. Returning to England, Lieutenant Timberlake followed the example of Sir Alexander Cuming, taking with him several Cherokee braves. The Cherokee travelers conducted themselves with dignity during their long journey to a land that surely seemed as strange to them in appearance and customs as had the Tennessee country to their British host.

By now, the well-marked Indian roads had led the first hunters into the Tennessee country. Returning to Virginia and North Carolina with glowing tales of the beauty and fertility of the lands across the mountains, these hunters came back again and again, leading parties of adventurous friends who wanted to see for themselves. Daniel Boone was the most famous of these "long hunters" —so named because they remained for such long periods of time in the wilderness. The hunters at once adopted the deerskin shirt and trousers costume of the Cherokee as well as the soft moccasins that were both silent and comfortable. It was inevitable that some of the hunters who found the Tennessee country so much to their liking would want to return and settle there. By the beginning of the Revolutionary War, several small settlements had grown up, and there were many scattered farms belonging to individual pioneer families.

It was John Sevier, one of Tennessee's greatest pioneer heroes, who led the force of these settlers who marched back across the mountains to defeat the British at King's Mountain in what is since regarded as a turning-point battle of the Revolutionary War. On the way home from King's Mountain, Sevier was warned by two white traders that the Cherokee were gathering, and were planning to attack the frontier settlements. Before this attack could be made, Sevier set out with one hundred of his men to find the Cherokee and head them off from the homes of the settlers. Finding the Indians camping near the French Broad River, Sevier attacked them at once and won a decisive victory. The Indians scattered to hide in the forest, while the settlers, who had been reinforced by the arrival of troops from Virginia, marched toward Chota and the other towns on the Little Tennessee River. The Cherokee were taken by surprise when Sevier's men crossed the river a mile or so below the town of Chota and attacked it unexpectedly from the land side. The size of Sevier's force so frightened the Indians that they abandoned their towns and fled to the mountains. The attacking settlers then burned every Cherokee town between the Little Tennessee and Hiwassee rivers. Returning to Chota, John Sevier held a two-day council with the Indians. The Cherokee gladly agreed to the terms of peace offered, and Sevier's men marched home.

One would think that the Cherokee might have

learned a lesson from this defeat, but they continued to make attacks on outlying farms and settlements in the years that followed. Each time, however, that they planned a really serious raid, John Sevier managed to hear of it in advance, and to prevent it by attacking the Indians first. Although they hated John Sevier, the Cherokee respected and feared him more than any other white man in the frontier country.

Now, the British had always believed that the best way to obtain land for their colonists to settle was to purchase it from its Indian owners; and after the Revolutionary War, the new government of the United States continued this treaty-purchase method of dealing with the Indians. The Cherokee were always more than willing to attend a treaty meeting, which they did in force, their chiefs in their best deerskin costumes ornamented with paint and feathers and jewelry of bone being followed by hundreds of warriors and braves to the place of meeting. In the course of several treaties, the Cherokee sold large tracts of land to the whites, but there was always a catch in the agreement. To begin with, negotiations had to be carried on through an interpreter, and it is quite possible that neither side really understood what the other had in mind. Then, too, the Cherokee had no written language, so it was impossible for them to take home a copy of the treaty in order to remember its provisions exactly. In addition, the terms of most Indian treaties were vague, and the boundaries called for in these treaties were unmarked, so that it was literally impossible for the settlers arriving from across the mountains to know whether or not the land they chose for settlement was really within the tract purchased from the Indians.

One of the most famous of all the treaty meetings with the Cherokee occurred in 1791, at what is now Knoxville. By this time, so many settlers had made their homes in the Tennessee country that the newly established government of the United States had designated this area as the Territory South of the River Ohio, and had appointed William Blount of North Carolina as its governor. William Blount was appointed also as superintendent of Indian affairs for all the land south of the Ohio. Governor Blount selected the spot where First Creek flows into the Tennessee River as his meeting place with the Cherokee, because this location was not far (thirty miles) from the Cherokee towns, and White's Fort (established by James White in 1786) was available nearby to house the Governor and his party.

William Blount had attended treaty meetings with the Cherokee before and he was aware of their love of ceremony. Accordingly, he ordered built on the bank of First Creek an elaborate pavilion where he himself would sit. He wore for the occasion his finest uniform trimmed with gold lace, and he insisted that the members of his party and the settlers from White's Fort who attended the meeting should be dressed in their showiest and best clothes to represent the importance and power of the United States. Twelve hundred Cherokee arrived for the meeting, and William Blount had been right. They were impressed with the pavilion, and the bunting, and the gold lace of the Governor's party. But they were no more impressed than were the whites at the sight of the Cherokee chieftains, tall and straight and wearing every bit of finery they possessed. Some of their ornaments had been gifts to them at previous treaty meetings, and one of the Cherokee chieftains came near to eclipsing the Governor himself, for he was wearing yards of silver lace, and was carrying a crimson parasol.

The Cherokee thoroughly enjoyed the negotiations, which continued for some days and ended with the purchase of much of the East Tennessee Valley and the promise to mark a boundary line which would show plainly the extent of the purchase. The ceremonial pipe of peace was smoked, and Governor Blount felt that his Treaty of Holston had secured to the settlers the peaceful enjoyment of their lands. The Cherokee, however, were immediately dissatisfied with the treaty. They claimed that they had misunderstood the amount of money to be paid them, and demanded five times as much as the treaty called for. The Cherokee's democratic form of government came in very handy on such occasions, for they invariably claimed that the chiefs who had signed a treaty they wished to change had done so without the consent of the people. The federal government in Philadelphia had had no experience with the Cherokee in treaty making and breaking, and, anxious to ensure the peace of the frontier, they granted the Indians the money they asked for. Nobody marked the boundary line for six years after the signing of the treaty.

Governor Blount began to receive a steady stream of complaints from the settlers that the Indians were a source of worry and a danger to them. Cattle were stolen; men who went on solitary hunting trips disappeared to be seen no more. Barns and dwellings were burned. The federal government at Philadelphia forbade the Governor and the settlers to strike back against the Cherokee, for the authorities believed that the Treaty of Holston could be enforced. However, in 1793 the protests from the Tennessee country were so numerous that the War Department decided to build a fort that would remind the Indians that they were dealing with a powerful government. William Blount had chosen the site of the signing of the Treaty of Holston for the capital of the Territory South of the River Ohio. Here he had built his "Mansion," the first two-story frame house west of the mountains, and had christened the capital "Knoxville" in honor of General Henry Knox, who was Secretary of War in President Washington's Cabinet. The new capital was growing rapidly, and it was here that the United States government built in 1793 a handsome blockhouse, manned by a small garrison of army troops.

The Cherokee, who had been joined by a war party of fierce Creek Indians from farther south, determined to attack the blockhouse. The Chiefs John Watts and Doublehead set out from the Cherokee towns with a large force. They were moving, under cover of darkness, toward the city from the west when they were seen by an army scout who alerted the garrison at Knoxville. When the Cherokee's scouts reported that the fort was in a bustle of preparation for defense, the Indian leaders decided not to attack Knoxville. However, they were determined to make a raid on white settlers somewhere, for the war party would have lost face had it returned to the Cherokee towns without fighting. They turned southward, then, toward the little settlement called Cavett's Station. This station, like so many others in this part of the country, was in reality a farmhouse sturdily built of logs, with slits in the walls through which rifles could be fired. There were only thirteen people in the station, all of them members of the same family. The first attack by the Indians was repulsed by the vigorous rifle fire of the Cavett family. The Indians then suggested, through one of their number who spoke a little English, that if the whites would surrender and come out of the building, their lives would be spared, and they would be exchanged for an equal number of Indian prisoners. This trick worked as well at Cavett Station as it had at Fort Loudoun, for no sooner had the settlers (men, women, and children) emerged from the station than they were set upon by the Creeks and were murdered and horribly mutilated.

At the very time of the massacre at Cavett Station, Governor Blount was in Philadelphia attempting to convince the government that the Cherokee must be controlled by force. Secretary Daniel Smith, who was in charge during the Governor's absence, decided that, regulations or no regulations, the Cherokee had to be punished. It is not surprising that it was John Sevier whom he authorized to lead an expedition against the Indian towns. Sevier and his men first captured the small Cherokee village of Estanaula in a night attack, going on the next morning to the larger and more important town of Etowah. The Cherokee chieftain at Etowah, Chief King Fisher, was killed in the battle for the town; and after his death the Indians fled into the forest, leaving their homes unprotected. Sevier burned Etowah to the ground and had its ashes scattered. It turned out that this was language that the Cherokee understood.

The five lower towns of the Cherokee, near present-day Chattanooga, continued to harass the settlers in Middle Tennessee; so in 1794, Governor Blount sent Major Ore with federal troops from Knoxville to the aid of the settlers in Nashville. Major Ore's detachment joined groups of volunteers from Middle Tennessee and Kentucky, and together they began the celebrated Nickajack Expedition in mid-September. They captured the large Cherokee town of Nickajack, which was inhabited by about two hundred and fifty families, killing seventy-six of the Indian warriors. Many of the Cherokee, including the women and children, escaped by swimming across the broad Tennessee River and hiding in the forest on the other side. All the remaining inhabitants of the town were taken prisoner.

From this time on, the Cherokee seemed inclined to abide by the treaties they continued to make with the whites. In each treaty they gave up more of their lands in return for gifts and payments until, in the last of their treaties, in 1835, they ceded to the United States government all their remaining lands east of the Mississippi.

Probably the United States government would not have been so anxious to purchase the Cherokee's last tract of land if it had not been for the gold fever of the 1830's. Gold had been discovered in the mountains of North Georgia in 1831, and mining interests were putting pressure on the government to force the Cherokee out of the whole mountainous district so that miners might search for further evidences of the precious metal without fear of Indian attacks. As it turned out, the gold was in such small quantities that it was impractical to mine it, but in the first enthusiasm of the discovery, the federal government completed the purchase of the Cherokee's land. It had become the policy of the government by this time to remove all the Indian nations from their native areas, and to concentrate them all in what was then called Indian Territory but what is now the State of Oklahoma. The treaty in which a small number of the Cherokee agreed to the sale of their

This Indian mound on The University of Tennessee's agricultural campus is mute evidence that the Cherokee were here first.

Blount Mansion, first two-story frame house in the West, was built by William Blount in 1792 and served as his capitol while he was Governor of the Territory South of the River Ohio.

lands required them all to leave the mountains within two years and go to make their home in Indian Territory.

The Cherokee people at once rejected the treaty, saying that the chieftains who signed it had done so against their wishes, and they refused to move. They appealed to the "Great White Father in Washington" as they had done before when treaties did not suit them. This time, however, was to be different; for the President of the United States in 1835 was Andrew Jackson, noted Indian fighter who hated the Cherokee and was glad to see them go. He listened to their complaints about the treaty, and then told them calmly that they would be better off in the West. Still they did not leave. After the two years had expired, no amount of peaceful persuasion could budge the Indians, and General Winfield Scott was ordered by President Van Buren to remove them by force to Indian Territory. General Scott's soldiers rounded up all the Cherokee they could find in the villages, the largest number of whom were women, children, old men, and the sick. Many of the Cherokee warriors had fled back into their beloved mountains, and there they hid themselves so well that General Scott despaired of finding them.

Finally, so the Cherokee say, General Scott offered compromise terms to the hiding braves. One of the General's soldiers had been killed by the Indians while on a searching trip into the mountains. General Scott's tempting proposition was that if the Indians responsible for the killing of the soldier would surrender to him for trial, he would allow all the other Cherokee braves to remain in the mountains and would not force them to accompany him to Indian Territory. Tsali, one of the Cherokee chieftains, with his two sons, voluntarily gave himself up for trial and execution so that the remnant of his people might be spared. Whether Tsali and his sons actually were the ones who killed the soldier none of the Cherokee would ever say.

General Scott then proceeded, although it was already late autumn, to take the Cherokee to Oklahoma. This forced march was at bayonet point, through the worst of the winter weather, and it was the weakest members of the Cherokee nation who were forced to make it. The sufferings of the Indians were acute; about one fourth of the Cherokee died before Indian Territory was reached. Those who survived the hardships of the journey were heartsick to find themselves in a flat land without the beautiful forests and sparkling streams that they so loved. By twos and threes many ran away and straggled back, carrying young children and the sick, to join the braves still hiding in the mountains of Tennessee.

It was the custom of the Cherokee occasionally to adopt a white man into the tribe, and rarely, to elect a particularly beloved white man as chief. It was one of these adopted Cherokee who came to the aid of the Indians hiding in the Great Smokies. Colonel William H. Thomas of North Carolina had some years before made a long visit to the Cherokee and had been elected a chieftain. He was alarmed by the plight of his friends in the mountains, and in 1842 he journeyed to Washington to appeal to the President on their behalf. He was able to persuade the Congress to give to the Eastern Cherokee their share of the money Congress had previously appropriated to pay the nation for their ceded lands. Then the Cherokee found themselves in a strange situation. They had the money with which to buy homes for themselves, but were not permitted by law to own property outside the Indian Territory. Once again Colonel Thomas came to their rescue, purchasing in his own name a tract of land in North Carolina which now comprises the Qualla Cherokee Indian Reservation. By 1866 he was able to deed the land to the Cherokee, for the Congress then made it possible for Indians to own property; but it was not until 1903 that an act of Congress finally confirmed the title of the Cherokee to this reservation.

Qualla Reservation is in the foothills of the Great Smokies on the North Carolina side, just outside the Great Smoky Mountains National Park on the main highway across the Smokies from Knoxville to Asheville. Each summer the Cherokee reenact there the touching drama of Tsali and the great Cherokee migration in the stirring pageant, "Unto These Hills."

It was while the Cherokee were still making and breaking treaties with the Tennessee settlers that a member of their race, Sequoyah, accomplished what no other man in modern times has been able to do. His statue stands in the Hall of Fame in the National Capitol building in Washington. He is claimed by Oklahoma and represents that state in the Hall of Fame, but Sequoyah was born in one of the Cherokee towns on the Little Tennessee River and spent most of his life in the mountains of East Tennessee.

No one would have chosen Sequoyah, as a boy, the Cherokee most likely to succeed, for his physical appearance and his parentage were much against him. Sequoyah was lame from birth, but he hunted and fished with the other Indian boys, not allowing his clubfoot to hamper him greatly. He was the son of a white father, who abandoned him, and a Cherokee mother, with whom he lived. The Cherokee had by this time acquired some cattle from the white settlers, and Sequoyah's mother operated a sort of dairy for the village. Growing up, Sequoyah served as herdsman and dairyman, but this work was not to his liking.

It was the fashion of the times for the Cherokee to wear a great deal of silver jewelry—bracelets, amulets, and necklaces were highly prized by the chieftains, and someone had to make these ornaments that were in such demand. Here was work that appealed to the young Sequoyah, and he became a skilled silversmith. Taking great pride in his finished jewelry, he wished to mark the pieces as his work. He therefore asked one of the half-breed Cherokee chiefs who was well-educated in English to write his name for him in English letters. Carefully, Sequoyah copied this signature, engraving it on his silver jewelry as part of the pattern of decoration.

Most of the Cherokee thought that the most remarkable accomplishment of white men was their ability to write down things that had happened. When this ability was discussed and praised by his fellows, Sequoyah always declared that he saw nothing so remarkable about it. He was fond of saying that he himself could probably figure out a way to write down the Cherokee language, and when he was about forty years old he actually set to work on the project. None of the Cherokee paid much attention to what Sequoyah was doing. A few of the Cherokee chieftains read and wrote English with facility, while the rest of the nation were content to have their reading and writing done for them by their better educated leaders.

Actually, Sequoyah's final accomplishment was most amazing because he knew no other language than the

Cherokee tongue and was totally ignorant of the English alphabet. At first, he planned to write down the Cherokee language by having one character for each word, but he soon realized that there would then be too many symbols to be easily learned. Finally, he determined to have one letter for each sound of human speech, and he developed a brand-new alphabet, or syllabary, of eighty-five characters, each representing a sound. The first characters drawn by Sequoyah very much resemble German script, and many of these he discarded as too complicated to be practical. One day, at the home of his brother-in-law, he saw an English Bible. Of course, he was unable to read its words; but, leafing through the pages, he copied out some of the letters to use as characters for his own alphabet. Since these English letters themselves had no meaning for him, he turned some of them on their sides, and used some of them upside down.

By 1821, Sequoyah had finished his phonetic alphabet, or syllabary. The beauty of this method of writing was its simplicity and the ease with which it could be learned. There were of course no schools for the Cherokee children, so Sequoyah undertook the teaching of his alphabet himself. He taught it first to his five-year-old daughter, then to his friends (who naturally could not admit that they could not master what a small child had learned). Children and adults learned it rapidly, for it could be studied as they worked or played. Many of the intelligent Cherokee learned to spell in a single day.

Now that the Cherokee language could be written down, the National Council of the Cherokee, many of whom were well-educated, decided to publish a newspaper. In 1825, they purchased a printing press and with the aid of

some white missionaries proceeded to print the first newspaper in an American Indian language, the *Cherokee
Phoenix*. The *Phoenix* was a weekly paper, printed in
English and Cherokee. Its appearance brought to the attention of the outside world the amazing accomplishment of
Sequoyah, who was invited to come to Washington in 1828.
The United States Congress voted him a gift of five hundred dollars in acknowledgment of what he had done for
his people, and the Cherokee nation gave him a medal.

Sequoyah's alphabet was so complete that he very
shortly realized that not only the Cherokee language but
any other Indian dialect could become a written language
through its use. He therefore left his home for the newly
established Indian Territory in Oklahoma to teach his
alphabet to the various tribes and nations gathered there.
The alphabet was as useful and as easily learned in Oklahoma as in Tennessee, and Sequoyah, a crippled half-breed
Cherokee Indian, had accomplished a feat unparalleled by
anyone in modern times. He had invented an alphabet for
his people, and in so doing had opened the way to literacy
for all American Indians. It is fitting that his name was given
to the Giant Sequoia trees of California, for because of his
accomplishment, Sequoyah stands head and shoulders above
all other Cherokee as the Sequoias tower over the other
trees of the forest.

Although the Cherokee have been gone from Tennessee for more than a hundred years, they have left behind
many things to remind us that this was once their beloved
home. Many towns in East Tennessee bear their ancient
Cherokee names with pride—Chattanooga, Etowah, Watauga, and Chilhowee are but a few of them. The State of
Tennessee itself rejoices in a Cherokee name. U. S. High-

way II E follows very closely the route of the great North-South Indian Warpath, while many of the cities and towns of the region owe their twisting streets to the fact that they were laid out following Indian trails. It is doubly appropriate that, in Knoxville, a fine example of an Indian burial mound exists today on Cherokee Boulevard in Sequoyah Hills!

When the Tennessee Valley Authority built its series of dams in East Tennessee, many sites of Cherokee towns were covered by the waters of the lakes thus created. The University of Tennessee's Department of Anthropology, under the able direction of Professor T. M. N. Lewis, raced against time to excavate these townsites to recover and catalogue scores of interesting relics and artifacts found in them. It was conclusively proven that the Cherokee were not the first tribe to hold this section of the country, and the presence of long-ago Indian visitors from as faraway as Montana or the Dakotas was evidenced by the finding of ceremonial pipes made of clays from those distant regions. Thanks to the Cherokee towns, The University of Tennessee now has the finest collection of Indian relics and artifacts in the East.

The rising waters of the TVA lakes have covered the entrances to many decorated caves along the steep rock cliffs that border the rivers of East Tennessee; yet small boys searching along the shores of streams, or farmers plowing their hillside acres, still find the fine flint arrowheads of the Cherokee.

The story of the Cherokee in Tennessee is a prelude to the story of Knoxville, for the city owes its very existence to the Cherokee nation. Why? Why, because its site is the one chosen by William Blount for the Treaty of Holston

and as the capital of the Territory South of the River Ohio
—a site convenient to the Cherokee towns on the Little
Tennessee River, only a day's journey away. As the city
has grown, it has been easy for those who have lived here
to understand how the Cherokee could so have loved this
beautiful country that *nothing* would induce them to leave
it!

CHAPTER TWO

William Blount

In 1790, President Washington was looking for just the right man to serve as governor of the newly created Territory South of the River Ohio. This was the second of all the federal territories and it comprised the western lands that had been ceded to the federal government by the State of North Carolina. There was no lack of available men of ability, and had the position been simply that of governor, the President's choice might very possibly have been his friend George Mason of Virginia. The job was difficult to fill because it was two-fold: its holder would, under the supervision of the State Department, be governor of the territory, but he would also, under the direct supervision of the War Department, serve as supervisor of its Indian affairs. Seeking a candidate who combined administrative ability with a knowledge of how to deal with Indian difficulties, the President was pleased to find a man who combined exactly these qualities in William Blount of North Carolina.

When William Blount accepted the appointment as Governor of the Territory South of the River Ohio, he had never set foot upon the land that he was to govern and was almost unknown to its inhabitants. Yet he was definitely the man for the job. At forty-three, he had already served a long apprenticeship in public affairs in his native state. He had fought in the Continental Army and for two years had held the difficult and thankless job of paymaster for the North Carolina militia as well as the Continental troops within the state. He had served in the North Carolina Legislature and in the Continental Congress. He had been speaker of the lower house of the North Carolina legislative body. He had been a member of the Constitutional Convention of 1787 and had signed for North Carolina. He had attended the important Treaty of Hopewell meeting in an attempt to secure concessions from the Indians for his state. In 1790, William Blount was already a man of national prominence, and so brought to his new position not only the experience gained in his previous public service, but also a dignity that was needed and wanted in the frontier area.

Even his early training had been the right kind for his new job. He was born in Bertie County, North Carolina, in 1749. His father, Jacob Blount, a prosperous farmer who had many business interests in addition to his large land holdings, insisted that each of his sons become acquainted with every phase of the family business. He insisted, too, that the boys not only learn how to do things themselves, but, which was to him even more important, that they learn how to get things done. William, growing up, learned therefore how to farm profitably, how to manage stores, foundries, mills, and so on. Best of all, he learned how to manage men.

With his father and his brothers, young William Blount formed a sort of family company which engaged in a wide variety of business enterprises. Jacob Blount understood farming best, so he managed all the farms. John Gray Blount was the practical businessman, and he supervised all the stores and factories. Thomas Blount was the family linguist and cosmopolitan, so he went to live abroad to handle the family affairs on foreign shores. And William? William was the family diplomat, and so he turned to politics, where his influence and position helped the family business, and where the family business supported him financially and furthered his political ambitions.

Although William Blount had never crossed the mountains into the Tennessee country, he owned large tracts of land there. It would have been rather surprising if he had not owned western land, for it was the thing in which every man of means was investing in his day. At the close of the Revolutionary War, North Carolina gave "land-warrants" to her soldiers who had fought in the war. These warrants entitled the holders to tracts of the public lands of the state beyond the Great Smokies. Few people had seen the land, which had been secured by treaty and purchased from the Indians, and most of the ex-soldiers had no idea of moving west. There were, therefore, great quantities of the "land-warrants" for sale, and they were bought by almost every well-to-do citizen as a speculation. Those who bought them usually turned over their warrants, sight unseen, to a land agent, whose business it was to locate the land the warrants called for and file the correct claims with the proper authorities. The Blount family, considering land to be, after all, the basic and practical investment, bought "land-warrants" right and left. They also acquired land under North Carolina's so-called "Land Grab Act" of 1783, which gave speculators the right to buy as much land as they wished for the equivalent of $5.00 per hundred acres. As the owner of many thousands of acres of Tennessee land, William Blount had therefore a proprietary interest in the development of the territory, and he had no idea that his land holdings would ever cause him the slightest trouble.

At the time of his appointment as Governor of the Territory South of the River Ohio, William Blount was considered a man of wealth, but, like other so-called "rich men" of his day, he seldom saw any hard cash. His was a wealth on paper, for he was a speculator who made most of his investments on credit. In a later era, William Blount would have bought common stocks on margin: in his own time, land was the great speculative investment. Although he owned thousands and thousands of acres of land in the Tennessee country, Blount was forced to delay his departure for the west in 1790 in order to put his business affairs in order. As usual, he had no cash in hand, and he needed cash to outfit himself and his body servant properly for the trip to the Tennessee country. As governor of the territory, William Blount in the future would be paid his salary in cash, so against this salary he borrowed sufficient money for clothes, horses, luggage, and spending money. He collected various accounts due him in North Carolina (not without difficulty, for his business associates were as short of funds as he was himself) and sold some of his slaves in order to raise enough to pay off his most pressing debts in North Carolina before leaving.

After providing himself with a wardrobe befitting the dignity of his new position (no fringed buckskin for William Blount!), he set out across the mountains in 1791 to take over the reins of government of the Territory South of the River Ohio. He went first to the comfortable log house of William Cobb, near the Watauga Settlement, where he visited for several weeks transacting such business as was brought to him. Those of his constituents who met him for the first time were much impressed with his appearance. He was a handsome man, with a full face and regular features; he had great dignity and was as formal in his manners as in his attire. He wore his hair powdered and clubbed; he dressed in rich fabrics, well-cut and ornamented with the added touches of gold lace and silver-buckled shoes. Always the diplomat, he was courteous but noncommittal, approving but not enthusiastic, deliberate but not dilatory—in short, the very man to set a standard for a frontier area. His dress and manner were in sharp contrast to those of the men who were accounted leaders in the territory he had come to govern, but so great was his charm and magnetism that, instead of mistrusting him as a stranger to their problems, they respected him as a man of substance and wisdom. So from the very first, William Blount found friends and admirers in the west.

He was given free rein by both the State and War Departments in the establishment of the new government, for there were no precedents for him to follow. It seemed to William Blount in 1790 that his job as supervisor of Indian affairs was of the most immediate importance. The

white settlers who were beginning to come into the area in
large numbers could not be sure that their cabins would not
be the object of immediate attack from the Indians because
they had been built on land which the Indians considered
theirs. Therefore, while visiting William Cobb, Governor
Blount planned the first important official act of his administration, a treaty meeting with the Cherokee.

White's Fort was the spot he chose for the all-im-
portant meeting with the Cherokee chieftains to settle the
land question. It was his previous experience with the
Indians at the Hopewell Treaty meeting that guided him
in his preparations for the reception of the chiefs. Knowing
their love of ceremony and display, William Blount put on
his most elaborate uniform, ornamented with gold lace. He
had built for himself an elaborate pavilion, where he sat in
state; and there he received the chiefs of the Cherokee
nation with the same courtesy and dignity he would have
shown to the emissaries of any foreign power. All this was
not lost on the chiefs. They liked this manner of doing
things, and they liked William Blount; so they signed the
Treaty of Holston, and the Blount administration was off
to an auspicious start.

Having (so he thought) settled the Indian question,
the Governor set about establishing a regular government
for the territory. The first step was the selection of a capital, and since White's Fort had been so good a choice for
the treaty meeting, it was selected as the site of the capital,
which would be named Knoxville in honor of General
Henry Knox. General Knox, who was Secretary of War in
President Washington's Cabinet, was Blount's immediate
superior in all matters dealing with Indian affairs, and by

naming the new city Knoxville the Governor hoped to interest the General in the welfare of its citizens. General Knox had made no secret of his feeling that the settlers had been at fault in their disputes with the Indians, and that they were not properly keeping the terms of treaties. He had fully approved the Treaty of Holston, and when it became apparent to him that in spite of this treaty, the Cherokee were continuing to harass the settlers, he was more sympathetic toward Governor Blount's efforts to protect the citizens of the territory. So, in 1793, there were federal troops at Knoxville to aid volunteers in fending off Indian attacks.

It was not that the Indians regretted their bargain in the Treaty of Holston; nor had they lost their respect for William Blount. They simply did not ever intend to be bound *permanently* by their promises, and this was a fact that William Blount had great difficulty in explaining to General Knox. The Indians came often to Knoxville to see their friend the Governor and to admire the fine house he had built for himself there. Sometimes they came on business, sometimes on purely social visits. At the height of the difficulties between the Cherokee and the inhabitants of Knoxville, a friendly Chickasaw named John Morris was visiting Governor Blount at the Blount Mansion. On the street in Knoxville, Morris was attacked and killed by two white settlers who mistook him for a Cherokee. This incident could have started a large-scale war between the Indians and the whites had not William Blount again treated the Indians with courtesy and diplomacy. He at once posted an offer of a $100 reward for the apprehension of the killer of John Morris. Then he ordered (and paid for) an elabo-

rate funeral for his friend, walking himself immediately
behind the casket as chief mourner, and the Indians *still*
liked William Blount.

By 1794, there were enough white settlers in the
Tennessee country to have a legislative body, and to take a
census with a view to petitioning the federal government
for statehood for the territory. The Governor proclaimed
the date for the election of representatives to the Territorial Legislature from the various counties, and the
legislature met in Knoxville in 1794. The legislators were
men who were leaders in their own communities, most of
them settlers who had come into the Tennessee country
several years before it became a federal territory. It would
have been quite possible for them to take a dislike to the
prosperous, elegant Governor from across the mountains,
but once again William Blount proved himself a master of
diplomacy. He announced (and stuck to it) that he had
no intention of interfering with the legislators, who were
perfectly capable of making the laws of the territory
properly. So the legislators, as well as the Indians, liked
William Blount, and they proved it by passing a bill to
establish a college in Knoxville which they named Blount
College in his honor.

In 1796, the territory having a population according to
census of more than enough people to entitle it to statehood, Governor Blount called a convention to meet in
Knoxville to frame a constitution for the new state. The
resulting document was patterned on the constitutions of
North Carolina and Pennsylvania; like them, it protected
rights and liberties. Once again, Blount's previous training
stood him in good stead, for he had been a member of the

Constitutional Convention and knew just how to secure the agreement of delegates to such a document.

With great reluctance, the Congress of the United States admitted the State of Tennessee to the Union in June of 1796. The presidential campaign between John Adams and Thomas Jefferson was a bitter one. It was well known in Philadelphia (then the national capital) that William Blount and John Sevier, the two most powerful men in the new state, would favor Jefferson, and the Adams faction opposed the state's admission in order to prevent the Jefferson side from gaining votes. William Blount made an enemy in John Adams, as Tennessee, by a narrow margin, became the sixteenth state in time to cast three votes in the electoral college for Thomas Jefferson. Tennessee, by a compromise which ensured her admission, was allowed only three electoral votes instead of the customary four.

Even before Tennessee was admitted to statehood, John Sevier was elected governor, while William Blount was chosen (with William Cocke) to be the state's first representative in the United States Senate. It was deemed most appropriate by Tennessee's citizens that the polished Blount should have the honor of going to Philadelphia, where he would be such a credit to his constituents. Arriving in Philadelphia to take his seat in the Senate, William Blount was a welcome addition to society in the national capital. But while his appearance and manner betrayed no hint of it, his financial situation had become critical. International disputes over the control of the Mississippi River had so depressed the values of western lands that, even on paper, William Blount was less than wealthy. His patient creditors began to press for a settlement of their claims, and the new senator, unable to raise cash to satisfy them, found it necessary to evade bankruptcy by the stratagem of deeding to his half-brother and secretary (Willie Blount) much of his land, all of his slaves, and even his household belongings. On the heels of this financial ruin came a blow that would have finished a lesser man than William Blount.

President John Adams would have had to be less (or more) than human not to have rejoiced over a letter sent to him shortly after the new senator from Tennessee had arrived in Philadelphia. At this time, Spain owned all of Louisiana, including the important port of New Orleans at the mouth of the Mississippi River. It was believed that these lands were about to be ceded to Napoleon, who intended to close the river to American use. People who owned lands in western Tennessee were alarmed at this prospect, since it would cut off the Mississippi River trade and would therefore make West Tennessee lands less valuable and less enticing to prospective settlers. Spain was at war with Great Britain, who was also interested in acquiring Louisiana, and many Americans felt that it would be to the advantage of the United States to have the mouth of the Mississippi under the control of England, whose policy would be to encourage trade with western states along the river. There was a movement on foot among the owners of western lands to support Great Britain in her war against Spain, although this was in violation of the United States' position of neutrality. The letter received by John Adams purported to be from William Blount to a man named Carey, and contained an outline of the plot to aid the British against Spain.

This letter was sent by President Adams to the Senate

on July 3, 1797. On that day, Senator Blount, becoming
bored with debates on consular salaries and taxes on parch-
ment, went out for a walk. On the steps of the Senate
chamber, he met the President's secretary, Samuel Malcom, carrying a document. Senator Blount stopped Malcom
and asked him what message he was bringing to the Senate.
The embarrassed secretary stammered that the message
was confidential and hurried on into the Senate, while Mr.
Blount finished his walk.

When he returned to the Senate chamber, William
Blount found every head turning to stare at him. There was
a motion to reread something that the clerk had just read
aloud. To his horror, Blount listened to a letter to James
Carey, signed William Blount. The Vice-President asked
whether he had written the letter. The stunned Senator replied that he had written letters to James Carey, but that he
could not identify this one. He asked for time to prepare his
answer and walked with dignity from the room.

In the confused days that followed, sentiment against
Blount was running high. He asked for an opportunity to
testify before the Senate, but the request was denied. His
personal effects and papers were seized by the senatorial
committee investigating his case. On July 8, after a cursory
hearing at which he himself was not asked to speak, William Blount was expelled from the United States Senate.
He was released under bond of one hundred dollars for
himself and five hundred dollars for each of his two securi-
ties, to appear at a later date to be tried for impeachment.
But William Blount had had enough. Bond or no bond, he
was on his way home.

Word of the events in Philadelphia had of course preceded him, and he must have had serious doubts as to his

reception in Tennessee's capital, but he need not have worried. As he approached the city, William Blount (ex-governor and now ex-senator) was met by James White, the city's founder, and a large group of its citizens. The people of Knoxville gave William Blount a rousing welcome and conducted him triumphantly home to his mansion.

As the time approached for Blount's trial before the House of Representatives on the impeachment charges, James Matthers, the Sergeant-at-Arms of the United States Senate, was sent to Knoxville to arrest ex-Senator Blount and bring him back to Philadelphia. Mr. Matthers found himself in a very strange position upon his arrival in the capital of Tennessee, for he was greeted by William Blount and everyone else as though he had come upon a purely social visit. Pleasant entertainments were planned for him by the state officials, and he was for several days the guest of William Blount at the Blount Mansion. Feeling that the time had come to return to Philadelphia with his prisoner, Matthers asked the United States Marshall to appoint a posse to act as escort. His request was treated with polite indifference. Appealing publicly for a posse, he found not a single man who was willing to be a member of it. The Sergeant-at-Arms reluctantly concluded that he would not be able to force William Blount to return to Philadelphia, and so he announced his intention of leaving alone. It seemed as if the posse so unwilling to escort William Blount out of Tennessee had no such reluctance with regard to James Matthers. A large group of citizens accompanied Mr. Matthers several miles on his way, assuring him firmly the while that William Blount could never be taken from Tennessee as a prisoner. Having impressed this point upon the

Sergeant-at-Arms, the posse then bade him a most polite farewell.

The truth of the matter was that the people of Tennessee *liked* William Blount and had confidence in him. As historian J. G. M. Ramsey wrote: "Whatever foundation there may have been for the impeachment of William Blount, and whatever truth there may have been in the charge preferred against him, there was no one in Tennessee who viewed his conduct as criminal, unpatriotic, or unfriendly to the true interests of the State or the West, and all refused to sanction the proceedings against him."

This attitude on the part of his neighbors was conclusively proved by what happened next. While the federal charges were still pending against him, William Blount was signally honored by the citizens of his own state. James White was serving in the State Senate as the representative of Knox County and as speaker. In 1798 he resigned those positions to serve as an Indian commissioner. The voters of Knox County immediately elected William Blount to the State Senate. At a called meeting on December 3, 1797, the Senate of Tennessee unanimously elected Senator Blount of Knox County to serve as its speaker. So it happened that at the very time that Blount was being tried for impeachment from the United States Senate, he was serving as Speaker of the Senate of the State of Tennessee.

When the impeachment proceedings finally began in the United States Senate, they were of short duration. The articles of impeachment charged that Blount had conspired to set on foot a military hostile expedition against the territory of the King of Spain in the Floridas and Louisiana, for the purpose of wresting them from Spain and conquering them for the English king. As soon as the attorneys for Blount were given an opportunity to speak, they pointed out to the august body that, the Senate having expelled William Blount, he was no longer a member of the Senate and therefore not subject to its deliberations or punitive jurisdiction. They also claimed that under the Constitution senators are not subject to impeachment. No trial on the charges was held. Instead, the impeachment trial was dismissed on the grounds of lack of jurisdiction. William Blount thus achieved the dubious honor of being the only United States senator ever to be tried for impeachment, for in his case a precedent was set.

It was not until 1835 that any explanation or vindication of William Blount's conduct was written, and even then it was not for the eyes of the public. In that year Willie Blount (half-brother of William) wrote a full account of the affair for the information of the Blount children. It was unnecessary in Knoxville to defend William Blount—like the Indians and the legislators, the people still liked him.

For two years after the impeachment trial, the Blounts lived in Knoxville, the center of a circle of devoted and admiring friends. William Blount was Speaker of the State Senate, and the Blount Mansion was still open to a constant stream of visitors. The children were growing up—the girls attending balls, the boys attending Blount College. On the surface, life at the mansion was polished and serene as ever, but there were differences. William Blount was the victim of recurring attacks of the fever and chills of malaria—so precarious was his health that his friend Dr. Fournier lived with the Blounts in order to keep a close watch over his condition. There were financial difficulties, too; for in spite of his disastrous experiences with land speculation, William Blount was still convinced that land was the only safe investment. He was buying more land in Middle Tennessee in an attempt to recoup his losses. Much of his former holdings had been seized for delinquent taxes. But western land prices continued to fall: the boom in land was over along with the general business boom, based on credit alone, that had made the Blount family appear wealthy.

Fever struck in Knoxville in 1800. Hardly a family escaped it, and the Blount family was no exception. Mrs. Blount's mother was the first victim of it in the Blount Mansion, then one of the Blount boys came down with it. William Blount watched beside the bed of his son for days and nights; then he himself had fever. He recovered enough to sit up and to feel that he needed no further nursing— then a sudden relapse brought the end quickly to a man who at fifty-three had spend his entire adult life in service to his country and his state.

Mrs. Blount survived her husband by only two years. After her death, Willie Blount, who had been his half-brother's secretary and protégé, took over the education of the children and called upon brother John Gray Blount in North Carolina for help in realizing as much as possible from William Blount's depleted estate. Even his family did not perhaps fully appreciate the affection and confidence the people had reposed in the Governor of the Territory South of the River Ohio, who is regarded with respect in Tennessee to this day. A simple marble slab covers his grave

in the churchyard of the First Presbyterian Church, en-
graved simply with the words: William Blount, died 1800,
age 53 years. John Gray Blount had written from North
Carolina to Willie Blount in Knoxville:

> As that is a new country the face of which will be in a
> few years totally changed I hope you will procure to be
> engraved on some lasting stone his name, age, etc., which
> will for a time point out the place of his interment.

CHAPTER THREE

The Founding of a City

When we think of a planned city, we remember Philadelphia, the brain child of William Penn, or Washington, the beautiful realization of L'Enfant's plan. We certainly do not at once think of Knoxville, Tennessee. Yet this, too, was a planned city, with a name, a drawing for lots, and even a newspaper established before the first house was built within its limits.

It was in 1785 that James White, a quiet, staunch Presbyterian of Iredell County, North Carolina, brought his family and household goods across the mountains, down the French Broad and Holston rivers, to near the site of Knoxville. James White had been here before. Two years earlier he had crossed the mountains in company with three friends and North Carolina neighbors, Robert Love, James Connor, and Francis Ramsey. They had found the spot where the Holston and the French Broad rivers join, and

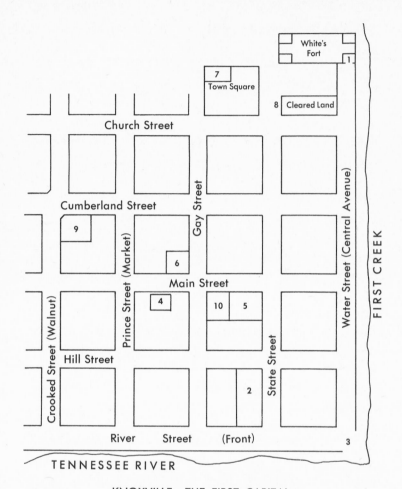

KNOXVILLE—THE FIRST CAPITAL

1—House built by James White, 1786. 2—Blount Mansion, built by William Blount, 1792. 3—Site of Blount's Treaty, 1791. 4—Blockhouse, 1793. 5—Court House. 6—First store on Gay Street (Cowan). 7—Blount College, 1794. 8—First Presbyterian Church and cemetery, on first land cleared by James White in 1786. 9—Sevier–Park House, built by John Sevier but never occupied by him. 10—Jail.

felt that this beautiful country was the very place to live in peaceful solitude. Back across the mountains they went to prepare for the move. Isolation would be complete—they must take with them everything they would need which they could not make for themselves. And these necessities must be kept to a minimum, for the trip across the Appalachians must be made with pack animals, since the only roads to follow were the narrow Indian trails.

After living for a year at the forks of the rivers, and attending the Constitutional Convention of the State of Franklin, James White decided to leave his friends and move to the site of Knoxville. He selected a spot where a large creek flowed into the winding Tennessee River. Following the creek upstream, he built a cabin on a wooded hill above it, and set about clearing land to plant his first crop. This first small plot of cleared land was planted in turnips, for thus the family was assured of an immediate crop of greens from the turnip tops and a root crop that would keep well through the winter. With wild game and fish so plentiful, they fared well from the first. James White had chosen wisely. His land was fertile, his water supply assured, his way of life well-suited to his new homeland.

This land on which White built his cabin and sowed his turnips was part of a large tract which he had purchased from the State of North Carolina under a land act of 1783. He probably knew that the lands directly across the river had been reserved by that law for the Cherokee Indians and that the Cherokee towns were only twenty-five miles away. However, the small cabin on the creek bank did not appear a threat to the Cherokee, and they left it alone.

But the settlers who were coming into the Tennessee country in ever-increasing numbers did not leave James

White alone. They agreed with him that he had found an ideal spot in the wilderness and insisted upon settling near him. Accordingly, the kindly White rebuilt his original cabin into a crude fort for the protection of his family and neighbors, and built for himself a small tub mill on the creek bank near the fort to grind meal from the corn which was the settlers' staple crop. This mill was the first evidence of industry in the new country.

James White would have been content to leave matters thus, but history decreed otherwise. In 1790, William Blount of North Carolina had been appointed governor of a new federal territory. North Carolina had ceded her lands west of the mountains to the federal government in payment of her Revolutionary War debt, and the federal government had organized these lands as the Territory South of the River Ohio. The governor of this territory was also to be superintendent of Indian affairs for the entire area west of the mountains and south of the Ohio. Settlers were moving in so rapidly that William Blount felt that the first thing his double duties required him to do was to conclude a treaty with the Indians which would define once and for all the boundaries of the lands owned by the government and open to settlement. A site for such a treaty meeting had to be found which would be close to the Indian towns on the Little Tennessee River, yet also accessible for Blount and his party; and it was necessary that there be some form of protection for the whites should the Indians who came to the treaty meeting prove unfriendly. White's Fort fulfilled these conditions exactly, and William Blount selected it as the spot for the important meeting with the Cherokee chieftains, at which James White's lands were at last legally acquired from the Cherokee.

Because the Treaty of Holston signed at this meeting was considered so successful, William Blount chose White's Fort as the site of the capital of the territory and planned a town to be built there. Of course, James White owned all the land on which Blount planned to build his capital city, but White agreed to sell the necessary ground, reserving certain portions of it for his own use.

The planning of the new town which would supersede White's Fort was to be a family affair for James White. In 1788, Charles McClung, a young man from Philadelphia, had journeyed south through Virginia to the Tennessee country. At White's Fort he had found much to admire, including particularly the eldest daughter of James White, Margaret, whom he married in 1790. He was commissioned by his father-in-law in 1791 to make a plan for the new capital of the Territory South of the River Ohio. He was first to survey the terrain, then to divide it into lots to be drawn for at a public lottery.

McClung laid out a town having sixteen blocks and sixty-four lots. It was bounded on the south by the river, and on the east by First Creek. The northern limit was the present Church Street, and it ended on the west at Crooked Street, which is now Walnut Street. The street along the river front was called with great logic River Street, while the street along the creek (Central Avenue) was Water Street. Included in this square were Hill Street, Main Street, and Cumberland Street; State Street, Gay Street, and Prince Street (Market Street). Some of these street names he borrowed from his former hometown, Philadelphia. Commons were reserved between First Creek and Water Street, and it was decreed that the boundary streets that marked the edge of the town (Church Street and Crooked

Street) should be very wide. That width was set at thirty-
three feet.

The lottery to determine the ownership of the sixty-
four half-acre lots thus created was held on October 3,
1791. The price of each lot was set in advance, and those
drawing the lots were requested to pay for them promptly,
on pain of a fine of five dollars. James White had retained
eight of the sixty-four lots for himself, and of these, he
gave one to the town to be used for a church. Considering
the character of James White, it was surely no accident
that the lot so designated for church use was the very one
which he had first cleared and which had been his turnip
patch. This lot, at the corner of State and Church streets,
is still occupied by the First Presbyterian Church, whose
churchyard was Knoxville's first cemetery. It seems particularly appropriate that James White who gave the land,
and William Blount who envisioned the city, both are buried there.

So well had Charles McClung surveyed and planned
the new town that he was asked by the Knox County Court
to survey a good road west from Knoxville to Campbell's
Station. He established his home, "Statesview," near the
western end of this road, and from it supervised the construction of this first good highway leading out of Knoxville, which is now called Kingston Pike. He also was one
of the commissioners who surveyed and marked the county's boundaries, and was a United States commissioner to
run the boundary line established by the Treaty of Holston.

Charles McClung's influence on Knoxville was not limited, however, to its actual physical appearance. He was
named clerk of the first Knox County Court in 1792 and
served as County Court Clerk until 1824. As a member of

the Constitutional Convention of 1796, he was chosen, with William Blount, to represent Knox County on the committee to draft the state's constitution and was one of Tennessee's first presidential electors in 1796, serving again in 1800. The first Territorial Legislature appointed him in 1794 one of the first trustees of Blount College, where his daughter Polly made history ten years later by entering as one of the nation's first five co-eds. All in all, it was most fortunate for Knoxville that James White's eldest daughter Margaret had chosen to marry a man who understood engineering and surveying. Presbyterian James White himself would probably have called it "providential."

Having arranged to acquire a lot at the corner of Hill and State streets as marked out on McClung's plan, William Blount proceeded to construct thereon his "Mansion," which was really the capitol of the territory, since he conducted his official business from the small office on the grounds of the house. The house was built in 1792, and in that year Knoxville became in fact as well as in name the capital of the Territory South of the River Ohio.

The name "Knoxville" had been given to the town before Charles McClung began to survey it, and the name itself was part of the plan. Blount had been appointed to the governorship of the territory by President Washington, but although federal territories were under the direct supervision of the State Department, it was the War Department that had charge of Indian affairs. President Washington's Secretary of War was Major General Henry Knox, a man who felt that the settlers in federal territories should be firmly controlled in their dealings with the Indians, in order that treaties with the Indians might be easier to make and to keep. It was therefore a very politic move on the part of William Blount to name the capital of the territory for his immediate superior in the realm of Indian affairs, in hopes of disposing General Knox more kindly toward the problems of the settlers.

In 1791, a newspaper was considered a mark of civilization and progress, and Blount was determined that his new capital city should have one. He therefore persuaded George Roulstone, a printer of Fayetteville, North Carolina, to move his press to the Tennessee country. Roulstone arrived across the mountains before the town of Knoxville was underway, so he set up his press first at Rogersville, where the first issue of the *Knoxville Gazette* appeared on November 5, 1791. This, too, was part of the plan; for the *Knoxville Gazette* was thus able to carry the result of the lottery for the town lots and to advertise the wares of Knoxville's first merchants as they appeared on the scene. In October of 1792, Roulstone and his press were established in Knoxville, where the *Gazette* was advertising J. Chisholm's tavern, Nathaniel and Samuel Cowan's stores in Knoxville and Jonesboro, and Charles McClung's "goods" for sale or trade.

These "goods" were coming into Knoxville by wagon, primarily from Virginia by way of Abingdon. There was considerable use of the river to transport the products of the town south and west, although Muscle Shoals made the use of the water route from Knoxville to New Orleans impractical for any but flat boats or rafts.

When he built his home in Knoxville, William Blount had every intention of building the finest house in the town. At great expense, and with great difficulty, he imported from North Carolina and Virginia materials for the

The First Presbyterian Church occupies the first cleared land in the Knoxville area, where the city's founder, General James White, planted his first crop of turnips in 1786. In its cemetery are the graves of James White, Hugh Lawson White, and William and Mary Blount.

Swan Pond, built about 1795 by Thomas Hope for Francis Ramsey, is one of the oldest houses in the area and has been restored by the Society for the Preservation of Tennessee Antiquities.

first two-story frame house west of the Great Smokies. Such an elaborate structure was most unusual in a frontier area, but from the beginning it was intended that Knoxville should be a city, and not just a frontier settlement. Although the remaining buildings constructed so hastily in 1792 were built of logs and "cat and clayed," or chinked with mud, frame and brick buildings were soon replacing them and Knoxville began to have the look of a real town.

As the capital of the Territory South of the River Ohio grew and prospered, log houses began to be considered beneath the dignity of its prominent citizens. After all, this was a spot where elegant building materials were easily available—the red clay soil was perfect for brick-making, fine marble was available for trimmings, field stones were plentiful and suitable for foundations and chimneys. The tall, straight forest trees of the Tennessee country were ideal for paneling, for wainscoting, for furniture making. There was no lack of materials or of skilled artisans, only a lack of design. This lack was remedied in large part by the arrival in Knoxville of Thomas Hope.

Thomas Hope was from County Kent in England. He had early proved himself a gifted woodcarver and cabinet maker and had been trained in London as an architect. He had come to Charleston, South Carolina, in order to plan and superintend the building there of a large house for Ralph Izard. He came with his family to Knoxville in 1794 and immediately began the building of a plantation home for Francis Ramsey at the Forks of the River, six miles east of the city. No doubt Thomas Hope was fascinated by the abundance and variety of building materials ready to his hand—this first of his Knoxville houses is built of blue limestone and red granite, in Gothic style. Was he homesick, in this empty countryside, for the ancient manor houses of England? Whatever influences were at work, Thomas Hope created a fine, sturdy "gentleman's house" for Francis Ramsey, and the owner christened it "Swan Pond." While supervising the building of the house, Hope lived on the estate in a log cabin, and further demonstrated his talents by making for "Swan Pond" an elegant tall secretary bookcase for the library and a "massive beaufet" for the dining room. In the fashion of the times, he carved elaborate cornices of wood for the house, painting them to resemble marble, although fine marble was being quarried only a mile away.

This house that he built for Francis Ramsey was such a splendid advertisement for his skills that Thomas Hope was in great demand among Knoxville's prosperous citizens to plan and construct their homes. Charles McClung secured his services for the building of "Statesview," ten miles west of the town at Ebenezer. Several years in the Tennessee country had left an impress on Thomas Hope, and he was developing a style less reminiscent of England and more specifically suited to this new land. "Statesview" he built of fine red brick, burned on the spot from the rich clay soil, and its lines were simpler and stronger than those of "Swan Pond." Within Knoxville itself, he planned a residence for Dr. Joseph C. Strong, at the corner of State and Cumberland streets. This house, too, was of red brick, and now Thomas Hope had learned to use real stone instead of painted wood for trimming. He was able also to execute some commissions for fine cabinet work while Knoxville was a-building—tradition has it that the mantel and wainscoting in the main room of the Chisholm Tavern were carved by his hand. Certainly he made the desk and furniture for the office of David Henley, War Department agent, in whose office Tennessee's Constitution was signed. Henley is commemorated in Knoxville by Henley Street and Henley Street Bridge.

Of course, not all the dignified houses built in the early days of Knoxville were planned by Thomas Hope. Most of them were built by well-trained slaves and artisans from plans in a book of architectural designs. But the influence of Thomas Hope was present even in the houses he did not build: his plain, uncluttered style, his use of beautiful red brick and white stone became the tradition of residential building for the Knoxville area.

In 1793, William Blount's diplomacy in naming the town for General Henry Knox paid off, for the War Department decided to build a blockhouse fort at Knoxville for the defense of the citizens from Indian attack. This blockhouse, located where the Court House now stands, was two stories tall and commanded a view of the opposite shore of the river for several miles. This substantial log building was large enough to house the small garrison sent to man the blockhouse and protect the town. It was surrounded by a stockade, within which the citizens of Knoxville could take shelter in case of Indian attack, and it boasted several small cannon, one of which was regularly fired at sunset and sunrise. All trees were cut down for several hundred yards around the fort on all sides, so that the view would be clear from the lookout and in order that no Indians might use the trees for cover in making an attack on the fort. Knoxville's citizens breathed easier with the coming of the federal troops, for, although the town was never actually attacked by the Cherokee, there were many alarms and several attacks on outlying stations in the area. The Indians continued to constitute a real threat to the settlers in East Tennessee until the time that they were removed to Indian Territory. The blockhouse itself served as the scene of social functions and governmental affairs as well as in its protective capacity. Here were held meetings of the first Territorial Legislature when it convened in Knoxville in 1794.

When the census of 1795 showed that the Territory South of the River Ohio had more than enough residents to entitle it to apply for statehood, Governor Blount ordered a convention to be held to draft a constitution for the new state. Excitement ran high—everyone knew that history was being made in Knoxville when the Constitutional Convention met there on January 11, 1796. The office of David Henley, at the corner of Gay and Church streets, was rented as a meeting place for the convention. On the second day of deliberations, the delegates "Resolved, that economy is an admirable trait in any government and that, in fixing the salaries of the officers thereof, the situation and resources of the country should be attended to." They then proceeded to reduce their own pay from the $2.50 set by the act providing for the assembly to $1.50 per diem!

Five delegates from each county had been elected to the Constitutional Convention, but it was seen at once that a smaller group would be better able to do the actual writing of the document. Then it could be discussed and voted upon by the entire group. Accordingly, a committee consisting of two delegates from each county was appointed to draft the constitution, with William Blount and Charles McClung appointed as the two members from Knox

County. Local tradition has always held that this committee gathered round a large table in the office of Governor
Blount at the Blount Mansion to do their work. That the
document echoed the phraseology of the constitution of
North Carolina was hardly surprising, since William
Blount had been a member of the earlier North Carolina
Constitutional Convention. Since several of the delegates
were former Pennsylvanians, it was natural that some provisions were borrowed from Pennsylvania's Constitution.

The constitution established Knoxville as the capital of
the new state until 1802, at which time the location of the
capital should be voted on again. Actually, with the exception of one day's session at Kingston in 1807, Knoxville
remained the capital until 1811, when the legislature set the
next meeting for the following year in Nashville. Once
more Knoxville was Tennessee's capital, in 1817–1818, but
the state's seat of government was destined to be located in
Middle Tennessee for reasons of geographical convenience,
first in Murfreesboro and later in Nashville, which was
designated Tennessee's permanent capital in 1843.

In 1793, Knoxville received her first internationally
famous and important visitors when Louis Philippe, then
the Duc d'Orleans, visited the city with his two younger
brothers. These sons of Louis XVI of France were then in
exile in the United States, and traveled widely about the
country. They were entertained at the Blount Mansion by
Governor Blount, and found accommodations for themselves and their retinue at the Chisholm Tavern. Years later,
when Louis Philippe had ascended the throne of France as
the Citizen King, he startled an American tourist from
Tennessee by remarking: "Tennessee—Ah, yes! Tell me,
do they still sleep three in a bed in Knoxville?"

In 1802, André Michaux, the great French naturalist, visited Knoxville on one of his botanical expeditions and left a brief description of the town itself:

The houses, in number about 200, are almost all, of wood. Although it has been built eighteen or twenty years, this little town has not yet any kind of establishment or manufactory, except some tanneries. Commerce, however, is brisker here than at Nashville. The stores, of which there are fifteen or twenty, are also better provided. The merchants obtain their supplies by land, from Philadelphia, Baltimore, and Richmond, in Virginia, and in return, send, by the same channel, the productions of the country, which they buy from the farmers, or take in exchange for their goods . . .

They also send flour, cotton, and lime, to New Orleans, by the river Tennessee; but this method is not much used, the navigation of this river being very much interrupted, in two different places, by shoals and rocks . . .

. . . Travellers, with their horses, are accommodated here at the rate of a dollar per day.

In 1853, the first real history of the Tennessee country was written by Dr. J. G. M. Ramsey, the son of the Francis Ramsey who arrived from North Carolina with James White in 1786 and who built his house "Swan Pond" at the Forks of the River. Because of the author's personal knowledge of persons and events in the Knoxville area, Ramsey's *Annals of Tennessee* is considered the definitive work on its early history. He sums up his chapter on Knoxville with these words:

It (Knoxville) became the seat of government of the state of Tennessee, and so continued to be for many years after. The sceptre has departed from her, but time, and change, and progress cannot deprive her of her ancient honors, nor make her less venerable for the proud associations that cluster round her early history. Here Chieftains of the Cherokee nation met Governor Blount in council, smoked the pipe of peace, and formed the Treaty of Holston;—here the pious White pitched his tent in the wilderness, lived his life in patriarchal simplicity and unostentatious usefulness; . . . Here too was born the infant Hercules—since become a giant—Tennessee. Tennessee looks back to Knoxville, and recognizes her as the home of her youth, and the fond centre of her hallowed recollections.

CHAPTER FOUR

John Sevier

In the Hall of Fame in the National Capitol in Washington, D. C. (not far from the statue of Sequoyah, the greatest of the Cherokee) stands the statue of the man who was the greatest Indian fighter of them all. His military prowess alone would have been enough to entitle him to a place in history, but fighting was only one of the things he did well. He was a pioneer in the best sense of the word; he was the first governor of the State of Tennessee; he was the first member of the United States Congress from the West; he was on an important mission for the President of the United States at the time of his death. His name was John Sevier.

John Sevier was born in the Shenandoah Valley of Virginia in 1745, and his first military service was as a captain of the King's troops in his native state. In 1772, he visited the new settlements on the Holston and Watauga rivers in upper East Tennessee, and he liked what he saw there. Back he came the following year with his wife, Sarah Hawkins Sevier, his parents and his brother to settle near the present site of Bristol, in an area which was governed by Virginia until 1779. About 1775, John and Sarah Sevier moved to the Watauga Settlement, located in the Indian country. A few years later, Sevier built for himself a cabin on the Nolichucky River which he called Plum Grove. Soon he was as much a part of the frontier country as the river itself, for he was known everywhere in the Tennessee country as "Nolichucky Jack." In spite of the honors he earned and received in later life, Nolichucky Jack he remained to the end. The very nickname tells a good deal about the man himself, for it was an affectionate one, used in friendship by the men of his time of high and low estate, and these were men who did not lightly proffer friendship. John Sevier was everybody's friend in the Watauga country, and he proved to be a good one.

The public career of Nolichucky Jack began with his election as one of the five commissioners of the Watauga Association. This was the first attempt at organized government in the new country, and John Sevier was therefore associated with the government of Tennessee from the very beginning. When the Revolutionary War began in 1775, the Watauga Association was reorganized and assumed the name "Washington District"—it was thus the first government division to be named for George Washington. John Sevier was a member of the District's "Committee of Public Safety," and later one of its representatives to a North Carolina convention. In this capacity he helped to frame the constitution of the very state from which he would later help to carve a new state.

But all the time that he was engaged on the one hand with the organization of a government for the new residents of the country west of the mountains, Nolichucky Jack was busy on the other hand protecting the residents from the original owners of the land. The Cherokee Indians were taking out their resentment against the encroaching settlers by attacking farms, setting up ambushes beside the narrow trails that led between the settlements, and making wild and savage attempts to destroy the settlements themselves. During one such raid occurred an incident that has been one of East Tennessee's favorite fireside stories during all the intervening years. The Cherokee, under their chief, Old Abraham, attacked the Watauga Settlement. As the Indians approached the fort, they surprised and almost surrounded Catherine Sherrill, a young white girl who was outside the stockade. As soon as she realized her danger, Catherine began to run toward the fort. She was very tall, and was sufficiently fleet of foot to outrun the Indians pursuing her, but she found her path to the gate of the fort blocked by another group of Indians. Turning swiftly to the right, she was able to scale the palisades of the fort with the aid of Captain John Sevier, who had been watching her frantic approach. A few years later Catherine Sherrill became Mrs. John Sevier after the death of Nolichucky Jack's first wife, Sarah Hawkins. As friendly and hospitable as her husband, Catherine Sherrill Sevier was greatly beloved and is still best known by the affectionate nickname "Bonny Kate."

It was in reprisal against Indian attacks of this kind that John Sevier made his several campaigns against the Cherokee during the Revolutionary War, burning the Indian towns and always coming off victorious in battle. From the Indians he learned new methods of fighting, well-adapted to the wild terrain, and from them he learned also the spine-chilling Indian warwhoop. By the end of the war, Nolichucky Jack had become the one man who was really respected and feared by the Cherokee.

After North Carolina had created Washington County in 1777, Sevier was appointed colonel of its militia. As the need for their aid arose, he sent his neighbors in several brief campaigns against the British and the Tories in western North Carolina. Because of the danger from the Indians at home, men were asked to volunteer for only one brief journey; as soon as the actual fighting was over, back they hurried to their real work of wresting farmland from the virgin forest and fending off marauding Indians.

In 1780, word reached Colonel Sevier that the British commander in North Carolina, Colonel Ferguson, was planning to cross the mountains and seize the frontier settlements, thus surrounding North Carolina and making possible easy British attacks on western Virginia. John Sevier and Isaac Shelby were the two colonels of militia in North Carolina's transmontine counties, and they arranged a meeting of volunteers for September 25 at Sycamore Shoals on the Watauga River. At this time the entire fighting population of this western district was less than one thousand men. When the appointed day dawned, it was found that every able-bodied man in the district had arrived at Sycamore Shoals! Shelby and Sevier agreed that it would never do to take with them all the available men, leaving the scattered homes entirely unprotected, so they arranged what was really the first military draft in United States history,

except that this was a draft in reverse—they conscripted
men to stay at home! Each colonel accepted only two hundred and forty volunteers, and with this small force they
started east to head off Ferguson's attack. They were joined
en route by Virginia troops under Colonel William Campbell and by other North Carolinians under Colonel Charles
McDowell. Steadman, who served under Cornwallis, says
of them:

> The enemy was composed of the wild and fierce in-
> habitants of Kentucky and other settlements beyond the
> Alleghenies, who had assembled from different places.
> . . . the men were well mounted on horseback, and each
> carried his own provisions in a wallet, and were not en-
> cumbered by wagons.

Goodspeed's *History of East Tennessee* has this to say of
them:

> Each man, each officer set out with his trusty Deck-
> hard (rifle) on his shoulder. A shot pouch, a tomahawk,
> a knife, a knapsack, and a blanket completed his outfit.
> The earth was his bed, the heavens his covering, the
> mountain streams gave him drink, and the forests yielded
> him food.

This was a force whose mobility was incomprehensible to
their British opponents, but it was from the Indians that
John Sevier had learned these lessons on how to travel
light in order to travel fast.

As the frontiersmen moved east across the mountains,
Ferguson retreated before them with his forces. Finally he
found a spot which he considered an advantageous one and
took up his position on an eminence which he named
"King's Mountain." To his horror, the mountain men did
not line up in proper battle array—they raised a blood-

curdling Indian warwhoop and attacked the mountain from all sides simultaneously! The wild and desperate fighting lasted only one hour, but it turned the tide of the Revolutionary War in the South. Ferguson was killed, and the baffled British troops surrendered unconditionally. The next morning, John Sevier and the mountain men were on their way home to see what the Cherokee had been up to in their absence.

After the Revolution was over, North Carolina determined on a plan to cede to the federal government all of her lands west of the mountains in return for cancellation of the state's debt to the federal government which had been incurred during the war. The North Carolina Legislature passed this Act of Cession in 1784, and most of the settlers west of the mountains were delighted. They had not been satisfied with their treatment at the hands of North Carolina, and they hastened to organize a government of their own, which they called the State of Franklin, hoping to be received into the federation of states when the population of the area was large enough. John Sevier was elected Governor of the State of Franklin, and excitement was high among its residents. At last they were going to run things in their own way—and they would see to it that there was protection from the Indians for every settlement and farmhouse in the region. Nolichucky Jack was the man to do it! But the happiness was short-lived, for this state of affairs did not suit North Carolina at all.

At the very time that the State of Franklin was being organized across the mountains, the General Assembly of North Carolina was busily regretting its hasty action in ceding this western territory to the federal government. North Carolina's legislators felt that the state had not been

adequately compensated for its expenses during the Revolution. Repealing the Act of Cession, the Assembly attempted to conciliate the Westerners by creating a new
Washington District for the Tennessee country, and to this
end they authorized courts for it and appointed John Sevier
as brigadier general of its militia.

Sevier himself was willing to accept this action of the
North Carolina Assembly, and he advised his neighbors to
abandon (at least temporarily) their plans to establish a
separate state. But even the influence of Nolichucky Jack
was not enough to change the minds of the men of the
Tennessee country, and they went right ahead with their
plans, tentatively adopting a constitution, establishing
courts, and making a treaty with the Indians. They appealed to Congress for admission to the Union, but the
Confederation government merely asked North Carolina to
repeat its cession.

When Governor Martin of North Carolina heard
news of all this, he sent a letter to John Sevier, asking what
in the world was happening in Washington District. An
official letter was sent back from the government of the
State of Franklin, then at Jonesboro, explaining what had
been done, and why. Governor Martin called an emergency
session of the North Carolina Legislature to consider the
problem, and issued a manifesto to the residents of North
Carolina's Washington, Sullivan, and Greene counties urging them to reaffirm their allegiance to North Carolina and
warning of dire consequences should they persist in trying
to form a separate state.

Even as the State of Franklin under its governor, John
Sevier, was establishing its new capital at Greeneville, the
North Carolina government was publishing proclamations

denouncing it. They stated that North Carolina desired to furnish proper civil government and proper representation for the counties across the mountains, and promised pardon for all those who would declare allegiance to North Carolina.

Many people considered it wise to return to the protection of North Carolina, but many others persisted in their efforts to establish the independent State of Franklin. For a time, the area had two conflicting governments, each making laws, issuing edicts, and holding courts. This conflict reached a climax in 1788, when John Sevier was leading an expedition against the Indians on the frontier.

Hearing of this, Governor Johnston of North Carolina issued an order to the sheriff of Washington County to arrest "John Sevier, who styles himself captain-general of the State of Franklin, (and) has been guilty of high treason, in levying troops to oppose the laws and government of the State . . . and . . . order him to be committed to the public gaol." In desperation, Sevier had also begun negotiations with the Spaniards at New Orleans in a final effort to save his "lost" state.

Some days later, Sevier was arrested, handcuffed, and taken across the mountains to Morganton, North Carolina, where a court was convened to try him for high treason. But the people of the Tennessee country had no intention of permitting Nolichucky Jack to be convicted of treason! Two of Sevier's sons, James and John, went with a few friends to Morganton, arriving singly and unnoticed among the crowds that had come to witness the trial. As court was adjourning in the evening, these friends created a diversion which attracted the attention of court officers and spectators. During the attendant confusion, John Sevier and his

sons rode out of Morganton and across the mountains beyond pursuit. Meanwhile, his old friend Colonel McDowell
had made bond for his release. The people of Morganton enjoyed this dramatic incident and sympathized with
it. Like the settlers across the mountains, they felt that John
Sevier was acting in the best interests of his neighbors no
matter what laws he might technically have been guilty of
breaking.

Although all hope of establishing a State of Franklin
was now abandoned, those who had supported the movement felt deep gratitude and admiration for its erstwhile
governor, Nolichucky Jack Sevier. In November, 1788,
North Carolina's General Assembly passed an act granting pardon to all those who had taken part in the Franklin
"revolt" *except John Sevier*, who was specifically barred
from any office of profit, honor, or trust in the State of
North Carolina. The very next year the people of Greene
County elected John Sevier to represent them in the Senate
of North Carolina. Nolichucky Jack had already arrived
in Fayetteville when the legislature convened November 2, 1789, but "on account of disabilities," he tactfully
delayed a few days before presenting himself to the Senate. During these days of waiting, the legislature repealed
the clause barring him from holding office, and reinstated
him as brigadier general for the western counties. Taking
his seat in the Senate of North Carolina, John Sevier voted
(of course) for the second cession in 1789 of the portion
of the state he represented. It is entirely possible that North
Carolina had found her western counties too hot to handle, for this time, in 1789, the legislature voted without
demur to give the western counties to the federal government—and this time they were not Indian givers!

The federal government itself was much better organized by this time and did not wait for the settlers to set up a form of government for themselves. The new lands were immediately organized as a federal territory and named as the Territory South of the River Ohio. The territory was placed under the jurisdiction of the State Department, and President Washington appointed William Blount as governor of the territory and supervisor of all Indian affairs south of the River Ohio. This could not have been very good news for the settlers, for they had never heard of William Blount, and they felt sure no one was so well qualified to deal with their problems as their old friend, Nolichucky Jack. Other people were more worried about the appointment of William Blount than was John Sevier —he was too busy. President Washington had appointed him Brigadier General of the Washington District militia, and he was keeping a sharp eye on the Indians. He had meanwhile been twice signally honored by the state that had once sought to try him for high treason. He was a member of the second convention called by North Carolina to consider ratification of the United States Constitution, and with his fellow delegates ratified the constitution on behalf of the state. Then, North Carolina having been divided for purposes of representation in the United States Congress into four congressional districts, John Sevier was elected to serve in the United States House of Representatives for the district comprising all of the counties west of the mountains. Thus he became the first member of Congress from the West, but had to resign when this district became a federal territory. He was now prepared to offer his assistance to William Blount in securing the best possible government for his friends and neighbors.

Governor Blount's first large item of official business was the conclusion of a treaty with the Cherokee, and he wisely asked John Sevier to act with him as one of the United States Commissioners at the Treaty of Holston. The advice of Nolichucky Jack would have been invaluable to Blount on this occasion. No man in the country knew more about the Cherokee, or better how to deal with them. His very presence at the treaty meeting was like a guarantee of safety to the Governor and the other settlers, for the Indians had a healthy fear of Sevier, who had learned to fight by their own methods and who had proved that he could beat them at their own game.

When Knoxville was selected as the capital of the Territory South of the River Ohio, John Sevier found himself spending more and more time away from Plum Grove, his home on the Nolichucky River. His advice and counsel were in great demand, but he was first and foremost the Brigadier General of the Washington District militia. In 1793, Nolichucky Jack made his last campaign against the Cherokee, and this final burning of the Cherokee towns impressed upon the Indians that it was best to let Nolichucky Jack, and his friends, alone. As a man already experienced in affairs of government, John Sevier was chosen one of the members of the upper house of the Territorial Legislature in 1794, and he was appointed by his fellow legislators to be one of the original trustees of Blount College which was chartered by the legislature.

Then in January, 1796, the Territory South of the River Ohio held a convention which drafted a constitution for the State of Tennessee. John Sevier, busy with military duties, was not a delegate. But since he had been a member of the Constitutional Convention of North Carolina, he no doubt sat in the office of Governor Blount to discuss with him the provisions of a constitution for the new state. Perhaps they discussed the new public offices to be filled. Without waiting for Congress to admit the new state, the Tennesseans adopted what became known as the "Tennessee plan" (recently copied by Alaska) and organized the state government months before it officially became a state on June 1, 1796.

Now that the people were allowed to choose their own governor, there was no doubt of their choice. Sevier they would have for the head of the government at home, and Blount should represent them in the East. So, although the rosy future predicted for the State of Franklin came to naught, John Sevier was governor of the new state when it entered the Union after all. The only difference was that its name was not Franklin, but Tennessee, which was the Cherokee name for a town on a branch of the great river that crossed and recrossed the domain.

Since Knoxville, which had been the capital of the Territory South of the River Ohio, was named the first capital of the State of Tennessee, it was necessary for the Seviers to move to the capital city upon his election as governor. This was no mean undertaking, for there were seventeen young Seviers, though at the time of the move several of the older children were grown and no longer living at home. Other men who came to Knoxville to make their homes were anxious to buy lots within the town as it had been laid out, so that they might have mutual protection from the Cherokee who, in spite of the Treaty of Holston, were entirely too close for comfort. Not John Sevier. He alone of all the newcomers built his house across the river from the town itself, five miles in the direction of the

Cherokee villages on the Little Tennessee River. This home
he built was much like the one he had left on the Nolichucky—it was of log construction and consisted of one
very large room with a sleeping loft above and a lean-to
kitchen. This was a far cry from the elegance of the Blount
Mansion within the town, but each of these early gover-
nors built the type of house that seemed suited to his needs.

Three times in succession his friends elected Nolichucky Jack for a two-year term as governor. The constitution Sevier had helped to frame limited any man's con-
secutive terms in this office to three, so someone else had
to be elected in 1801. Archibald Roane, a brilliant and well-
educated lawyer, thereupon became Tennessee's second
governor, serving from 1801 to 1803. Then there was no
reason why John Sevier could not be governor again, for
another three terms if he and the people saw fit. Everybody agreed that this was a good idea—everybody, that is,
except Archibald Roane who liked being governor and
decided to run for a second term himself.

The supporters of Roane agreed that the only way to
overcome the tremendous personal popularity of Nolichucky Jack was to discredit him in some way that would
make him unacceptable to the voters. They hit upon the
same tactics that had been successful in removing William
Blount from the United States Senate, and they publicly
accused John Sevier of dishonest dealings in public lands.
Roane's advisers overlooked one thing. The people of Tennessee had not believed the charges against William Blount.
They did not believe the charges against John Sevier, either. This was the same Nolichucky Jack that they had
elected to the North Carolina Senate in the face of charges
of treason against him, and they elected John Sevier to a

fourth gubernatorial term by a large majority. Archibald Roane was both out of luck and out of office.

Yet the campaign left its scars. Bitter and acrimonious things had been said on both sides, and men who had been friends ended up as enemies. Andrew Jackson, at this time Superior Judge for East Tennessee, had supported Roane in the election and had supplied him with the evidence on which the land fraud charges were based. Shortly after Sevier's inauguration, while Jackson was holding court in Knoxville, the two men met in the public square. Sevier violently denounced Jackson to his face for his part in the campaign; the fiery Jackson replied in the same vein. James Phelan's *History of Tennessee* describes the encounter:

The two men had many points in common. Both had a gracious and winning suavity of speech and gentleness of manner when calm. Both were subject to frantic outbursts of fury. And both, when enraged, were like madmen. They stormed. They blustered. They swore loud and boisterous oaths. Their faces and lips grew white. Their eyes glistened like melted glass. And like wild beasts, the first impulse of each was to strike, to wound, to tear. But each had also a reserve of prudence that was rarely extinguished even in the most violent paroxysms. Jackson's anger flamed out at (a) reference to his wife, and he made desperate efforts to reach Sevier, but was restrained. Jackson, seeing his antagonist with a drawn cutlass, and having only a cane himself, prudently yielded to the remonstrances of the bystanders. The next day, he sent a challenge. Sevier returned a mocking reply, accepting for any time and place "not within the State of Tennessee." Jackson insisted on the meeting taking place in the neighborhood of Knoxville, since the insult had been passed here. Sevier declined. "I have some respect," said he, "for the laws of the State over which I have the honor to preside, although you, a judge, appear to have none." Charges and counter-charges were hurled back and forth, verbally and in writing. Jackson suggested several times and places for the duel, Sevier refused them all, not even opening Jackson's letters. Jackson went to Southwest Point, near Knoxville, at the time he had appointed in one of his letters to meet Sevier, but Sevier did not come. On the way back to Knoxville, Jackson and his party met Sevier riding with a group of friends.

Enraged, Jackson charged upon him with his cane. Sevier dismounted. Pistols were drawn. But Jackson had lost all stomach for the fight, and Sevier had never had any. Friends interfered. After some wrangling, an indifferent peace was patched up between them . . . Sevier had seventeen children alive. Sevier's death at Jackson's hands meant also Jackson's death at the hands of Sevier's sons, who were proud, brave, and devoted to him. This undoubtedly had much to do with the hair-splitting niceties of the correspondence by which a meeting was successfully evaded.

These two men were so much alike that it was a case of "flint striking flint."

After the excitement of the election of 1803 had subsided, John Sevier went right ahead, as everyone had expected, serving another three successive terms as governor. Being the governor of Tennessee was really a much easier task in those days than it is today, for there was very little business, and almost no public money to administer. In all the years that the state capital remained at Knoxville, the thrifty East Tennesseans never felt it necessary to construct a special building for the state capitol. The capitol was the governor's house, and often his office was his pocket where he kept any official papers he had on hand. Wisely, John Sevier never attempted to live as governor in the same style that had characterized the administration of his predecessor, William Blount. He knew that his frontier neighbors and friends expected of him unfailing hospitality, but hospitality of a simple and unfeigned kind that they could accept without embarrassment. The Seviers continued to live in the log house five miles from Knoxville during part of his term of office, but this was really rather inconvenient, and there is a tradition that he lived for some time in a house on Central Avenue. He also began the building of a brick residence at the corner of Cumberland and Crooked (Walnut) streets in Knoxville. It was a handsome house, but it was still unfinished at the time of John Sevier's death. Occupied for many years by the Park family, it is now the property of the Knoxville Academy of Medicine and houses an interesting small medical museum of early day medical instruments and paraphernalia.

It is possible that, having served six terms as governor of his state, Nolichucky Jack felt in 1811 that it was time for a change. Anything he wanted was perfectly all right with the voters of Tennessee, who happily elected him to the United States House of Representatives. Re-elected in 1813, he served during both of his terms in Congress on the military affairs committee of the House of Representatives. This was an important committee post, for the War of 1812 against the British was in progress, and the hero of the Battle of King's Mountain was a natural choice for such a position. So able did he prove himself as a member of the Congress, and so wide was his fame as a man who knew all there was to know about Indians, that President Monroe appointed him in 1815 to a very important special government mission.

Andrew Jackson, who had become a military hero dur-

ing the War of 1812, had just completed his famous campaign against the Creek nation of Indians in Alabama. In
the treaty of peace that ended the Creek War, a boundary
was agreed upon, but was unmarked. For the task of running the boundary line and marking it unmistakably, President Monroe felt that John Sevier was the very man.

In the late summer of 1815, Nolichucky Jack, with a
detachment of United States Army troops, set out for the
last time to protect the rights of settlers against the Indians. Shortly after his departure, he was elected to a third
term in the Congress. This news never reached him, for
on September 24, at the Indian town of Tuckabatchie, John
Sevier died suddenly of a fever. He was buried near Fort
Decatur, Alabama, by his soldiers, who erected a cairn of
stones above the spot on the banks of a slow-moving stream.
For more than eighty years, Tennessee's first governor lay
in an isolated grave in another state.

It wasn't that the people of Tennessee had forgotten
John Sevier—not at all. He was a legend in his own state,
and people still talked about him, described him to their
children. He was a tall man, they said, well built, blue-eyed
and fair skinned, with firm, chiseled features. He walked
rapidly; he claimed to be the best rider in the country and
spent much time on horseback to prove it. The force of
his personality was such that people, seeing him for the
first time, said to themselves: "This must be Nolichucky
Jack." His was a natural dignity that was the result of ability and accomplishment, and he was a great man for a
state to claim as her first governor.

In 1897, the legislature of Tennessee appropriated
funds to remove the body of John Sevier from its secluded grave in Alabama and inter it on the Court House

lawn at Knoxville. A special train, bearing dignitaries of the state and the city, went to Alabama and returned with the flag-draped casket. The ceremonies were the most elaborate that Knoxville had ever seen, but there was about them a simple dignity that would have pleased the man they honored. He would have been pleased, too, with the fact that his final resting place is the Court House Square in the heart of town, for John Sevier was always a man who liked to be in the center of whatever was going on.

CHAPTER FIVE

✿ *Hugh Lawson White*

It is a common fallacy to think of a man who is well known in history as having moved through the great events of his life and his times alone. Rarely do we picture such heroes against the background of a wife and children. We say: "In 1786, *James White* arrived from North Carolina to build a log house on the present site of Knoxville." We can imagine the house, and the brave pioneer, James White; but we find it impossible to people the imaginary wilderness with Mrs. White and the children. Yet they were there. And from this shadowy background of the founding of the city emerges the figure of a man who was to be perhaps Knoxville's most brilliant citizen: James White's son, Hugh Lawson White.

Born in North Carolina in 1773, Hugh Lawson White was twelve years old when he came with his father to the Tennessee country. Surely his enthusiasm had been fired by the glowing accounts of his father and the friends who accompanied him on a trip of exploration two years earlier. For a boy of twelve, this removal of the family to the very edge of Indian territory would have been adventure unexcelled! The next year, at thirteen, he probably was old enough to help with the actual construction of the log house his father raised on the bank of First Creek. Undoubtedly he helped construct the other cabins and the stockade that turned the family home into White's Fort the following spring. It might even have been the hand of Hugh Lawson White that guided the plow over the first cleared land in the area—the "turnip patch" where the First Presbyterian Church now stands, and in whose churchyard James White and Hugh Lawson White himself are buried. Here, then, was a boy who was helping to make the exciting kind of history that was to be the Tennessee country's heritage.

James White was a busy man as White's Fort was taking shape. He had enough to do, it would seem, clearing the land, building shelters for his family and the settlers who persisted in joining him, raising a crop, erecting a tub mill, fending off the Indians, and so on. But James White was also a family man, with responsibilities along that line, too. Here was Hugh Lawson, growing up in frontier country where there were no schools. The boy was obviously possessed of a brilliant mind, and something had to be done about his education.

Fortunately for the Whites, father *and* son, one of the first persons to settle in the vicinity of White's Fort was the Reverend Samuel Carrick, a Presbyterian divine, who was a preacher of note and the possessor of a classical education, and who was destined to become an educator of

distinction. At the age of fifteen, Hugh Lawson White be-
gan the study of Latin and Greek with the Reverend Dr.
Carrick, and an apt pupil he proved indeed. In order to receive instruction, it was necessary for the boy to live in
Dr. Carrick's home during the winter months, for Dr. Carrick had taken up a grant of land several miles east of
White's Fort, where he was pastor of "Lebanon in the
Forks," the first Presbyterian Church in this part of Tennessee. It is a tribute to all three—to James White, to
Hugh Lawson, and to Dr. Carrick himself—that under
such circumstances they embarked upon an educational
plan of such scope and difficulty. In his capacity of minister, Dr. Carrick was often away from home preaching to
groups of settlers in widely scattered new settlements.
When this occurred, Hugh Lawson White worked with
yet another well-qualified tutor, whose name was Archibald Roane. Archibald Roane was a young lawyer, a graduate of Dartmouth College, who had come to carve a place
for himself in this brand-new country. He was living about
twelve miles west of White's Fort, and since there were as
yet few courts to require his talents as a lawyer, he was
available to assist in the education of Hugh Lawson White.
Roane was regarded by his contemporaries as the best educated man in the territory, and James White must surely
have been pleased that two such able teachers were present
and willing to supervise the classical education of his brilliant son.

All three of the persons directly involved in the education of Hugh Lawson White played an important part
in the history of Knoxville and of Tennessee. Dr. Carrick
organized the First Presbyterian Church of Knoxville,
preached the opening sermon of the first Territorial Legis-

lature, and was the first president of Blount College (which is now The University of Tennessee). Archibald Roane was one of the ablest lawyers Tennessee has produced, serving also as a district judge in Knoxville and as the second governor of the State of Tennessee. As for Hugh Lawson White, that is a longer story.

During these early years of Hugh Lawson White's growth and training, John Sevier was carrying on his various campaigns against the Cherokee. Sevier lived five miles south of White's Fort, across the river in the direction of the Indian territory. He was an impressive figure, the man most greatly admired by Indians and settlers alike. It is hardly surprising that any young man of the area would want to be identified with him. Hugh Lawson White, unlike his father, was not of a soldierly disposition, but the romantic appeal of Indian fighting was strong. When John Sevier was gathering a group of volunteers to accompany him on what was destined to be his last campaign against the Cherokee, Hugh Lawson White was one of those who volunteered. He served as Sevier's aide and was by his side when the band of settlers moved against the Cherokee town of Etowah. Sevier reported later that the great chief of the Cherokee, King Fisher, was leading the Indian defense of the town, and that when Chief King Fisher was killed by a bullet from the gun of one of the settlers, the Cherokee were so frightened and disorganized that they fled to the forest, abandoning the town.

What Sevier did not report was that the bullet which killed Chief King Fisher came from the gun of Hugh Lawson White, who was not a soldier and who had no stomach for killing. After the rout of the Indians from the town, Sevier ordered Etowah burned and its ashes scattered, as a lesson to the Indians that the white men would stand for no more attacks upon their towns. The death of King Fisher at his hand and the subsequent scene of the burning of the town were shocking and horrifying to sensitive young Hugh. So ashamed was he of his part in the battle that he never thereafter discussed it, nor allowed it to be mentioned in his presence. Sevier's young aide had discovered that whatever his future career was to be, it would have nothing to do with fighting.

By the time he was twenty, Hugh Lawson White had completed his education at the hands of Samuel Carrick, Archibald Roane (and John Sevier). He was ready to put this education to use. Accordingly, about 1793, he became private secretary to Governor William Blount, who was directing the business of the Territory South of the River Ohio from the Blount Mansion in Knoxville. White's Fort had become the capital of the territory and was rapidly growing into the town Governor Blount had in mind when he established his home there in 1791. For a year, Hugh Lawson White handled the official correspondence of the territory, and then decided that he needed further education.

In 1794, he journeyed north to Philadelphia, where he spent a year in the study of practical and higher mathematics. Then, before returning home, he went to Lancaster, Pennsylvania, for a year of intensive study of the law. Feeling at last that he was qualified to make his way in the world, Hugh Lawson White returned to Knoxville in 1796 to enter the practice of law. He proved to be an able lawyer, and so distinguished himself in the profession that after five years he was elected a judge of the state's highest court. He served as superior judge for six years, resigning in 1807 to enter the field of politics as a State senator.

By the time Hugh Lawson White retired from the State Senate in 1809, the court system of the state was in the process of revision. A State Supreme Court was created, and Hugh Lawson White was promptly appointed one of the justices, which position he held until 1814, when he resigned the office.

It was not that Judge White did not like the law, or that he disliked being a judge; he had embarked upon a new career for which his education had peculiarly fitted him. In 1811, the Bank of the State of Tennessee had been established as one of the great series of banks handling the financial affairs of Tennesseans during this period, and Hugh Lawson White had been elected president of the state bank although he was serving on the State Supreme Court at the time. For three years he managed to fill both positions, but in 1814 he resigned from the court in order to devote his full time to the bank, which he considered to be his primary duty. Because of his financial genius, the bank prospered under his direction, and he served as its president until 1827.

What was happening meanwhile to the town where Hugh Lawson White had helped his father clear the first land and build the first house? With its industry, its trade, and its outlying farms, Knoxville was growing and changing with the times. New residents were attracted to the little city because it offered, along with the beauty of its situation and the mildness of its climate, excellent business and educational opportunities.

Knoxville had become the first capital of the State of

Tennessee almost automatically, since it was already the capital of the Territory South of the River Ohio, and it had continued as the capital until 1812, except for one day in 1807, when the Legislature met in Kingston. In the absence of any actual building to house the state government, the capitol had actually been the home of its governor, whoever the governor happened to be. Space was rented for the meetings of the State Legislature in the blockhouse at Knoxville and later in the Knox County Court House. This simple arrangement worked very well during the terms of John Sevier and Archibald Roane, but it was felt to be a little old-fashioned in 1812 during the third term of Willie Blount (William's half-brother) as governor.

The capital moved to Nashville in 1812, but returned to Knoxville for two years, 1817–18, before going to Murfreesboro. By this time farms and towns were dotting Middle Tennessee, and even West Tennessee, acquired from Indians in 1818, was building up. West Tennessee's delegates to the legislature had to ride for weeks over muddy, well-nigh impassable roads to reach the sessions in Knoxville. People in the western portions of the state began to say that if the State of Tennessee did in reality extend from the Great Smokies to the Mighty Mississippi, then her capital should in all logic be located about halfway between the two.

So Tennessee's peripatetic capital had been on the move among Knoxville, Kingston, Nashville, and Murfreesboro from 1796 until 1826, when it settled back once more in Nashville. It had moved irretrievably to the central section of the state in 1818 and was finally officially located in Nashville in 1843.

Of course, Knoxvillians did not like the idea of giving

In 1897, the body of John Sevier was brought home from an isolated grave in Alabama and interred here on the Court House lawn. The smaller monuments are to his wives, Sarah Hawkins (left) and Bonny Kate (Catherine Sherrill).

The Sevier-Park House, built by John Sevier while he was Tennessee's first governor, is responsible for the jog in Walnut Street that earned it the early name of "Crooked Street."

The Tennessee School for the Deaf now owns the house built about 1815 by Melinda White Williams and her servants as a surprise for her husband.

up the distinction of being the state's capital, and even as late as 1840 there was a strong movement afoot to bring the capital back to East Tennessee. But in the early days, there was only the distinction to be considered. There was no expense involved in moving the capital, and no one in the chosen city really profited by having it located there except the innkeepers. Had they been touched in the pocket by the move, canny Knoxvillians would no doubt have fought harder to keep it.

The man in Knoxville whose judgment was most respected on all matters was Hugh Lawson White. Was he not the best educated man for states around? Had he not studied higher mathematics and the law? Had he not already been lawyer, judge, state senator, and president of the state bank? Did he not rejoice in the well-earned title of Hugh Lawson White the Just? If he were to say that the thing to do was to let the capital go, then his Knoxville neighbors were willing to take his word for it that it would be all right. Hugh Lawson White said just that. He reminded his neighbors that it would be much fairer for everyone if the capital were placed where it would be equally accessible to all parts of the state. He reminded them, too, that Knoxville did not have to be the capital of Tennessee in order to be a distinguished city. She was that already—the educational and cultural center of East Tennessee, and the center of trade and industry for a very large area which included parts of other states. So, somewhat reluctantly, and with an occasional backward glance, the capital of Tennessee moved west.

His neighbors had good reason to call their distinguished fellow citizen Hugh Lawson White the Just. They were fond of reminding each other that it had been he,

brought up in a staunch Presbyterian household, and educated by a Presbyterian minister, who had given the ground
and much of the money for the new little Methodist
Church built in 1816 on Hill Street, the first of its denomination in strongly Presbyterian Knoxville.

As early as 1820, Banker White began to talk of re-
tiring. His health, he said, was poor. But a man of his capa-
bilities simply could not be spared. In 1821, while he was
still president of the Bank of the State of Tennessee, he was
appointed by President James Monroe to be one of the
three commissioners of claims for the transfer of Florida
from Spain to United States rule. This was another kind of
court, where claims against the United States government
arising out of the treaty provisions were heard and settled,
and the legally and financially astute Hugh Lawson White
was a splendid choice for it.

In 1825, Banker-Commissioner White, his work on the
Claims Commission completed, was elected to serve in the
United States Senate. He replaced Andrew Jackson, with
whom he had become well acquainted during the years
when both of them were lawyers and judges in Knoxville.
White served his constituents well in the Senate—everyone
in Tennessee knew him as well-educated, wise, and honest.

In 1835, Andrew Jackson's second term as President
of the United States was drawing to a close. He was anxious
that his policies should be carried out by his successor and
decided that Martin Van Buren was the man who should
follow him. This high-handed decision was not well received in the South, where it was thought that the Presidency should be occupied by one man for no more than
two terms, and that no president should attempt to influence the voters who were choosing the next president.

Nowhere were these sentiments more strongly held than in Andrew Jackson's home state. Accordingly, the General Assembly of Tennessee passed resolutions formally nominating for the Presidency of the United States Hugh Lawson White. A storm of protest arose from Jackson and James K. Polk, who had been White's close friends and political associates; White himself held the same view as the men who had nominated him, and he agreed to make the race. Senator White had little chance of actually being elected President of the United States, and he knew it. He consented to be a candidate for the office in order to make clear his stand upon a matter of principle. He and his principle were both approved by the people of his state, for in the election, in spite of the bitter opposition of all the party leaders within the State of Tennessee, Presidential Candidate White carried his state in 1836 by a majority of ten thousand votes. In 1836 in Tennessee, a ten-thousand vote majority was astounding.

It was over a matter of principle again that Senator White and the Legislature of Tennessee finally disagreed. He had not resigned his seat in the United States Senate in order to be a candidate for president, and thus was still a senator from Tennessee in 1839.

The General Assembly of Tennessee contended that, in the United States Senate, the representatives from Tennessee were chosen by the State Legislature, and, therefore represented the state itself rather than the people of the state. The legislature then undertook to instruct the state's United States senators how to vote. This was a point of principle upon which Hugh Lawson White's feelings were very clear. Government in the United States was by and with the consent of the governed. He was representing the people of Tennessee, and only them. To make his point clear to the people, he resigned his office and published his reasons for so doing. Then at last, in 1840, twenty years after he had first wished to do so, Hugh Lawson White retired from public life and returned to Knoxville to live. As it turned out, he never did really retire, for he had barely arrived in Knoxville when on April 10, 1840, Hugh Lawson White died.

Did he then do all these things by himself? Who was with him while he was lawyer, judge, state senator, bank president, claims commissioner, presidential candidate, and United States senator? The drama of the public career of Hugh Lawson White was played against a somber background of tragedy in his private life.

In his early youth, while he was a student living in the home of the Reverend Dr. Samuel Carrick, Hugh Lawson White first met his future wife. Elizabeth Carrick was the very attractive and intelligent daughter of his teacher, and the match was an eminently suitable one. In 1798, when they were married, Dr. Carrick was president of the newly opened Blount College and pastor of several Presbyterian churches, including the First Presbyterian Church in Knoxville. He was a citizen greatly admired and respected. James White, Hugh Lawson's father, having sold the property on which the town of Knoxville was built while retaining his remaining land-grant acres, was one of the wealthiest and most influential citizens in the new State of Tennessee and held the rank of general in the state's militia. Hugh Lawson and Elizabeth White were well born and well educated, and their future looked bright.

They became the parents of twelve children, of whom two died in infancy. The White children inherited their

Above: The Craighead-Jackson House, built in 1818, houses the Toms Memorial Collection of fine furniture and silver.

Below: Knoxville's oldest house continually occupied as a residence was built in 1823 by Drury P. Armstrong, and named "Crescent Bend."

Knoxville's City Hall occupies the building erected in 1848 for the Tennessee School for the Deaf. It was used as a hospital during the Civil War, first by the Confederates and later by the Union Army.

parents' intelligence and charm, but Elizabeth White was always delicate and so were her children. The eldest son, C. A. Carrick White, followed his father into the practice of the law, and people said that he might even be the better lawyer, so brilliant was his mind and so great his knowledge of legal principles. He was married and the father of two children when, in his middle twenties, his health began to fail. There was no cure in the 1820's for Carrick White's malady, which was "consumption." Elizabeth and Hugh Lawson White were crushed by the death at twenty-seven of this brilliant and promising son. His young widow, Nancy Park White, returned with her children to live in the house her father had bought unfinished from John Sevier, and the Hugh Lawson Whites journeyed to Washington where duties in the United States Senate awaited him.

But one by one the White children, just growing up or in their early twenties, fell ill with the dread tuberculosis, for which there was neither treatment nor cure. Eight young Whites died of it within a short six years, and with each death Hugh Lawson and Elizabeth White grieved the harder.

The journey to Washington on which Elizabeth White accompanied her husband several times was long and difficult. Because of the precarious state of her own health, Elizabeth carried with her on all her travels a small trunk which contained the clothes in which she wished to be buried, and it was on a return trip from Washington that the need for the trunk and its contents arose. The Whites were traveling by carriage, but a wagon followed loaded with the trunks and boxes that held their belongings. They halted for the night at Natural Bridge, Virginia, and in the morning, Elizabeth White was too weak to go on; it was there that, after several days of desperate illness, the delicate Elizabeth died. A coffin was procured, and servants brought from the wagon the trunk, whose packing she had supervised, so that she might be dressed in the burial clothes from the much traveled little trunk. It is said that Hugh Lawson White himself drove the wagon on which his wife's coffin was transported back to Knoxville, in order that in traveling the long, rough road the body of the gentle Elizabeth should not be "rudely shaken."

And now Hugh Lawson White, bereft of wife and all but two of his twelve children, was a desperately lonely man. He devoted himself anew to his duties in the Senate, remaining in Washington for long months at a time. After several years had passed, he was married to Mrs. Peyton, a charming widow in whose select boarding house lived many of the famous senators and representatives of the day.

When he returned to Knoxville to enter retirement in 1840, his wife, Ann Peyton White, accompanied him home. From his father, James White, he had inherited a "plantation" east of Knoxville and had built his home upon the eminence that was called Flint Hill. Knoxville welcomed its distinguished citizen with anticipation of entertainments renewed in the White home that had been visited so often by tragedy, but the greetings of old friends had hardly been offered when death came for Hugh Lawson White.

Although he was a man of strictest rectitude and uncompromising principles, Hugh Lawson White was affiliated with no church. He had never joined the Presbyterian denomination in which he was born and educated, nor the Methodist Church to which he had donated its first site within the city. His funeral was held at his home, and he was buried in the churchyard of the First Presbyterian

Church. This was a day when all of Knoxville mourned. Immediately behind the bier, his favorite horse, Rienzi, followed his master in the funeral procession. Then came the dignitaries of church and government, the judges, the members of the bar, the students of East Tennessee College of which he was a trustee, the school children of Knoxville, and the people. It was like going back in time as the cortege passed slowly through the thriving town, for Hugh Lawson White was going back to the first cleared land in Knoxville—land he had helped his father clear and plant before a city was imagined, and before there was any thought of a State of Tennessee. So back to the very spot where Knoxville began came the man who had watched its beginning and who had brought it honor with his exemplary career— Hugh Lawson White the Just.

CHAPTER SIX

The War Between the States

With the approach of the War Between the States, the people of East Tennessee found themselves torn by conflicting loyalties. They were Southerners, many of them slaveowners; but they were the descendants of John Sevier's mountain men who had fought for the independence of the Colonies, and they were not many generations removed from the men who had struggled for Tennessee's admission to the Union. They were convinced that the preservation of this Union, rather than the question of slavery, was the most important consideration.

Of course, many East Tennesseans, notably those large segments of the population that were of German or Dutch descent, objected to slavery on moral and religious grounds, but there were many more who opposed the secession of the State of Tennessee for reasons other than the dislike of slavery. In fact, almost all of the most prominent East Ten-

nessee Unionists were slaveholders themselves. For example, William Brownlow first achieved national prominence
in his Philadelphia debates with the Reverend Abram Pryne,
in which Brownlow defended the institution of slavery
with the same fiery oratory he later used in defense of the
Union.

If this attitude is difficult to understand, it is because
we have forgotten some important facts about East Tennessee. The actual terrain did not lend itself to a plantation-
type economy, and there were very few really large landowners. There were many more slaves in East Tennessee's
towns and cities than on her farms; the reverse, of course,
was true in most of the rest of the state. From the beginning, East Tennessee had industries, and slaves were not so
inexpensive nor so capable a source of labor as the white
workers who could be hired by the owners of mills, mines,
and foundries. This meant that the slaves owned by East
Tennesseans were principally house servants or skilled artisans who worked alongside their masters in trade or business. There was therefore a very close relationship between
master and servant in this section of the South.

It was because of this unusual set of circumstances that
Tennessee, after her secession, raised 100,000 troops for the
Confederate Army but also sent 30,000 volunteers into the
Union Army. Goodspeed's *History of Tennessee* says of
these Union volunteers:

> . . . unlike the volunteer from the Northern states,
> the Union soldier from Tennessee was not tempted to
> enlist by a munificent state bounty, nor impelled by the
> force of public opinion, but on the contrary, to do so, he
> was forced to escape from an enemy's watchful guard at
> night, and leaving his home and all he held dear to the

mercy of a hostile foe, make his way across the bleak and cheerless mountains to the Union camps in Kentucky.

The intensely patriotic people of East Tennessee, whose enthusiastic response to the call for volunteers in the Mexican War had earned Tennessee her title of the Volunteer State, found themselves in a very strange position at the outbreak of hostilities. After the fall of Fort Sumter, President Lincoln's call for troops, and Tennessee's secession, Andrew Johnson who was elected from this district was the only senator of a seceded state left in the United States Congress. Tennessee had left the Union as a result of an election held on June 8, 1861, to determine whether or not Tennessee would declare its independence and join the Confederacy.

Andrew Johnson, Thomas A. R. Nelson, William G. Brownlow, Connolly F. Trigg, and Horace Maynard were the acknowledged leaders of the Unionist sympathizers in Tennessee. All of them were from the eastern portion of the state, and four of the five were from Knox County. One month before the scheduled state election on the question of secession, a convention was held in Knoxville which was attended by delegates from all the counties of East Tennessee. This convention adopted strong resolutions opposing both secession and the support of the Confederacy.

At the June election, however, the eastern district of the state was outvoted by Middle and West Tennessee, and the State of Tennessee left the Federal Union and joined the Confederacy. Even in 1861, the City of Knoxville and Knox County were not seeing eye to eye in the matter of politics. At this time, the vote within the city favored secession, but the vote of the county was overwhelmingly in favor of remaining within the Union. This same divergence of opinion exists today, the city consistently voting Democratic, the county regularly voting Republican.

Three days after this election (in which 32,962 votes were cast by East Tennesseans to remain in the Union) Judge Nelson called the East Tennessee convention to meet again on June 17 at Greeneville, home of Andrew Johnson. This convention adopted a resolution appointing a committee to appear before the State Legislature ". . . asking its consent that the counties composing East Tennessee . . . may form and erect a separate state."

Although the legislature did not act upon this resolution, its presentation caused the Confederate authorities to realize that East Tennessee was a danger spot, and Confederate troops were at once dispatched thither. General Felix Zollicoffer was in command of these forces, and had his headquarters at Knoxville where the fairgrounds two miles west of the city had been made a Confederate military camp. It must be understood that not all East Tennesseans were Union sympathizers. At least one regiment of Confederate infantry and two regiments of Confederate cavalry were recruited in Knoxville and the surrounding area. Meanwhile, East Tennessee's Unionists were streaming into Kentucky to join the United States forces there.

A situation somewhat similar to this had existed in the extreme western portion of Virginia, where the overwhelming Union sentiment of the people made possible the formation of the new State of West Virginia which remained in the Federal Union. The sentiments of West Virginians and East Tennesseans were the same, but the situations were otherwise very different. While West Virginia had federal territory on three sides, East Tennessee was surrounded entirely by Confederate states except for a short section of Kentucky border. Had East Tennessee been permitted by the legislature of the state to form a government of her own, it is not likely that such a government could have survived for long. In the end, it was probably more advantageous to the Union forces to have East Tennessee in the Confederacy, a small but vigorous island of sympathy and aid for their cause.

However, two years went by before Union strategists took advantage of this situation in East Tennessee. Meanwhile, General Zollicoffer, who had lived in Knoxville for a time some years before while working as a journeyman printer, was finding the city a hotbed of dissension. There were prominent men on both sides of the struggle in Knoxville, and it was fortunate for all concerned that the commanding officer of the Confederate forces was a man who knew and understood the people and their problems. Jefferson Davis, President of the Confederate States of America, had ordered all citizens of East Tennessee to take an oath of allegiance to the Confederate government or leave the country by October of 1861. Many Unionists left; many took the oath without the slightest intention of being bound by it; many others categorically refused either to take the oath or to leave. In November of 1861, Union sympathizers burned five strategic East Tennessee bridges, but failed at Strawberry Plains. The Confederate government, abandoning its policy of trying to win over to the cause of the Confederacy the powerful opposition in the Knoxville area, placed the city under martial law and imprisoned many prominent Unionists suspected of having a hand in the burning of the bridges.

The residents of Knoxville were having an increasingly hard time as the war progressed. Both sides had predicted that the conflict would be of short duration, and everyone was dismayed and discouraged as weeks stretched into months, and months lengthened into years of war. Certain foodstuffs, which had formerly been imported from abroad, disappeared from the stores throughout the South. Stocks on hand in Knoxville of coffee, tea, and spices were gone early in 1861. Salt became so scarce that it was necessary to establish a Salt Agency to control its distribution, while the price of this most valuable commodity rose from two cents to thirty cents a pound, when available. Confederate military hospitals were opened in Knoxville by Dr. Francis Alexander Ramsey and Dr. Richard O. Currey, and for this purpose they commandeered the buildings of East Tennessee University, the Deaf and Dumb School, and the Court House.

It was not until June of 1863 that Colonel William P. Sanders of the Union Army came down from Kentucky to destroy the East Tennessee railroads that were supplying the Confederacy. He struck first at Lenoir City, capturing there a small Confederate force. He then turned toward Knoxville, his men destroying the railroad as they moved along it by tearing up gaps in the tracks, one mile apart.

The main body of Confederate troops stationed at Knoxville was absent at the time, and when word reached the city of Colonel Sanders' approach, it was necessary for the Confederates to attempt to defend Knoxville with the few volunteers they could muster. Hastily, they posted their eight cannon on Summit Hill, Mabry's Hill, and College Hill, expecting the attack to come from the west; but the Union troops skirted the city and attacked from the north. Colonel Sanders ordered his men to take shelter in houses, and sent out sharpshooters to pick off the Confederate artillerymen. Union artillery shelled the battery on Summit Hill, killing its commander, Colonel Pleasant Mc-Clung. Then, making no attempt to occupy the city, Colonel Sanders moved off in the direction of Strawberry Plains, destroying the railroad as he went.

Three months later, General Ambrose Burnside moved into Knoxville with 10,000 Union troops, which included four divisions of infantry and a troop of cavalry. In the face of such numbers, the Confederates made no attempt to prevent their taking the city, and the Union forces were deployed in all sections of the town, with headquarters in a house on Gay Street. General Burnside had decided to make Knoxville his headquarters in order to head off General Longstreet, who was moving north from Chattanooga with a large Confederate force. As Longstreet's men approached, there were sharp, though brief, engagements south and west of the city. General Burnside, on advice from General Grant's staff, determined to hold Knoxville at all costs. All Union troops were drawn back within the city, and artillery was placed on all the hills between College Hill and Summit Hill. On the bluffs south of the river, several forts were established. These forts consisted of earthworks, but their position and the cannon they had mounted formed a large part of the defense plan.

Since the city was to be protected on the south by this line of forts crowning the hills across the river, it was considered essential that a bridge be constructed at the mouth of First Creek which would connect these forts to the city proper, so that they might be supplied with food and ammunition. This bridge would serve, too, to bring in supplies from the farms lying south of the city in Knox County. Accordingly, engineers took up a pontoon bridge which had been built across the river at Loudon and, loading it on flatcars, transported it to Knoxville by railroad. No sooner was it placed in position at Knoxville than reports came in that the Confederates were constructing a heavy raft at Boyd's Ferry, a few miles up the river. They planned to float the raft downstream to destroy the pontoon bridge by ramming it. To prevent this, U. S. Army engineers stretched an iron cable across the river above the bridge, and this was augmented later by a boom of logs above the cable. Hearing of these defenses, the Confederates abandoned the idea of trying to attack the bridge from upriver.

On November 17, scouts reported that General Longstreet's army was advancing up the Kingston Pike. Preparations to defend Knoxville were nowhere near complete, so General Burnside decided upon a delaying action. General William Sanders (the same man who had previously destroyed the railroad and shelled the city) was a member of Burnside's staff, in command of a troop of cavalry. He was ordered to dismount his troops and move westward to meet Longstreet, skirmishing if necessary, to ensure time for the fortifications to be finished. Accordingly, at nightfall of the seventeenth, Sanders' men dug themselves in alongside Kingston Pike, near the residence of Robert H. Armstrong. Early on the morning of November 18, Confederate General McLaws arrived and took up a position directly in front of the house. Throughout the day, Sanders' men fiercely defended their position, knowing that each hour was of the utmost importance to General Burnside's engineers in completing their preparations. By three o'clock in the afternoon, however, McLaws' attack had become so determined that General Sanders, according to one account, rode forward to rally his men and to organize their retreat. A conspicuous figure on his snow-white horse, he was the target for a Confederate sharpshooter concealed in the tower of the Armstrong house. Mortally wounded, General Sanders was carried by his men into the city and taken to the best hotel, where he died the following day. General Wolford succeeded in withdrawing Sanders' forces safely into the city. On the night of November 18, General Sanders was buried by moonlight in the churchyard of the Second Presbyterian Church, with General Burnside and all the officers of his command present at the ceremony.

No lights were permitted at General Sanders' funeral, and no volley was fired over his grave, for on the morning of November 18, the siege of Knoxville had begun. General Longstreet's forces had completely surrounded the city, except for the south side which lay along the river. The position of the Union forces was serious, but the gallant delaying action of General Sanders had allowed the engineers to complete a fort just west of the city, which was promptly christened Fort Sanders in his honor. Built atop a steep hill, the fort was surrounded by a deep ditch. In front of the ditch, a network of telegraph wire was fastened to the sharpened stumps of trees and saplings which had been cut down to build the fort. As a further precaution, both First and Second creeks had been dammed by the engineers, thus flooding the low ground around them and providing protection from the east and from the west for the center of the town, which lay between the two creeks on high ground.

Realizing the extreme importance of the forts across the river, the Confederates ferried over a force of some thousand men in an attempt to gain control of these heights overlooking the city. They succeeded in taking only Cherokee Heights, which was located somewhat downriver from Fort Dickerson, their primary objective, but which was still close enough to be within cannon range of portions of the town. Placing an artillery battery there, the Confederates used this position to shell the city, slightly damaging the buildings of East Tennessee University which lay almost in range of the guns.

So, the position of the Union forces seemed serious when the siege of Knoxville began. The Confederates, in force, were blocking the north and west sides and had taken Cherokee Heights to close the south, but neglected to blockade the French Broad River to the east of the city. However, General Longstreet depended on an erroneous map which showed the French Broad joining the Holston below Knoxville. Knoxville was in the center of the area sympathetic to the Union cause, and staunch Unionist farmers lived along the French Broad River. William Rule's *History of Knoxville* puts it thus:

As is well known, the object of General Longstreet was to starve the Union forces into surrender, in which he would certainly have succeeded had he cut off all supplies from reaching the fort; but large quantities of provisions were continually brought down the Holston River from the vicinity of the French Broad under cover of the darkness and the fog, the river not being carefully guarded by the Confederate forces, and at the close of the siege, when an attack was made upon the fort, there were within the fortifications a sufficient supply to last the Federal army ten days. These supplies were freely furnished by the citizens in the immediate sections of the country, who were loyally disposed to the Government of the United States. It was therefore this faithfulness on the part of the people of East Tennessee that saved the city and caused its final abandonment by the Confederate forces. They (the supplies) were sent down the Holston by Captain Doughty and his company, who remained on the French Broad during the siege.

In the final analysis, it was not the Union Army who won the battle for Knoxville, but the people of East Tennessee; for without them, Knoxville might very possibly have been another Vicksburg.

Now that the siege was actually underway, the residents of Knoxville found themselves living under strict military regulations. Many private homes and almost all the public buildings had been taken over to house the soldiers. Knoxville's Market House, which had been built in 1853, of course had no produce for sale in its stalls, since all the food coming into the city by way of the pontoon bridge or rafts was received and distributed by the military authorities. Since the Market House was so centrally located, it was made the powder magazine for the Union forces, and in it were stored large quantities of ammunition for distribution to the various sections of the city as it was needed for defense. Even under military siege, the city fathers of Knoxville were not pleased with such high-handed commandeering of public property. Calling an emergency meeting of the city's Board of Aldermen, they instructed the Mayor to call on General Tillson, who was in charge of the ammunition supplies for the Union forces, with the request that he take the ammunition out of the Market House and distribute it to the several forts and batteries. They asked the Mayor to tell the General that he should not store all his explosives in one place, and particularly not in Knoxville's valuable Market House. If an explosion occurred there, they said, it would not only destroy the Market House itself, but would also endanger the lives and damage the nearby property of Knoxville's loyal citizens. While they were at it, they further complained that Federal troops had removed the stalls and benches of the Market House to the outside, where they had suffered damage from the weather.

The siege was several days old when, on November 25, General Longstreet was advised by General Bragg that his troops were needed back at Chattanooga: Bragg urged him to move in at once and take the fortifications by force. After a few days delay Longstreet decided to comply, not knowing that it was now too late to return to Chattanooga, for Bragg had already lost the battle there. The time of the attack was set for Sunday morning, November 29, at dawn. Lieutenant General A. P. Stewart, in his sketch of the Army of Tennessee, gives this moving account of the battle:

The weather was bad, misty and freezing. A large number of the Confederates were barefooted and thinly clad . . . calmly but quickly with fixed bayonets and with the precision of dress parade, the assaulting columns moved through the mists of the early morning toward the bastions of the dimly outlined fort. The distance was short. The garrison was fully aware that the assault was to be made at daylight and every man was at his post. The embrasures of the fort bristled with twenty pound Parrotts and twelve pound Napoleon guns, which had been double and triple shotted with shot and shell; and which, almost from the moment the columns moved, had full play upon them. Yet proudly, confidently, heroicly, and defiantly the gray, grim and grizzled veterans moved into the "jaws of death." Suddenly the head of the assaulting column was broken, the men pitching forward and falling over each other. They had struck the invisible telegraph wires stretched from stump to stump. The guns of the fort belched forth thunder and lightning into the disordered ranks. Quickly reforming under the galling fire, the Confederates rushed for the fort, when once again they halted. They had reached the deep wide ditch about which they were misinformed, and over which they had no way to cross. Only for a moment they paused. Apparently endowed with superhuman activity and determination they crossed the ditch, while volley after volley of artillery and musketry was poured upon them from above, and while "twenty pound shells with fuses cut to explode them at twenty seconds were hurled from the fort into the living mass below." Still onward was borne the flag of St. Andrews. The parapet was reached, only to find it covered with ice. Undismayed the boys in gray attempted to scale the slippery sides. A few reached the top only to meet instant death or capture. Three times the cross-barred flag of the Confederates was planted on the parapet to float only for a moment. . . . The assault had failed.

The battle for Fort Sanders had lasted twenty bloody minutes; the Confederates had lost eight hundred and thirteen men, killed, wounded, or captured.

General Longstreet's attack was directed at the weakest point of the fort, the northwest corner, which was in effect a "blind" corner. If the attackers could reach the ditch surrounding the fort, they would be out of reach of the fort's cannon. But the artillery commander within the fort, Lieutenant Samuel N. Benjamin, resorted to a stratagem which helped save Fort Sanders from capture. He had available a considerable number of spherical cannon shells of the type ignited by time fuses. When the attackers managed to get through the telegraph wires and came into the ditch, Benjamin and the others of his command lighted the shells with the fuses and tossed them over into the ditch as if they were hand grenades. The attackers thought they were being fired on by their own artillery. So did Longstreet. Consequently, he ordered the artillery, which was in fact raking the flanks of the Federals, to cease firing.

Of perhaps even greater importance than the "hand grenades" was the ditch that surrounded the fort. General Longstreet erroneously believed that this ditch was not more than three feet deep. He had, through field glasses, watched Union soldiers walking easily across the ditch while the fort was being built, and he assumed that his attacking soldiers would find the ditch equally easy to cross. What the General did not know was that the Union soldiers had been crossing the ditch on planks which reached from side to side under the surface of the water of a moat which was from six to eleven feet in depth. He therefore sent his troops into the attack on the fort without ladders or any other aids for scaling the sides of the ditch and the embankment towering above it on the fort side. Floundering in the icy water of the moat, the Confederates found it impossible to gain a firm foothold on the frozen mud of the embankment, and were at the mercy of the murderous gunfire pouring down upon them from the parapet above. As if this were not enough, the defenders of the fort had during the night poured water over the sides of the parapet. Freezing temperatures had then coated the parapet with a thin sheet of ice to make the assault upon the cleverly fortified fort truly hopeless.

The need for hospitals to care for the wounded of both armies was now acute. In addition to the buildings earlier used by the Confederates for this purpose, the Union Army now took over the Baptist, Methodist, and First and Second Presbyterian Churches, all the city's hotels, and the buildings of the East Tennessee Female Institute.

In their hasty retreat from Fort Sanders, Longstreet's men were forced to abandon many wounded Confederates and the bodies of their dead. The Union soldiers dug shallow trenches into which a great many bodies were piled; but the Union soldiers, too, were so concerned with the defense of the city from further attacks that they had little time for the burying of their own dead, much less the fallen Confederates. Two businessmen of Knoxville, visiting the battleground a few days after the battle had taken place, were horrified at the sight of the Confederate dead half buried in their shallow graves. They felt that Christian charity demanded proper burial for any soldier fallen in battle; they therefore commissioned a Knoxville undertaker to make simple pine coffins for these dead, who were reinterred in Knoxville's Bethel Cemetery. Ninety-two Confederate soldiers were reburied in this way, the businessmen paying four dollars to the undertaker for each such burial. Three hundred soldiers had already been buried in Bethel Cemetery by the Confederate military authorities. Three hundred and ninety-two Confederate dead from this one battle are known to be buried in this cemetery; many of the graves are unmarked.

Several days had elapsed after the battle when Confederate scouts captured a Federal courier who carried letters from General Grant to General Burnside. The letters contained the information that Union troops were on the way to the aid of the beleaguered city from the north, the south, and the west. Upon receipt of this news, General

Longstreet concluded that it would be best to give up all idea of taking Knoxville, and he consequently withdrew his troops in the direction of Virginia on the night of December 4, 1863, thus ending the siege.

General Longstreet left not a moment too soon, for the dispatches he had captured were correct in stating that the arrival of fresh Union troops was imminent. All of the Union generals were worried about General Burnside's command, expecting momentarily to hear that he had been forced to surrender the city, for they could not imagine how his troops could long survive without supplies. It was General William Tecumseh Sherman, bringing a large Union force to the relief of Knoxville by forced marches from the vicinity of Chattanooga where he had helped defeat Bragg's army, who was the first of the generals to arrive. As he hurried into Maryville on the morning of December 5, he was met by the news that the siege had been lifted only the night before. Supposing that the withdrawal of the enemy troops might be a trick of some sort, General Sherman left the main body of his troops in Maryville and pressed on to Knoxville with two divisions. Crossing the river on the pontoon bridge that had been provided for their convenience by General Burnside's busy engineers, General Sherman's men rode into the "starving city." The first sight that met the eyes of the astonished General Sherman as he rode ashore into Knoxville was a large pen filled with fine fat cattle. General Sherman was escorted to the headquarters of General Burnside, whom he found living with his staff in a beautifully furnished large mansion (tradition has it that Burnside's headquarters at this time were in the residence of Colonel Perez Dickinson on Main Street). General Burnside presided over a belated Thanksgiving dinner, featuring roast turkey, and served in a style which ran to fine silver and delicate table linens. While General Sherman and his staff were feasting at headquarters, his cold and hungry relief troops were warmed and fed by the soldiers to whose relief they had come. The amazed Sherman at last blurted out the fact that he had thought the defenders of Knoxville were starving.

General Burnside explained the unusual circumstances of Knoxville's defense. Sherman and his staff listened open-mouthed as they heard how provisions for the city had floated nightly down the river on many rafts, under the very noses of the Confederates. They heard with amazement how the loyal East Tennesseans had provided the citizens and troops at Knoxville not only with necessities, but with luxuries and delicacies unimagined by troops in the field. After discussing the situation thoroughly, the generals agreed that there was very little danger that the attack on Knoxville would be renewed—General Burnside asked for no more than one extra division to be left with him to strengthen his command. So General Sherman returned to Maryville to lead his troops back to Chattanooga, quite bewildered by the strange siege he had attempted to alleviate, and convinced that had he only known the facts he need not have hurried to help Knoxville.

Just to make doubly sure that Knoxville was safe from further attack, General Philip Sheridan was ordered with his troops to the French Broad River country. His men found it easy to support themselves with the provender freely furnished to them by the residents of Sevier and Cocke counties, and they continued to send supplies down-river to the garrison at Knoxville. General Sheridan was no less surprised than General Sherman at the situation in East

Tennessee, of which he was ignorant until he found himself in the midst of it. He paid tribute in his *Memoirs* to the people of East Tennessee by saying that "the intense loyalty of this part of Tennessee exceeded that of any other section I was in during the war. The women were especially loyal. . . . So long as we remained in the French Broad region, we lived on the fat of the land. . . ." Unfortunately for the comfort of General Sheridan and his men, it was soon felt that all danger to Knoxville was past, and he was told to withdraw his troops toward the north. Union forces were left in undisputed possession of Knoxville until the end of the war.

The War Between the States ended in 1865, but it was not really over in Knoxville for a long time thereafter. All the city's churches, the University buildings, the School for the Deaf, and many private homes had been used by the opposing armies in turn. These buildings had seen service as headquarters, barracks, hospitals, and even stables, and some of them were in unusable condition when they were finally turned over to their rightful owners. Those that were in better condition were restored, and many of them still stand today. It took a long time to erase the scars of battle; it took even longer to wipe out the bitter feelings of the people.

The siege of Knoxville had one pleasant effect upon the area which still may serve as daily reminder of the period. Before the Civil War, there were no wild mockingbirds in the Valley of East Tennessee, for this section of the state was not on their route of migration. Mockingbirds were highly regarded as pets, however, and there was hardly a porch in the city that did not boast a mockingbird cage. These were special cages, long instead of tall, having rounded tops, and made of fine wickerwork. Because mockingbirds eat only insects when they are roaming free, the caged pets could not be fed on sunflower seeds or pepper grass as could other types of captive birds; so the pet mockingbirds of Knoxville subsisted on a diet of hard-boiled eggs. When the siege of the city was underway, there were no eggs to waste on mockingbirds. Reluctantly, the ladies of Knoxville opened the doors of the mockingbird cages and freed their pets. It was a happy surprise to them that, instead of flying away, the mockingbirds made themselves very much at home, sometimes migrating in winter but returning each year in ever-increasing numbers.

The final chapter in the story of the Battle of Fort Sanders was written in 1890. In October of that year, veterans of both armies who had taken part in the battle held a reunion in Knoxville. A large number of former Union soldiers came; most of them were members of the 79th New York Highlanders who had been responsible for the defense of Fort Sanders on the day of the battle. There were three days of speeches and reminiscences, of band concerts and poetic readings. General Longstreet himself was present and had prepared an address for the occasion, but the address was read for him by a friend. A bullet wound

KNOXVILLE IN 1863

1—Fort Sanders. 2—Fort Dickerson. 3—Battery atop College Hill. 4—Battery on Summit Hill. 5—Battery on Mabry's Hill. 6—Armstrong House. 7—Parson Brownlow's House. 8—Perez Dickinson's Main Street House. 9—Perez Dickinson's Island Home. 10—Cowan and Dickinson Store. 11—Second Presbyterian Church and Cemetery. 12—Market Square. 13—The School for the Deaf (presently City Hall).

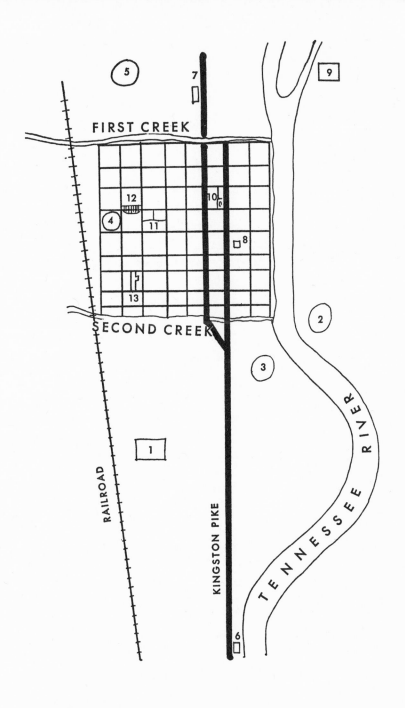

FIRST CREEK

SECOND CREEK

RAILROAD

KINGSTON PIKE

TENNESSEE RIVER

in the neck received during the war had made it impossible for the General thereafter to speak above a whisper.

That, then, was the end of the war as far as Knoxville was concerned, except for the lingering stubborn convictions of her citizens. When the State of Tennessee, the last state to leave the Union and join the Confederacy and the first among the Confederate states to reapply for statehood, was readmitted to the Federal Union, the people of East Tennessee expressed these convictions by sending a series of Republican representatives to the United States Congress— a habit they persist in to this day. The Second Congressional District (in which Knoxville is located) has not been represented by a Democrat in Congress since 1854, and the First Congressional District (upper East Tennessee) has broken the tradition only once. Records of the War Department of the United States were found to show, after the Civil War was over, that these two congressional districts of Tennessee had furnished more soldiers for the Union Army per capita than any other two congressional districts in the entire nation!

East Tennesseans, remembering the bitter battleground that was made of this loyal area, might agree with the old Knox Countian who was asked by his grandson who won the War Between the States. "Son," he replied, "it don't really make much difference *who* won the whole war—in East Tennessee, everybody lost!"

CHAPTER SEVEN

William G. Brownlow

In the twentieth century, the saying "Life begins at forty" has become as much a truism as "A rolling stone gathers no moss." In the 1840's, however, a man of forty was considered middle-aged, and the public expected him to be already well-established in his chosen profession, if he ever hoped to amount to anything. William G. Brownlow, who arrived in Knoxville in 1849, was a man who cared not a whit for public opinion, unless it happened to agree with his own.

When he came to Knoxville, William Brownlow was forty-four years old, and he was well launched on his second career. His first, in which he had achieved a rather widespread reputation in the South, was that of minister of the gospel. Lest anyone should think that this implied a mildness of manner and a kindliness of speech, let it be said at once that Parson Brownlow was a Methodist circuit-

riding evangelist, a master of vitriolic oratory, and a passionate advocate of temperance. In short, he was the kind
of minister most greatly admired in the South in his day—
a real "hell-fire-and-damnation" preacher.

In his late thirties, the Parson became convinced that
the pen was not only mightier than the sword, it was also
mightier than the tongue. He did not so much leave the
ministry as add to his preaching a new career, that of
newspaper editor. He first published a small newspaper,
the *Tennessee Whig*, at Elizabethton in 1839, moving to
Jonesboro in the following year. But Knoxville, in the
1840's, was larger than either of these towns and a more
progressive city. Deciding that such a spot would offer
greater scope for his talents as editor and publisher, William Brownlow moved his family and his printing press to
Knoxville and began the publication of *Brownlow's Knoxville Whig*.

The *Whig*, from the very first issue, was no ordinary
newspaper. It carried advertisements, to be sure, and it reported local news and events of national significance; but
here its resemblance to the other newspapers of its day
ceased. The *Whig's* real reason for being was its editorial page, and it was for these editorials that it was
bought and read. It was customary for newspapers at this
time to carry upon their mastheads mottoes descriptive of
the policies they advocated. Two of the mottoes often
used by the *Whig* were: "Cry aloud and spare not," and
"Independent in all things, neutral in nothing." These were
the exact sentiments of the *Whig's* editor. Sometimes it
seemed to his readers that he must have dipped his pen in
acid instead of ink to write his editorials, but this was the
kind of journalism they most enjoyed. So the *Whig* was

an instantaneous success. Its fame spread through the state and the South until its circulation had reached the phenomenal figure, for that day, of twelve thousand copies. Thus the *Whig* became one of the very few papers in the annals of American journalism to have a circulation greater than the total population of the city in which it was published.

If an election was coming up, the *Whig* was passionately partisan. If a public servant betrayed his public trust, the *Whig* was violently vindictive. If an issue was at stake, the *Whig* could be relied upon to present one side of it only.

Now, William Brownlow was a staunch Unionist, and he was an equally strong believer in the institution of slavery. This was true of many of his neighbors in East Tennessee, although the two beliefs were considered absolutely incompatible by the rest of the country. The proslavery bias of the *Whig* accounted for a large measure of its popularity in the South and was responsible for its editor's first taste of national prominence. In 1858, he was invited to Philadelphia to engage in public debate with the Reverend Abram Pryne on the slavery question. The debate itself lasted for five days, and much Scripture was quoted on both sides by the two ministers. Mr. Brownlow, favoring slavery, delivered himself of some fine periods of oratory that were reported in the press of the nation. The entire debate was afterward published in book form and was widely read in the North as well as in the South.

In the presidential campaign of 1860, there was a candidate precisely to the liking of William Brownlow. This was his close personal friend (for whom one of his sons was named) John Bell. John Bell was campaigning on the single platform: Preservation of the Union. As an uncompromising Union man, this was a situation ready-made for the editor of *Brownlow's Knoxville Whig*. The *Whig* thundered warning from its pages of the dire consequences of electing to the Presidency of the United States any man whose first concern was not to preserve the Union at all costs. In the famous four-way presidential race, John Bell and the *Whig* carried the State of Tennessee, but Abraham Lincoln was elected President.

After the election of Lincoln, South Carolina's convention passed the first Act of Secession, and William Brownlow was galvanized into frantic action. As he had years before denounced South Carolina's Nullification Acts, so he now excoriated her secession. He called it stupidity. He called it treason. In other parts of the South, subscribers cancelled their subscriptions to the *Whig*, and refused to accept copies that arrived for them at their local post offices. In Knoxville, William Brownlow's neighbors read the *Whig* with nods of approval. And subscriptions began to pour in from the North! It must be clearly understood that the majority of the *Whig*'s subscribers in East Tennessee agreed thoroughly with the opinions of its editor (though they might not have expressed those opinions so strongly), and that they stood by him loyally in the crises that were to follow.

In spite of the efforts of the *Whig* and William Brownlow's fellow Unionists in East Tennessee, the State of Tennessee seceded from the Federal Union in June of 1861. An attempt to create a new state in the eastern district of Tennessee came to naught. A less courageous and determined man would surely at this point have called it quits and capped his inkwell for the duration. But nobody ever called William Brownlow a quitter, though his enemies had some very fancy names for him. In the teeth of the Act of Secession, the *Whig* continued to carry editorials every bit as pro-Union as those of newspapers in New York or Boston. And William Brownlow, when the Confederate troops occupied Knoxville, kept the Stars and Stripes floating from a flagpole above his house on East Cumberland Street.

This flag and the popularity of Brownlow himself were sorely trying to the Confederate authorities, as well as to the many Southern sympathizers among the citizens of Knoxville. Tension was building up. One day, while Mr. and Mrs. Brownlow were away from home, a group of Confederate soldiers gathered in the street outside the house and demanded that the flag be taken down, or they would take it down themselves. One of the Brownlows' young daughters, Sue, was at home. With a courage that would have done credit to her intrepid father himself, Miss Sue stepped out upon the porch brandishing a pistol and invited any man who wanted to be shot to come and get the flag. The flag stayed put.

With the occupation of the city by Confederate forces in 1861, it was no longer possible to send copies of the *Whig* to its thousands of subscribers in the North, and Confederate authorities promptly banned the circulation of the incendiary *Whig* in the Southern states. By October of 1861, Parson Brownlow realized that, temporarily at least, it would be necessary to suspend publication. The final issue of the *Whig*, dated October 24, announced in an editorial that the editor had received information which led him to believe that he was about to be arrested. He supposed, he said, that if he were willing to take an oath of loyalty to the Confederate States of America, he would be

permitted to go free. He announced his intention of refus-
ing to take such an oath and that he expected to be sent
to jail. He said also:

> I shall in no degree feel humbled by being cast into
> prison, whenever it is the will and pleasure of this august
> government to put me there, but on the contrary I shall
> feel proud of my confinement. I shall go to jail—as John
> Rogers went to the stake—for my principles. I shall go,
> because I have failed to recognize the hand of God in the
> work of breaking up the American government, and the
> inauguration of the most wicked, cruel, unnatural and
> uncalled for war, ever recorded in history! I go, because
> I have refused to laud to the skies the acts of tyranny,
> usurpation, and oppression, inflicted upon the people of
> East Tennessee, because of their devotion to the Consti-
> tution and Laws of the Government handed down to
> them by their Fathers, and the liberties secured to them
> by a war of seven long years of gloom, poverty, and
> trial! I repeat, I am proud of my position, and of my
> principles, and shall leave them to my children as a legacy
> far more valuable than a princely fortune, had I the latter
> to bestow!

As it turned out, he did not immediately go to jail. A
few days after the publication of the *Whig*'s final issue,
Parson Brownlow deemed it wisest to leave Knoxville to
seek political asylum in the strongly Union counties of
Blount and Sevier. The wild and rugged Wear's Valley
was the spot he chose to hide in, and there he lived upon
sweet potatoes and wild game. Meanwhile, in Knoxville,
Confederate authorities posted a notice that two thousand
dollars would be paid for information leading to the ap-
prehension of William G. Brownlow.

The Unionists in Sevier County knew exactly the

whereabouts of Parson Brownlow, and they knew, too, that his hiding in the mountains was causing great embarrassment to his political enemies. Word went round that on a certain Sunday morning, the Parson would speak in the Court House Square at Sevierville. By wagon and buggy, on horseback and muleback, and on "Shanks' mare"—East Tennessee's phrase for just plain walking!—the people came down from the hills and the coves and the valleys. On that Sunday morning, the Court House Square was packed with the men and women of the back counties who formed the hard core of Union resistance in East Tennessee. To these, his friends, Parson Brownlow made a stirring speech. He told them what they wanted to hear—that the Federal Union could not fail to win in the end. Back to the hills and the coves and the valleys went Parson Brownlow's friends. Every one of them knew that there was a price upon his head, for he had told them so. Nobody claimed the reward, and William Brownlow went back to Wear's Valley.

News of this meeting, and the stiffening resistance of the Unionists in the mountains, reached Knoxville. The Confederate military authorities sent a message to Sevier County. They wanted to make a deal with the fighting parson. If he would agree to go to the North, and stay there, they were prepared to offer him safe conduct through the lines for himself and his family. When he heard this, Parson Brownlow decided to accept the offer. He left his hiding place in the mountains and returned to Knoxville to make preparations for the long journey. But his departure was not to be that simple. When he arrived in the city, he was immediately arrested and placed in the city jail by Knoxville's strongly Confederate civil authorities. The Confederate military authorities had kept their promise—a

safe-conduct pass for the Parson and his family was ready
and waiting—but they were unable to persuade the district
attorney or the judge who had jailed William Brownlow
that his imprisonment was making a martyr of him in the
eyes of his political adherents.

From the jail, Parson Brownlow wrote a letter that
was to be responsible for his ultimate release. The letter,
addressed to Judah P. Benjamin, Secretary of War for the
Confederacy, explained that the Parson had come to Knoxville in good faith to accept a proposition made to him by
duly constituted military representatives of the Confederacy. He told of his arrest and imprisonment by the
civil authorities, and asked that pressure from Richmond
be brought to bear upon the local judge to allow him and
his family to leave Tennessee. "If you will help me in this,"
he said, "I will do more for your Confederacy than the
devil himself, for I will leave it."

During the time that it took the letter to reach Judah
P. Benjamin in Richmond, and his directive to arrive in
Knoxville, Parson Brownlow had been removed from the
jail, where he had contracted a serious illness, to his home.
He was still under house arrest, and an armed guard was in
attendance in his sickroom at all times. Word came from
Richmond that it would indeed be to the best interests of
the cause of the Confederacy if Parson Brownlow left the
South. The civil authorities released him to the military,
who promptly made good their promise to send the entire
Brownlow family through the lines to safety in the North.

They arrived by train in Cincinnati, where the Parson
made an impassioned speech to the large crowd that had
gathered to greet him. In the crowd was a Union general
who was charged with the responsibility of obtaining

From the brick tower of "Bleak House," now Confederate Memorial Hall, a Confederate sharpshooter fatally wounded General William Sanders on the first day of the battle for Knoxville in 1863. General Longstreet had his headquarters here during the seige of the city.

View from Fort Dickerson, built by Union forces to protect Knoxville from Confederate attack by river. The earthworks fort, remarkably preserved, is now a city park.

volunteers for the Union Army on his recruiting trip through the North. At the end of Parson Brownlow's address, the General jumped to his feet and called for volunteers. So great was the response to his call that the General abandoned his own planned tour of the Northern states and followed William Brownlow on *his* tour, asking for volunteers at the conclusion of each Brownlow speech.

The Parson's bitter denunciations of the cause of the Confederacy were music to the ears of his Northern hearers, and great crowds assembled whenever he was scheduled to speak. As soon, however, as word reached him of the Union occupation of his city, William Brownlow set out for home and the resumption of publication of the *Whig*. The *Whig* took up again where it had left off in 1861, with an addition to its title. From this day forward, it was known as *Brownlow's Knoxville Whig and Rebel Ventilator*. By November of 1863, Parson Brownlow was back in the newspaper business in time to report upon the siege of Knoxville and the Battle of Fort Sanders.

But the most interesting incident about the Battle of Fort Sanders was not reported in the *Whig*, or anywhere else. It concerns the only Confederate soldier who actually got into Fort Sanders. Lieutenant O'Brien, of Louisiana, was leading his men in the charge on the fort. Through murderous fire, he had traversed the wire entanglements and the deep ditch, and had clambered up the icy side of the parapet. As he stood erect upon the parapet for one moment, a rifle bullet hit him. Pitching forward, he fell face first into the fort itself, to be seized and taken prisoner. Although he was seriously wounded, Lieutenant O'Brien managed to convey to his captors the information that he had a sister living in Knoxville, and asked that she be notified. And the name of the Lieutenant's sister? *Mrs. William G. Brownlow!* The Brownlows hurried to the fort and took Lieutenant O'Brien to their home, where his sister nursed him back to health. So it was that, during the siege of Knoxville, the city's most passionate Union partisan was harboring in his home a lieutenant in the forces of the Confederate States of America. Even the family of Parson Brownlow had its problems of divided loyalties.

With the fall of Nashville to the Union forces in 1862, Tennessee started on the long road back to statehood. That Tennessee escaped the full horror of the Reconstruction Era is well known, but the reasons for the preferential treatment accorded her are not always clearly understood. As soon as the Confederate state government had been forced to abandon the capital at Nashville, President Lincoln appointed a military governor for the state. His choice for this office was a logical one, for it fell upon Andrew Johnson, that lone senator from a Southern state who demonstrated his loyalty to the Union by remaining in his Senate seat on the fateful day when the other senators and representatives from the South left the halls of Congress. Andrew Johnson had been governor of Tennessee before his election to the Senate, in the 1850's. That he accepted the new assignment was a tribute to his bravery and devotion to duty, for no man could have found himself in a more equivocal position. As a Tennessean whose home area had felt the scourge of battle and alternate occupation by the warring forces, he had the deepest sympathy for the citizens of the state he was called upon to govern. The very title "Military Governor" made him cordially hated in every corner of the territory he administered. The people of Tennessee, and most especially those of Middle and West

Tennessee, looked upon him as a renegade and a traitor, and flouted his authority on every possible occasion. This made necessary more stringent measures of control than Johnson would otherwise have used. He was rescued from this untenable position by his nomination to the Vice-Presidency in 1864, when Mr. Lincoln was running for his second term.

The selection of Johnson as a running mate for the President was not a popular one. It is said to have been the choice of Lincoln himself, who felt that Johnson, a native of the South and a man who had experienced the anger of the defeated Southerners in his capacity of governor of a conquered state, would be able to give wise counsel about the rehabilitation of the South when the war came to an end. Certainly, Abraham Lincoln and Andrew Johnson were not thinking in terms of the same punitive measures advocated by many statesmen in the North. Each of them was convinced that the South, having already suffered greatly during the war, would suffer sufficiently in defeat without additional punishment from her victor.

Andrew Johnson was one man who was determined to get his state back into the Union without delay, and on the most favorable terms possible. The other man who had this as his primary objective in the closing days of the war was William G. Brownlow. Johnson and Brownlow, although formerly bitter enemies, had been leaders together of the Unionists in East Tennessee in 1861, and they determined to use the loyalty of this section of the state as the entering wedge to secure the entire state's readmission to the Union. They agreed upon the general course of action, but, as in the past, they did not always see eye to eye on the means to be employed to gain the desired end. It

was while Andrew Johnson was serving as Military Governor that he made a public speech to which Parson Brownlow took immediate and violent exception. Johnson, ad-
dressing a meeting of Negroes in Nashville, announced the
freeing of his personal slaves on August 8, 1864, and called
himself the hope of the colored people of the South. He
went further. He likened himself to Moses, who would
lead them "out of the house of bondage." In Knoxville,
Parson Brownlow addressed an equally large crowd of
Negroes, but the tenor of his remarks was quite different.
Brownlow informed them that if Andrew Johnson proposed to be their Moses to lead them to the Promised Land,
he, Brownlow, would be their Pharaoh to drive them right
back again. These two speeches created great amusement
in the North, and Parson Brownlow chose to keep the
amusement, and the controversy, alive for years by referring to himself often as Pharaoh Brownlow. Although these
two men were so often divided in opinion, together they
accomplished what seemed impossible to many contemporary observers. They saved their neighbors many years of
bitter oppression at the war's end, and they were doubly
detested by many for their pains.

With the cessation of hostilities, William G. Brownlow
was elected governor of the exhausted state of Tennessee.
He took office in 1865, faced with the improbable task of
pleasing the diametrically opposed factions of the state.
Soon afterward, upon the assassination of President Lincoln, Andrew Johnson became President of the United
States.

Almost the first act passed by Tennessee's newly reorganized legislature was a law denying the franchise to

former Confederate sympathizers for five to fifteen years. Most of the voters qualified under this law were from East Tennessee, and there was naturally a storm of protest from the rest of the state. So bitter was the opposition to this first postwar government that the term "Brownlow's Legislature" was used as an epithet of hatred.

Governor Brownlow, who was looking for the first favorable opportunity to apply for the readmission of Tennessee to the Union, recognized such an opportunity in 1866. The Fourteenth Amendment to the Constitution had been sent to the various states for ratification. The Radicals in Congress had implied that the acceptance of this controversial piece of legislation by the legislature of a seceded state would be a strong point in favor of its readmission to the Union. Six days after the passage of the bill in Congress, Governor Brownlow called a special session of the legislature of the state to consider its ratification. Even in 1866, the Fourteenth Amendment was destined to cause trouble.

The amendment was, of course, wholly unacceptable to the State of Tennessee at large, and President Johnson had advised the Southern states to reject it. Even William Brownlow, the most avid of pro-Union men, found it very difficult to swallow. The duly elected members of the legislature wanted no part of it, and they decided to avoid any action upon it. Enough of the legislators stayed away from the special session to prevent the bill's passage for lack of a quorum to act upon it. Governor Brownlow was incensed. This was Tennessee's chance to avoid much greater difficulties than the Fourteenth Amendment would imply, and he was determined that the amendment should be ratified. The next step taken was one which accomplished the Governor's purpose, but enraged the citizens of his state.

Enough of the absent members of the legislature to constitute a quorum were actually arrested and brought to Nashville, where they were announced to be in attendance, and a quorum was declared present. The Fourteenth Amendment was then voted upon and passed, although the members brought in by force refused to vote. Governor Brownlow telegraphed the news of the ratification to the Radicals in Congress, and Tennessee became the third of all the states, North or South, to ratify. Largely on the strength of this decision, Tennessee (the last state to secede from the Union and join the Confederacy) became the first Southern state to return to full statehood.

East Tennesseans breathed a sigh of relief to be back in the Union. They realized that there would be no further military occupation of the state, that the Freedmen's Bureau would henceforth have less than total power, and that their university could profit by the Federal Land Grant Acts of 1862. The rest of the state was categorically opposed. The Ku Klux Klan was organized and stirred the discontented in Middle and West Tennessee. Lawless acts and demonstrations became the rule rather than the exception, and Governor Brownlow was forced to take action. Declaring that a state of emergency existed in Middle and West Tennessee, he placed nine of the state's counties under martial law.

Even in East Tennessee, things were not running smoothly. There were many families who had ardently supported the Confederate cause, and many other families whose loyalties were divided. There was, for instance, the case of Abner Baker.

A few years earlier, Harvey Baker, the father of Abner, was a Confederate sympathizer who had been killed by soldiers in his own home at Ten Mile Creek, west of Knoxville, during the war. The Bakers, people of substance and position, were just as proud of their convictions as William Brownlow was of his. During the Brownlow regime, Abner Baker made a trip one day to the Court House in Knoxville. Did he try to vote? Did he object to the amount of his taxes? Whatever the cause, he quarrelled with the County Court Clerk. Abner Baker was a small man and slight of stature, while the clerk stood over six-feet tall and weighed more than two hundred pounds. Furthermore, the clerk, as was his habit, was carrying a cane. When the argument reached fever pitch, the clerk struck little Abner Baker across the face with his cane. Very few men went unarmed in those early postwar days, and Abner Baker was no exception. Whipping a pistol from his pocket, he shot his antagonist, who fell dead before the eyes of a crowd of people gathered in the Court House. There was no arrest for Abner Baker and no semblance of a trial. The courthouse crowd instantly became a mob and dragged their quarry to a tree on Hill Street, at the corner of the property of Colonel Perez Dickinson. A rope was placed about his neck, and then someone asked him if he had any last words to say. There was nothing small about Abner Baker but his size. Drawing himself up to his full height, he shouted: "Yes! Now watch a rebel die!"

William Brownlow was perhaps the only man in Tennessee who would have sought re-election to the governorship under such pressures. He conceived it to be his duty to see his state through her hour of deep distress. He was re-elected in 1867, but resigned the office of governor in order to accept his election by the State Legislature as United States senator from Tennessee. In the Senate, he continued his struggle to have his state take an equal place in the Federal Union of sovereign states, but there was one strange thing about his service in the Senate. During his entire term, William Brownlow, one of the foremost orators of his time, made not a single speech upon the floor of the Senate! The reason was obvious to those who knew him well. Illness had left him with a permanent throat disability, and he was unable in the last years of his life to speak above a whisper. The voice of William Brownlow may not have echoed in the Senate chamber, but his words were heard, nevertheless. His speeches were written and, although the vigor of his style was not one whit abated, they had to be read aloud for him by the clerk of the Senate!

His term in Washington completed, Senator Brownlow returned to Knoxville and to the newspaper business. He had sold the *Whig* at the close of the war, and he now purchased a half interest in the *Knoxville Daily and Weekly Chronicle*, and wrote some editorials for it. But Parson Brownlow was tired. He had fought, and he had won; he had lived to see the attainment of full statehood for Tennessee. It was time to let others take on the task of "binding up the wounds of war."

This was the man who was perhaps the most controversial figure in the history of Knoxville, and he loved every controversial moment of it. There was, for example, the incident which occurred when President Andrew Johnson was being tried for impeachment. The only count upon which the vote was taken was the one which accused him of removing from office the Radical Secretary of War,

Edwin M. Stanton, in contravention of the Tenure of Office Act. History records, of course, that his impeachment failed by a single vote, but in the midst of these solemn proceedings, there was humor—and that humor was injected by Parson Brownlow. During the trial, the personal honesty of Andrew Johnson was assailed. From Knoxville, his old political opponent, William Brownlow, telegraphed to Washington that, although he had fought Andrew Johnson on every stump in East Tennessee on every question that had arisen, and although he had pointed out all of Johnson's faults of omission and commission, which were legion, the personal honesty of Andrew Johnson was above question. The telegram was signed: "Pharaoh Brownlow"!

During the 1870's, two buggies, one large and one small, regularly met each train that pulled into the railway station at Knoxville. The smaller buggy carried passengers to the hotels; the larger conveyed travelers to the home of William Brownlow on East Cumberland Street. It was a rare day when at least a double dozen friends and associates of the Parson were not surrounding him on the porch or in the parlor.

In 1877, William G. Brownlow died in Knoxville and was buried in Old Gray Cemetery. Even after the Parson's death, the stream of visitors to his house continued. Every President of the United States who visited Knoxville in the period from Johnson to Taft paid his respects to the widow of William Brownlow, who lived to be ninety-five. The great and the near-great called upon Mrs. Brownlow, and there was a constant flow of humble people who simply wanted to tell her that they had known her husband, and liked him.

William Brownlow was a man whose tools were words, and words are fleeting things, not destined to endure. The greatest tribute to him was the deep personal affection for him in the hearts of his friends and neighbors. It might truly have been written of William Brownlow that "he who never made an enemy, never really made a friend."

CHAPTER EIGHT

Perez Dickinson

After the War Between the States, Knoxville returned rather quickly to her former position as a city of industry and business, but something new had been added. This was to be the era of the great wholesale houses, and Knoxville's location made it a natural center for a widespread wholesale trade that reached not only East Tennessee, but also western North Carolina, western Virginia, Kentucky, South Carolina, Alabama, and Georgia. Transportation and communication were slow, and it was not practical for country merchants to come themselves to Knoxville to select their merchandise from the wholesale center, so the wholesale firms sent "drummers," or salesmen, with their sample trunks throughout the area by horse-drawn hack to call on the customers. In such a system, it was necessary that the local merchants have the utmost confidence in the wholesale firms with which they

131

were dealing, and that their confidence be justified. Knoxville was fortunate in having businessmen of acumen and
honesty at the head of her wholesale houses, and this type
of business tided the city over the period of reconstruction
and business reorganization that lasted until the end of the
nineteenth century. Such firms as Cowan McClung and
Co., Daniel Briscoe Bros. and Co., M. L. Ross and Co., and
W. W. Woodruff and Co., made Knoxville the wholesale
center of the South.

This type of business had its beginning before the war
and attracted many able businessmen to Knoxville. A community is, after all, a reflection of the people who influence
its life, and nineteenth-century Knoxville was influenced
by its business leaders who were also its leaders in civic affairs. For example, there was Mr. Perez Dickinson who
arrived in Knoxville by 1830 from Amherst, Massachusetts.

It was not business that brought Perez Dickinson to
Knoxville, for his coming was a family affair. In 1827,
Joseph Estabrook had come to Knoxville to serve as principal of the East Tennessee Female Institute, and had
brought with him his young wife, Nancy Dickinson Estabrook, her mother, and her brother, Appleton Dickinson.
Two years later, the family was saddened by the death at
the age of twenty-one of the brilliant Appleton Dickinson,
who had already graduated from Amherst College before
coming with his mother and sister to Knoxville. A younger
brother, Perez, had stayed behind in Amherst to complete
his education, but in 1830, at seventeen, he too was graduated from Amherst, and journeyed south to join his family. As it happened, 1830 was soon after the reorganization
of the old Hampden-Sydney Academy in Knoxville, which
had been founded in 1806 as a school for boys and had

been part of East Tennessee College during the 1820's.
When it was decided to separate the school from the college in 1830, the trustees of the academy were delighted to
secure the services of Mr. Estabrook's young brother-in-
law as teacher. For two years, Perez Dickinson taught the
classics at Hampden-Sydney Academy and served as its
principal, but he was looking around at Knoxville all the
while. What he saw was a small city that had many business opportunities for a young man with capital and talents
to invest.

His sister Lucinda had married James H. Cowan,
whose uncles had been Knoxville's first merchants when
the town was established in 1791. James Cowan had a flourishing store and was not averse to taking a partner. So, in
1832, Perez Dickinson resigned his post at the Academy to
go into business with his brother-in-law. The new firm,
Cowan and Dickinson, built a two-story brick store on the
corner of Main and Gay streets and prospered mightily.
In 1858, the brothers-in-law branched out into a new field,
the wholesale business. With Charles J. and Frank McClung,
they formed the new Cowan, McClung and Co., which
was destined to become an outstanding firm in the wholesale field.

The Dickinson family was now thinking of Knoxville
as home. Nancy's husband, Joseph Estabrook, had been
made president of East Tennessee College in recognition of
his prowess as an educator. So prosperous were the affairs
of Cowan and Dickinson that it was not many years after
the firm's founding that Perez Dickinson was able to build
for himself and his mother a beautiful house on Main
Street (two blocks from the store). The house was a veritable mansion with a columned portico, wide and spacious

rooms, broad porches, and deep cellars. One of the cellars, and the porch above it, would later be of the utmost importance.

Then Perez Dickinson took a bride. In 1845, he returned to Boston to marry the lovely Susan Penniman of New Braintree, Massachusetts. The wedding took place on April 10, and the Dickinsons started at once for Tennessee. From Boston, by way of New York and Washington, they traveled to Raleigh, North Carolina. This much of their long journey they accomplished in the comparative comfort of railroad cars and steamboats, but the rest of the trip was not an easy one. Boarding a stagecoach in Raleigh, they jolted slowly westward to Greensboro, to Salisbury, to Asheville, to Warm Springs. Finally, through the glorious spring green of East Tennessee's countryside, they approached Knoxville.

A joyous welcome awaited them at the house on Main Street, and they began a pleasant and leisurely life. Susan loved flowers, and she liked the country. She enjoyed especially the drives in the comfortable carriage to see the nearby farms, the rugged hills, the views of the river and of the mountains in the distance.

They should build a summer home, Susan suggested, on a hill where there would be spacious lawns and great trees, and a garden filled with flowers. It would be nice to have enough flowers to share with friends. Perez Dickinson agreed and listened smilingly as Susan planned the house. It should be square and white, of the simple New England architecture she admired, and within, it should be spacious and comfortable, with large rooms suited to the entertaining she planned to do there. Perez had such a large family connection and so many friends that Susan felt sure they would entertain a great deal. As soon as they had decided on precisely the right spot, Perez promised, they would build the house and plant the gardens just as she said.

A year sped happily by, and even greater happiness was anticipated. There came the day when a baby was born in the house on Main Street, but the next day, Susan Dickinson and the baby both were dead.

The house had been built for a family, and Mr. Dickinson and his mother must have found it echoingly large when only the two of them were living in it. The time was rare, however, that they were there alone. It was a hospitable house and fairly running over with Estabrook and Cowan nieces and nephews, to say nothing of New England cousins who, after the long journey to Tennessee, made visits lasting months. Emily Dickinson, the family poetess, whose shy and unmaterialistic nature was delighted by the beauties of nature, enjoyed the returned travelers' descriptions of East Tennessee. Mr. Dickinson's sisters, Mrs. Estabrook and Mrs. Cowan, died during the 1840's, and his house became home for his motherless nieces. His own mother died in 1855, and from that time, his nieces Miss Mary Cowan and Mrs. Lucy Cowan Alexander managed the household affairs for him.

Perez Dickinson was a man of firm convictions. As a transplanted New Englander, he found the institution of slavery most displeasing. With interest, he read *The Liberator*, which advocated the absolute abolition of slavery and was published first in 1831 by a fellow native of Massachusetts, William Lloyd Garrison. It seemed to Perez Dickinson that an anti-slavery paper should logically be published in the South as well as in the North, for such a Southern paper would have a better chance of being read by slave-

owners who might be influenced to free their slaves. In
1838, Mr. Dickinson found himself dissatisfied with the
editorial policy and the literary style of Knoxville's weekly
newspapers, and he felt inclined to start a new and different type of paper, to be issued two times a week.

There were other young men in Knoxville who agreed
with him, and the group decided to finance such a newspaper. They were firmly agreed that the new newspaper
must be one of literary merit which would do credit to a
city with some pretensions as an educational center. But in
the year 1838, abolitionism was still considered very radical thinking, even in Massachusetts. In the Southern states
it was called unparalleled affrontery. Upon mature reflection, one after another of the group withdrew their names
and their financial support from the newspaper venture.
Finally, only Perez Dickinson was sufficiently determined
to underwrite the cost. In the summer of 1838 he journeyed
east to Philadelphia, where he purchased the best available
printing press, and then traveled on to Boston in search of a
printer. There he found James C. Moses, who was highly
recommended and who was willing to come to Knoxville
as foreman for the proposed *Knoxville Times*. In choosing
the editor for his paper, Mr. Dickinson followed a family
connection, for Editor Thomas Humes was the half-
brother of James H. Cowan, Mr. Dickinson's brother-in-
law and business partner.

Thomas Humes and Perez Dickinson had no intention
of producing an incendiary paper like *The Liberator*. They
stressed the fact that the new bi-weekly paper (Knoxville's
first to appear oftener than once a week) was intended to
be something more than a collection of news items and
advertisements; it was to be a real literary effort. The

Times had therefore the distinction of being printed on the very best of paper and written in the very best literary style. Even its advertisements were couched in elegant terms. In this form, disguised to be sure but still recognizable, appeared Perez Dickinson's idea of an abolitionist newspaper for the South. Its anti-slavery views were partially hidden in general moralization, but they were there, a strange anomaly in Knoxville, Tennessee. Perhaps this was the first straw in the wind to tell what Knoxville's role was to be in the bitter struggle of the 1860's.

After some months , the *Times* was allowed to merge with its rival, the *Knoxville Register*. The *Register's* name was retained, but James C. Moses became owner and editor of the combined papers. It was James C. Moses who suggested, in 1843, the formation in Knoxville of a Baptist church. He himself had never joined the church, although he had been raised a Baptist; and when he, with his brother John L. Moses and others, was successful in organizing the First Baptist Church, he was the first person baptized into its fellowship and served as the first superintendent of its Sunday School.

Meanwhile, Perez Dickinson had decided that it was too soon for even a watered-down version of abolitionism in Knoxville, but his own convictions upon the subject remained unchanged.

In the days immediately preceding the Civil War, Perez Dickinson was an avowed Union sympathizer. This is not surprising for a man of his New England background and education. He was not, as was William Brownlow, primarily interested only in the preservation of the Union, although of course this entered into his thinking. The difference was that Mr. Dickinson had kept right on being anti-slavery to the point of being an abolitionist. Needless to say, this was a position that was bitterly unpopular in any Southern state in the 1850's, and even in East Tennessee it was best to make no mention of such views. Yet Mr. Dickinson was a man whose convictions drove him to action, and action he took. To this day there are portions of his actions that remain shrouded in secrecy, and are destined to remain so, but a part of the story is this:

Generations of Knoxville's small boys and adventurous young men have told tall tales about a cave beneath the Tennessee River, extending from side to side, and having an entrance on the bluffs on the south side. Some have claimed to have made an underground journey all the way from the Cherokee Bluffs to Chilhowee Park. Others have hotly denied the existence of such a passage beneath the river, calling it "geologically impossible." No one has ever denied, however, that a network of underground caverns does underlie the center of the city itself on the north bank of the river, and Perez Dickinson put this natural phenomenon to a most unusual use.

His house on Main Street, with its extensive cellars, was a scant two blocks from the north bank of the river. At some undetermined time, and with unparalleled secrecy, a tunnel was constructed under the Main Street house, connecting one of its large cellars with a natural underground passage extending almost to the river's edge. A small "servants' house" was built over the opening of the passage beside the river. It may not be true, as many people thought, that Mr. Dickinson's tunnel connected with the cave that crossed under the river to the bluffs, but it would certainly have been relatively easy for a raft or a small boat to be floated downriver from the Dickinson property to come to rest across the river in the vicinity of Cherokee Bluffs, where a large cave certainly exists.

Once the tunnel was completed, Mr. Dickinson's nieces were sometimes called to sit with their needlework upon the porch which covered the cellar opening upon the secret passage. Who would suspect, seeing them thus peacefully sewing there in plain view of passers-by on Main Street, that below the floor on which their chairs rested, frightened black men waited for the darkness of night before attempting the fearful passage through the tunnel and the perilous crossing of the river to hide in the great cave on the bluffs?

With the secession of Tennessee from the Union, and the arrival of Confederate troops to occupy Knoxville, the Dickinson household found itself in the gravest of danger. Their distress was increased by a division of loyalties, for one of the Dickinson nieces, Miss Lucy Cowan, had married Charles Alexander who promptly volunteered for the Confederate Army and was commissioned a major in the Southern forces. Mr. Dickinson had living with him, at the time hostilities opened, his nieces and their children—babies who had been born in the Main Street house, and of whom he was very fond. His reputation as a Union sympathizer and a foe of the institution of slavery placed every member of his household in danger from the Confederate soldiers. There was only one thing to do—the family must go to the North.

A hack was heaped high with the luggage necessary for the travel of adults and infants, and a cow was tied behind the hack to furnish the children with milk during the journey. Thus Mr. Dickinson and his family traveled as far as Jonesboro, where they reached a portion of the railroad that was not in Confederate hands. Abandoning the hack, but *not* the cow, they transferred to the railroad for the long trip to Syracuse, New York, where they remained until it was safe for them to come home again.

After the publication of the Emancipation Proclamation, the Dickinson household returned to Knoxville. There had been many changes in their absence: Major Alexander was dead, and the Main Street house had been occupied first by Confederate, then by Union forces—a tree near the corner of the property was soon to serve as gallows for the hanging of the unreconstructed rebel, Abner Baker, for Knoxville was embarking upon the bitterness of reconstruction. In renovating the house, Mr. Dickinson decided to leave the tunnel. It might have its uses. And, as it turned out, it did.

Business affairs in the city were in a state of confusion during the closing days of the war. Banks prosperous before the war had been forced to close as Knoxville found herself the scene of hostilities. In order to re-establish Knoxville as a business center, one of the first steps was seen to be the formation of a good bank which could extend needed credit to merchants. Perez Dickinson and William Brownlow were both aware of the need for a sound new bank, and they, with several other Knoxvillians, joined in establishing the First National Bank in 1864. Mr. Dickinson was made president of the bank and served in that capacity for four years. During his term of office, the First National was famous for the fact that all dividends were paid to its stockholders in gold. Mr. Dickinson apparently wished to prove that the stock in *his* bank was truly "gilt-edged." In 1870, Mr. Dickinson was one of the organizers of Knoxville's Board of Trade, forerunner of the Chamber of Commerce, and served as its first president. The Board of Trade was anxious even then to secure for the city the best possible transportation at the lowest possible cost.

There was much interest in East Tennessee in rebuilding the land of the area's war-ravaged farms. Perez Dickinson was a leader in the new movement toward scientific farming and the rotation of crops, and in this leadership he found a rewarding new hobby. Purchasing an island in the Tennessee River just above the city, he bought also a mile or two of land along the south bank of the river near the island. He decided to build a country home on a hill overlooking the island, where there would be spacious lawns and great trees, greenhouses, and garden walks. The house, which went up quickly, was beautiful with the architectural simplicity of New England and Perez Dickinson was delighted with it. He planned an avenue of overarching trees to border the carriage drive that led through his property to the house itself, and he named the new house Island Home.

As a member of the Second Presbyterian Church, Mr. Dickinson quietly assumed the responsibility of furnishing flowers for its services. Each Sunday morning, his carriage arrived from Island Home bringing the best of whatever was blooming in the greenhouse. He found that in order to fill the two marble urns on the pulpit a good many flowers were required. Experience taught him that exactly enough flowers for the urns could be brought in an oval cardboard hatbox, and it became a familiar sight, on Sunday mornings, to see the hatbox of flowers arriving at the church in time for morning worship. To furnish these flowers regularly for five years, or ten, would have been an admirable example of devotion to purpose, but Perez Dickinson was not a

man of short-lived intentions. He furnished his church with
flowers for nearly half a century!

As the years passed, the trees arched over the carriage
drive exactly as Mr. Dickinson had planned. The shrubs
and the flowers bloomed on the lawn and in the greenhouse, and Perez Dickinson took great delight in driving
out to Island Home with visitors, and in bringing its abundant flowers in to town for his friends to enjoy. Though
he visited Island Home often, when the evening shadows
lengthened, Mr. Dickinson always turned back to the beautiful house on Main Street; although no other Knoxville
house was the scene of more entertainments or sheltered
more distinguished guests, Island Home's owner never
spent a night beneath its roof.

In postwar Knoxville, Perez Dickinson had become
one of the city's most beloved residents. His side had won
the war, and his convictions regarding abolition had become law; he wasted no time in saying "I told you so," but
worked harder than anyone to repair the ravages of the war
for his city. So much was his attitude appreciated by his
fellow Knoxvillians that in 1867, when he returned from
a several weeks' trip to the east, he was greeted at the station by a brass band playing "Welcome, Welcome Home."

In 1866, the General Assembly of the Presbyterian
Church had decided to organize churches for the Negroes
in the South. The Reverend G. W. LeVere, formerly the
chaplain of the 20th U. S. Colored Volunteer Infantry,
was sent as a missionary to Knoxville. He found here a
small group of colored people who had, before the war,
been members with their white owners of the First and
Second Presbyterian Churches. The Reverend LeVere
organized this group as the Shiloh Presbyterian Church and

set about finding a place to hold services. Historic First Presbyterian Church, which had served as a hospital during the battle for Knoxville, had been turned over to the Freedmen's Bureau for use as its headquarters, and Reverend LeVere's congregation first met in the basement of this church. But plans were being made to move the Freedmen's Bureau to another location and restore the First Presbyterian Church to its former owners, and the Shiloh Presbyterian Church needed another meeting place.

It is not surprising that this first of the Negro churches to be organized in Knoxville found a friend in Perez Dickinson. There was at the time a decided prejudice against Negro churches, but Mr. Dickinson's convictions had never permitted him to be influenced by public opinion. He promptly offered to the Reverend LeVere the use of the rear porch and lawn of his Main Street house for the services of the Shiloh Church, and there they were held until (with the financial aid of Perez Dickinson and his friends) a lot was finally purchased and a church built.

And what about the tunnel? These were still troubled times. Although Knox County was not one of the Tennessee counties placed under martial law by Governor Brownlow at the time of the rise of the Ku Klux Klan, the Klan was active here. Many times Mr. Dickinson's nieces and their children were requested to sit upon the side porch of the Main Street house when one of the family's colored friends was in trouble. The frightened ladies once more sat and stitched while the secret cellar and the secret tunnel offered escape to frightened men below.

But times were changing. Not even the bitterness of an internecine war can last forever, and people were learning

to live together once again. In the 1870's, young men of
Knoxville organized a company of rifles and entertained
themselves with drilling and with the more congenial pursuits of picnics and supper parties. These young men represented not only those families that had favored the Union
cause, but also families who had been ardent Confederate
sympathizers. They called themselves the Dickinson Light
Guard, and Perez Dickinson was named their honorary
colonel. He was pleased by the compliment, and responded
by entertaining the group often. Soon everybody was calling him Colonel Dickinson, and very much the Southern
Colonel he looked, with his twinkling eyes, his pleasant
smile, his broadbrimmed planter's hat.

The wholesale business was booming in Knoxville, and
Island Home had been converted into a prosperous farm.
Colonel Dickinson was always a man to be undeterred by
distances. He had gone to Boston for a printer, to Philadelphia for a printing press, to Syracuse to seek sanctuary
for his family; and he sent to Switzerland for a farmer to
manage Island Home. Under the supervision of Henry
Ebnoether, Island Home prospered as never before. There
was increasing interest in agriculture and the production of
fine livestock in these quiet years of the 1880's, when the
new University of Tennessee was stressing proper agricultural practices, and thereby hangs the tale of Colonel Dickinson's hog.

Island Home farm had produced a hog that was the
wonder of East Tennessee. This giant porker is said to have
weighed more than a thousand pounds and was the envy
of neighboring farmers. A parade of fine livestock was arranged in Knoxville, and it was a foregone conclusion that
Colonel Dickinson's hog would have a place of honor in

the line of march. Now, Gay Street was unpaved at the time, and its surface was pitted with mudholes on the day of the parade. Down the street came fine horses, cows, chickens, and pigs, and, the cynosure of all eyes, Colonel Dickinson's thousand-pound hog. As the parade reached the corner of Gay and Clinch streets, in front of the present site of the Farragut Hotel, the weary hog paused to wallow in a convenient mudhole. But the exertion of the march had been too much for him, and in the sight of hundreds of spectators, he turned on his bulging side, and died!

A businessman, a farmer, and a devoted churchman was Colonel Perez Dickinson. He was also interested in the educational and civic affairs of his city. In 1879, East Tennessee University was elevated to the status of a state university and became The University of Tennessee. Colonel Dickinson, former teacher and brother-in-law of a famous early president of the institution, was at once appointed as one of the new State University's first Board of Visitors. He responded by offering medals for superior scholarship among the students and made it a habit to entertain each year's Senior Class. As many as two hundred guests attended these banquets in honor of the University's graduating class, which were held at his home on Main Street, only a few blocks from the University itself.

Also in the year 1879, Knoxville took another step toward "culture." For several years, the city had had a Library and Reading Room, open to members only and supported by subscriptions. In this year it was decided that the privileges of the library should be extended to all the citizens of Knoxville, and that the library should be greatly expanded. In fact, the committee responsible for the change avowed for the new library the object of collecting within it every book and pamphlet ever published in Tennessee! When the Public Library was established, the chairman of its board was none other than Colonel Perez Dickinson. Later, in 1886, its librarian was his former editor, Thomas W. Humes, who in the meanwhile had been, successively, an Episcopal clergyman, an author, and president of the University.

As time passed, the aging Colonel Dickinson was still one of Knoxville's most beloved citizens, always interested in what was going on in his town, and always ready to lend his moral and financial support. In 1889, he served as a member of the commission to raise funds for the transfer and reburial of the body of another beloved citizen of Knoxville, John Sevier. Perez Dickinson made the journey on the special train to Alabama to escort home the body of Tennessee's first governor. He sat on the platform on the Court House lawn on the great day of the erection and dedication of the Sevier monument. This was a great day for Knoxville, and Colonel Dickinson was glad, as always, to have had a part in it; but he was growing old. More and more he limited his activities to church and home and to visiting with his friends and family. Island Home was the scene of hundreds of picnics and parties for church and civic groups; always the hospitable Colonel Dickinson was happy to entertain the Dickinson Rifles, the students of the University, his friends, and his family. Still the hatbox of flowers came each Sunday to the Second Presbyterian Church. And on his eightieth birthday there came an interesting reversal. A friend brought eighty lilies as a birthday gift to this man who had given so many flowers to so many friends for so many years.

In 1901, Colonel Dickinson died. His tombstone in

Old Gray Cemetery tells little: "Perez Dickinson, Born Feb. 25, 1813, Died July 17, 1901. A resident of Knoxville for 71 years." These seventy-one years, though, were full of importance for Knoxville.

Perez Dickinson would no doubt be pleased that his beloved Island Home is now the East Tennessee School for the Deaf. The house, the shrubs, and many of the old perennial flowers are still there, though nothing remains of the greenhouse except its foundations. He would be pleased that all these are enjoyed by children, whom he loved and to whom he was invariably kind. The Main Street house is gone along with the troublous times it symbolized, and the tunnel is forgotten. Actually, nothing is left of Perez Dickinson except his influence on the city in his time.

CHAPTER NINE

✿ *Lawrence D. Tyson*

July 4, 1861. What did the South do about Independence Day during the War Between the States? Probably there were speeches drawing a parallel between 1861 and 1776. Probably small Southern boys shot off the traditional firecrackers, if any were available. It would be hard to ignore such a holiday as the Fourth of July. On that day, on his father's plantation near Greenville, North Carolina, was born a man destined to become important to the United States and to have great influence upon the City of Knoxville, Tennessee, though both these destinies would have seemed improbable in North Carolina on the day of his birth.

This was Lawrence D. Tyson. Until he was seventeen years old, he lived on the plantation of his father, Richard Tyson, a former officer in the Confederate Army. Only four when the Civil War ended, his childhood was spent in the Reconstruction Era, in which North Carolina was not so fortunate as neighboring Tennessee. At seventeen he went to nearby Salisbury, where he intended to work as a clerk; but it would have been a pity to waste a Lawrence Tyson behind a counter or over a ledger, and Fate took a hand to prevent it. In Salisbury, he heard of a competitive examination for appointment to the United States Military Academy at West Point. Mathematics was to be the principal subject of the examination, and Lawrence had always been good at mathematics, so he decided to try for the appointment. He spent some weeks in cramming for the examination. When the marks were posted, Lawrence Tyson had made the highest grades among all of the applicants and was awarded the appointment.

The West Point attended by Cadet Tyson from 1879 to 1883 looked not too unlike the military academy of today, but the course of study was a little different. The plans and strategy of Grant and Lee were the last word in military tactics, and considerable attention was given to methods of Indian fighting. Graduates could choose their branch of the service from among the artillery, the cavalry, and the infantry.

Newly graduated Second Lieutenant Lawrence Tyson chose the infantry. He was ordered to Cheyenne, Wyoming, where he was attached to the Ninth Infantry Regiment. Wyoming, in 1883, was a federal territory and was still in the throes of Indian wars. The murderous Apaches to the south of the territory were a constant threat to the few white settlers who were courageous enough to live within its borders, and the great Apache leader, Geronimo, was at the height of his fame. Here was the place for Lieutenant Tyson to put into practice all he had learned at West

Point about fighting Indians. With his troops, the Lieutenant went south to Colorado and New Mexico to join the
long campaign to capture Geronimo. This was enough Indian fighting to last any man a lifetime.

Back in Cheyenne, the handsome Lieutenant was a
great favorite with the ladies. One day he was chatting with
a charming belle on the front porch of a house on "Officers'
Row." Down the dusty street galloped a high-spirited
horse, ridden by a lovely young lady. And Fate stepped in
again! Just in front of the porch where the Lieutenant was
sitting, the skittish horse reared, and the lovely rider was
thrown into the dust. Dashing down the porch steps, Lieutenant Tyson lifted her gently and carried her off to the
home of her sister, where she was visiting. The first young
lady waited in vain upon the porch for his return.

As it happened, the governor of the Wyoming Territory at the time was Colonel George Baxter, from Tennessee. Mrs. Baxter, coming all the way out to Cheyenne
to take up her duties as Governor's Lady, had brought with
her her young sister, Miss Bettie McGhee, from Knoxville.
Miss McGhee might not have been the most accomplished
horsewoman in Wyoming, but in the eyes of the young
Lieutenant who rescued her on the day of the accident, she
was the loveliest thing that had ever happened to the territory. The courtship continued during Bettie McGhee's
visit with the Baxters, and when she went home to Knoxville it was to make preparations for her wedding.

In 1886, Lieutenant Lawrence Tyson arrived in Knoxville for the first time, but he had not come to stay. After
the marriage, and an elegant reception at the McGhee home
on Locust Street, the young Tysons returned to the West.
Colonel Charles McGhee was not at all sure that his daugh-

ter Bettie would be safe and comfortable in an Army post, and the letters that arrived in Knoxville from her added to his fears instead of allaying them. Young Mrs. Tyson described her new home as "remote" and "primitive," words which sounded rather ominous back in Knoxville. Then she wrote that her husband had been ordered on a foray with his troops, leaving her behind at the post with her half-breed Indian servant. Although she described the situation as an adventure, Colonel McGhee was more than ever worried about his Bettie. This was not at all the same thing as having a daughter in Wyoming as the wife of the governor of the territory!

Fortunately for Colonel McGhee's peace of mind, a letter soon arrived with the heartening news that Lieutenant Tyson had been ordered east to New York State. This was not bringing Bettie really close to home, but at least New York was considered civilized. A telegram brought word that a son, McGhee Tyson, had been born to the Lawrence Tysons in 1889 at Clifton Springs, New York, and there was great rejoicing in Knoxville at the news. Now the Tysons began to talk of settling down in one spot. This constant moving around required by the Army was not, they felt, really good for children.

Back in Knoxville, Colonel and Mrs. McGhee felt it would be nice for Bettie to come home to live. At the Colonel's request, Lieutenant Tyson was appointed professor of military tactics at The University of Tennessee in 1891. The Tysons found themselves really settled at last in a city that welcomed them both warmly for their charm and their talents. Lieutenant Tyson decided it would be better to leave the Army than to leave Knoxville. While serving as professor of military tactics, he was studying law at the University. In 1895, he resigned his position on the faculty and his commission in the Army, and entered the law firm of Lucky and Sanford, but the Army was not to be so easily put out of his life.

When war with Spain was declared in 1898, West Point graduates were urgently needed to train recruits quickly. Volunteering at once, Lieutenant Lawrence Tyson found himself a colonel. He was assigned to command the Sixth United States Volunteer Infantry, which he himself was expected to recruit. His men were all from Kentucky and Tennessee—mostly Tennessee, for he found recruiting easy in the Volunteer State. After hasty training, the Sixth Infantry was ordered to Puerto Rico, where they spent the rest of the brief war. When the war was over, Colonel Tyson remained in Puerto Rico for some months as Military Governor.

In 1899, it was once more possible for Colonel Tyson to leave the Army, but he did not return to the practice of law. Instead, he went into manufacturing, organizing not one but two mills (the Knoxville Cotton Mills and the Knoxville Spinning Co.) and was president of both. He was interested, too, in coal mining and in various iron works, and he became a prosperous businessman of Knoxville. The Tysons purchased a handsome house on Temple Avenue and, facing the frame structure with soft yellow brick, they added columns, terraces, balustrades, a porte cochère. There they lived with their children, McGhee, whose birth had influenced their coming to Knoxville, and their lovely daughter, Isabella, who was born here.

Mrs. Tyson was chairman, in 1897, of a Ladies' Committee to bring to Knoxville the building erected by the City of Knoxville for the Tennessee Centennial Exposition

Colonel Perez Dickinson's Island Home, the scene of lavish entertainments in the late 19th Century, is now the home of the Tennessee School for the Deaf.

In the garden at Confederate Memorial Hall, a miniature Grecian temple commands a view of lake and mountains.

in Nashville in 1896. The ladies felt that the building was worthy of preservation and belonged in Knoxville, but such a move would cost money. The city, having appropriated the money to place the building in Nashville, felt that further expense was not justified. Businessmen saw little future and no profit in such a venture. So it was up to the ladies, who hit upon a sure-fire money raising project. Knoxville's most renowned cooks were invited to contribute their favorite recipes for publication in the *Knoxville Cookbook*. Knoxville's cooks bowed to none in the culinary field, and ladies were pleased and flattered to be urged to divulge their secret recipes. Copies of the book sold like the proverbial hotcakes, and the Women's Building was brought home from Nashville and came to rest on Main Street, across from the Court House.

Desserts must have been especial favorites in the Tyson household, for Mrs. Tyson was represented in the cookbook by no less than eight—pie crust, lemon pie, molasses custard, lemon custard, suet pudding, pineapple jelly, delicate cake, and Quaker sponge cake. Oh, the recipes are mouth-watering! It is no wonder that Mrs. Tyson was acclaimed as one of Knoxville's finest hostesses, for as the *Knoxville Cookbook* puts it: "I can teach sugar to slip down your throats a million ways." The cookbook contained not only recipes but suggested menus, and judging from these it is surprising that Knoxvillians were not all noted for excess poundage. The following menu, by no means the most elaborate, is for

A Simple Evening Supper

(The true essentials of a feast are only fun and feed)

Chicken consommé

Sweetbread *patés*

Rolled Sandwiches Tied with Red Baby Ribbon
Jellied Chicken with Beet Decorations
Celery Salad Served in Rosy Cheeked Apples which are not
Pared
Macedoine of Fruits Served in Orange Baskets Tied with
Red Ribbon, and Whip Cream on Top
Candied Cherries   Coffee
O tempora, O mores!

In 1903, a committee of Colonel Tyson's friends called upon him with the request that he consider it his duty to run for the State Legislature on the Democratic ticket. This he consented to do and, upon his election, was chosen Speaker of the House of Representatives.

These were halcyon days for Knoxville, between the turn of the century and the First World War. Life was leisurely, and the pleasant amenities were happily observed. The city was prosperous in an era that combined manufacturing and wholesale payrolls to provide a comfortable economy. The Tysons and their friends were entertaining with receptions and garden parties, and the Tyson children's many friends were always welcome at the hospitable house on Temple Avenue. McGhee Tyson was growing up— he went east to St. Paul's School and then to Princeton University. After his graduation, he returned to Knoxville to join his father in business.

On January 10, 1917, occurred an event that was of particular significance to the Tysons, and to Knoxville. This was the opening and dedication of the handsome marble Lawson McGhee Library, which was henceforth to be a free public library supported by the city. In 1885, Colonel Charles McGhee, who had already established at his own expense St. John's Orphanage for Knoxville, decided to make another gift to the city. He wrote a letter to the president of the Knoxville Public Library Board inviting this small library to become part of a large one he intended to create. "It has been generally understood for some time," he said, "that I intend to erect on the (northeast) corner of Gay and Vine Streets a building to be used as a library, and to be at the same time a memorial to a beloved child." The child of whom he spoke was his daughter, Lawson McGhee (Mrs. Shelby Williams) who had died two years before at the age of twenty-three. The Knoxville Public Library was happy to transfer its books (and its debts) to Colonel McGhee, who built for his library a building that served not only as its location, but which also provided its endowment. The first and third floors of the building were rented for income purposes, while the library itself occupied the second floor. This building burned in 1904. Although *The Knoxville Journal* reported the following day that "All that is left of the handsome Lawson McGhee Library building, long the pride of the citizens, is the blackened and warped walls and smoking ruins," many of the library's books were rescued. Quarters for the library were rented, and the Gay Street building was rebuilt entirely as a business property in order to provide the necessary income for its maintenance. However, the library needed a building designed especially for its purposes, and the city was prepared to accept the financial responsibility for its operating expenses. So it was that in 1916, after the death of Colonel McGhee, the Gay Street property was sold and the proceeds used to build the new Lawson McGhee Library. Upon the day of the dedication of the building, Colonel L. D. Tyson, representing the McGhee family, formally presented the building to the city and became president of its Board of Trustees. He looked upon the library as a family responsibility, and Lawrence Tyson was never a man to shirk responsibilities.

A fellow trustee of the library was Calvin M. McClung, whose first wife was also a daughter of Colonel McGhee. He, too, felt a family responsibility, but he loved the library for its own sake. Calvin McClung, a man of literary tastes, amassed a collection of historical and genealogical books and papers that was outstanding in the South. Upon his death in 1919, his personal library was presented by his widow, Mrs. Barbara Adair McClung, to Lawson McGhee Library, in which he had been so interested. This became the famous McClung Historical Collection.

But the golden age of peace and prosperity for Knoxville was drawing to a close. The dedication of Lawson McGhee Library preceded by only a few months the declaration of war upon Germany, and here was another responsibility for Lawrence Tyson. He volunteered his services immediately, and President Wilson appointed him the only Brigadier General from Tennessee.

It was an interesting coincidence that the 59th Brigade, which General Tyson commanded, was trained at Camp Sevier in South Carolina, near the site of the Battle of King's Mountain. These were worthy successors to the mountain men. Landing at Calais in May of 1918, the 59th Brigade was the first group of American soldiers to enter Belgium. The famous Battle of Ypres, fought there on July 4, was General Tyson's birthday celebration for the year 1918. Tyson's troops were constantly under fire in Belgium and France until September 29, which was to be a great day for America and for Lawrence Tyson.

On the evening of the 28th of September, General Tyson made a speech to his men. He told them that they were facing one of the decisive battles of history, and he was right. For it was on the following day that the 59th Brigade, under his leadership, penetrated the "impregnable" Hindenburg Line, the stronghold of German defense. When the Hindenburg Line broke, the resistance of Germany broke with it, and the war ended a short six weeks later. It was possible for Lawrence Tyson once again to leave the Army and return to Knoxville. General Tyson received a hero's welcome, but he received it with humility and personal sorrow.

Young McGhee Tyson had volunteered for his country's service as soon as had his father, but he did not follow his father into the infantry. This was a new century, and there was to be a new kind of warfare. McGhee Tyson was one of the first to enlist in the Naval Reserve Flying Corps. He received instruction in flying at Boston and Pensacola, was commissioned an ensign, and was sent overseas with his outfit to England in August of 1918.

Flying was new in 1918—new and uncertain, and more than dangerous. On a mission over the North Sea on a cold autumn day, Lieutenant McGhee Tyson's plane was shot down. Official notice of his death was sent to General Tyson in France and to Mrs. Tyson in Knoxville. It was presumed from the circumstances of the accident that his body could never be recovered.

It was in the midst of the battle for the Hindenburg Line that General Tyson received the news of his son's death. Under such circumstances, even grief must wait. Nothing could interfere when the outcome of a great war hung in the balance; but as soon as the 59th Brigade had penetrated the Line, the General received leave to go to England to search for his son's body. It was cold on the coast of England in the fall of 1918, and the waters of the North Sea were icy, but there was a sorrowful duty to be done. Procuring a small boat, the General went back and forth along the coast, and out into the sea, searching for signs of the wreckage of a Navy plane. Several days passed without incident, but finally the father's diligent search was rewarded. The body of McGhee Tyson was found and identified, and started on its long journey home to Knoxville, a journey that was to require months to complete.

A strange coincidence attended the final stage of the journey. James M. Meek, one of McGhee Tyson's boyhood friends, had served in the infantry during the war. He was released from the Army at Camp Lee, Virginia, and boarded the train there for home. As he waited to take the train, he saw loaded upon it a flag-draped coffin. When the train pulled into the station at Knoxville, James Meek saw from the window a guard of honor standing at attention, and he stepped from the car to join the group waiting to receive his closest friend, McGhee Tyson, whose body he had unknowingly accompanied home. Full military honors attended the burial in Old Gray Cemetery of McGhee Tyson, first Tennessee aviator to fall in battle, whose body would not have been found but for the diligent search of his father.

On Armistice Day of 1919, Knoxville's returned soldiers paraded down Gay Street to the strains of "Over There" and "It's a Long, Long Way to Tipperary." Tents were pitched on the Court House lawn for a detachment of infantry that would be featured in the parade. And Tennessee's only Brigadier General, recipient of the Distin-

guished Service Medal, rode tall and straight at the head
of the procession.

The Tyson's lovely daughter, Isabella, had married
a young Air Force officer, Kenneth Gilpin, and had gone to
live in Virginia. After the wedding at St. John's Episcopal
Church, the house on Temple Avenue was the scene of the
wedding reception. The guests overflowed the reception
rooms on the first floor and the stately ballroom on the
third floor, and walked and chatted in the gardens. So, as
Knoxville once more took up peaceful pursuits, the General and Mrs. Tyson were living alone in their hospitable
house; but they were far too busy to have time to be lonely.

The General entertained many visitors from out of
town. He was most interested in the American Legion and
welcomed many military dignitaries, including General
Pershing, who came to Knoxville. The formal gardens of
the Tyson home served often as the setting for amateur the-
atricals, dance recitals, and garden parties.

Already they had made their first of many gifts to
the city. The Knoxville Cotton Mill and the Knoxville
Spinning Co. (of both which mills L. D. Tyson was president) had decided that there was a need for a settlement
house in the Dale Avenue area to care for the children of
mothers working in the mills, and to provide a community
center for the neighborhood. In 1918, while General Tyson
was in France, such a settlement house was constructed in
accordance with plans he had approved before his departure. Mrs. Tyson presided at the formal opening of the Dale
Avenue Settlement House, in the absence of her husband.
She spoke of the importance of doing well whatever was
undertaken, however humble the task might be. The making of a really fine cup of coffee, she said, was as much a

real achievement as painting a picture or designing a building. This was language that appealed to the people the Settlement House was built to serve, in whom Mrs. Tyson continued to take a real personal interest. The General, when he took up again his duties as president of the two mills, continued to be regarded with respect and affection by his employees. He was a kind man, who cautioned the managers of his mills that no employee should be allowed to want for medical care, or for any necessities. Many people were helped through the Settlement House, many others by General and Mrs. Tyson directly; but always the assistance was given quietly and confidentially.

There was much talk of airplane travel. Newspapers carried stories of "long-distance flights" and predicted that it would not be long before the nation would be served by a network of airports. There was a feeling that Knoxville should not be left behind when other cities were preparing for the coming of the "air age." So General and Mrs. Tyson felt that a fitting gift from them to their city would be an airport, which should bear the name "McGhee Tyson" in honor of Knoxville's first flying officer. They presented to the city a tract of level land on Sutherland Avenue in West Knoxville, and McGhee Tyson Airport became a reality.

People were beginning to be interested in the appearance of their cities, and a City Beautiful League was formed, in which Mrs. Tyson was very active. Unsightly houses and sprawling businesses had sprung up along the riverfront, and the City Beautiful League felt that the improvement of a riverside drive should be undertaken at once. Harrisburg, Pennsylvania, had just completed a beautiful river parkway, and the mayor of Harrisburg, Vance Mc-

Cormick, was invited to Knoxville to explain what his city had done, and how they had done it. Municipal improvement is usually a slow process. In the meanwhile, the Tysons decided that Knoxville needed a new city park. They selected and gave to the city a tract of land along a winding creek in West Knoxville, to be known as Tyson Park in memory of their son. Mrs. Tyson selected shrubs and perennial flowers for the park and directed their planting. She planned as the final horticultural achievement in the park a circular garden, to be located at the top of the western slope, which would copy faithfully in color and design a Dresden dinner plate. The planting of this Dresden garden was deferred because of something else that happened.

As though he were not busy enough with his two Knoxville mills, his business interests in other towns, and his civic affairs, General Tyson had purchased a newspaper. *The Knoxville Sentinel* prospered under his direction and, of course, supported his candidacy when, a few years later, he was persuaded to run for the Senate on the Democratic ticket.

The planting of the Dresden garden had to wait, for the Tysons were moving to Washington. Knoxvillians were proud of their representative in the Senate. Here was a man of dignity and business ability, with a wonderful record of Army service. Washington welcomed the Tysons, who bought a splendid house there and entertained many new friends and many old friends, too. Senator Tyson concerned himself especially with legislation that would protect veterans, and the American Legion was still a major interest with him.

In 1929, Knoxville was preparing to build a new junior high school. It was to be located on Kingston Pike, near

Tyson Park, and the School Board agreed that it should be called Tyson School in honor of Knoxville's distinguished senator, but Senator Tyson was not to see the school.

When the Senate recessed for the summer in June of 1929, the Tysons returned to Knoxville. The Senator did not look well, and he complained of the heat. He announced his intention of going, later in the summer, to French Lick Springs for a rest. But first, he said, he had to go to Greeneville to make a speech. The American Legion was having its Tennessee state convention there, and he had agreed to be the principal speaker. Against the advice of his friends, he kept the engagement, for he considered it a responsibility. Ill in Greeneville, he was worse when he returned to Knoxville. A visit to specialists in Philadelphia was advised, and for a time his condition seemed improved. He died unexpectedly in Philadelphia, his Senate term uncompleted, but secure in the knowledge that he had never failed to meet his responsibilities.

After Senator Tyson's burial in Old Gray Cemetery, his newspaper and his mills passed into other hands. Into other hands, too, went the Dale Avenue Settlement House, which was deeded to the Junior League of Knoxville by the two mills which had built it. A portrait of Senator Tyson was placed in the school which bears his name. Upon Mrs. Tyson's death, the beautiful Tyson House was given to St. John's Episcopal Church and The University of Tennessee.

During the depression years, Tyson Park was more than ever needed. With W.P.A. labor, a bandstand and several tennis courts were constructed, and later city administrations have added outdoor grills and picnic tables, and a wading pool for very young visitors. The Dresden garden was never planted, but even without it, Tyson Park has proven a green oasis in the midst of a growing city.

And what about the airport? The air age, when it did arrive, was a bigger thing than even McGhee Tyson would have predicted, and it was soon discovered that the site on Sutherland Avenue was much too small and too near the heavily populated areas to handle the increasing volume of landings and departures. The city government decided on a new site in nearby Blount County, where the airport would serve the great Aluminum Company of America plants as well as Knoxville sixteen miles away. There was some talk of calling this the Knox-Blount Airport, or simply Knoxville Municipal Airport. However, Tyson Park had been given to the city with the understanding that the city's "principal airport" would always be called "McGhee Tyson." So the airport changed its location, but not its name. The former airport site became what would have pleased its donor best—the armory for the National Guard.

CHAPTER TEN

The University of Tennessee

When William Blount called together the first Territorial Legislature in 1794, the problems facing the inexperienced lawmakers were many and varied. They had to deal with Indian affairs, create counties, incorporate towns, establish a tax system, and enact other laws for the government of the territory. It is to the everlasting credit of Tennessee's first legislative body that, in the face of such pressing problems, it found time to consider and pass an act which, in the interest of educating its citizens, created two colleges within the territory. One of these institutions of higher learning was to be at Greeneville. The other, to be located at Knoxville, was at once named Blount College in honor of His Excellency, William Blount.

Blount College was not the first college established within the boundaries of what is now Tennessee, for in 1785, the Reverend Samuel Doak had founded Martin Academy, near Jonesboro, which was subsequently char-

164

tered by the Territorial Legislature of 1795 as Washington College. But Blount College has the distinction of two much more important "firsts." A most unusual feature of the legislative act creating the college is the following paragraph:

And the trustees shall take effectual care that students of all denominations may and shall be admitted to the equal advantages of a liberal education, and to the emoluments and honours of the college, and that they shall receive alike fair, generous, and equal treatment during their residence.

This short sentence made Blount College the first non-sectarian college in the Southwest, and Tennessee authorities maintain that it was the first college in America whose non-denominational status was guaranteed by the legislative act granting its charter.

James White, Knoxville's founder, was named one of the first trustees of Blount College. Through his efforts, the town square was made available for the use of the college and there, on the corner of Gay and Clinch streets (present site of the Burwell Building) a two-story frame building was constructed which was paid for by public subscription. The legislature appropriated no money for the college at any time.

Meanwhile, the college had operated for a time at the home of its president, the Reverend Dr. Samuel Carrick, at the Forks of the River, where he had been conducting a seminary. Dr. Carrick added this presidency to numerous other duties, for he was already pastor of several Presbyterian churches scattered over a wide area. Yet such was his remarkable industry that, as soon as the Gay Street quarters were ready, new students were enrolled and the college reopened its doors. The price of tuition was $8.00 per session of five months, and board cost $25.00 per session, and from these fees the college was self-supporting!

Unfortunately, the records of the college for its earliest years have been lost, although there was in existence as late as 1879 a record book for the period 1804 to 1808, for it was used by Moses White in writing his *Early History of the University of Tennessee* published that year. White found on the enrollment list, probably for the year 1804, five names which entitle the institution to be called the first co-ed college in America. William Blount's daughter Barbara, along with Polly McClung, Jennie Armstrong, and Mattie and Kittie Kain were among the students at that time. These were destined to be the last co-eds in the state until the University again admitted women students, but that did not occur until ninety years later! In honor of these real pioneers in education, five women's dormitories at The University of Tennessee today are named Barbara Blount, Polly McClung, Jennie Armstrong, Mattie Kain, and Kittie Kain.

In 1807, the name of the school was changed to East Tennessee College. The change was necessary in order to take advantage of a land-grant act passed by the United States Congress in 1806, which promised to support the college through the sale of public lands. As the lands to be sold were priced at the then high figure of $2.00 an acre, and as they were already firmly occupied by squatters, very few acres were sold, and the college received almost no money. Lack of funds forced East Tennessee College to close following the death of President Carrick in 1809, and it did not reopen until 1826.

In 1828, East Tennessee College moved to the present

main campus of the University, occupying a two-story college building. By 1835, three one-story residence halls had been built to form a square atop Barbara Hill (named for Barbara Blount). In 1834, Joseph Estabrook had become president of the college and proceeded to make sweeping changes. Mr. Estabrook, a graduate of Dartmouth College, had an idea that East Tennessee College should offer a program comparable to that to be had in the very best Eastern colleges, and to that end he revised the course of study, brought in a fine faculty of well-educated and dedicated teachers, and insisted on quality work by the students. So well did he labor that, in 1840, the college, having achieved larger scope, was given university status by the legislature. In 1842, new and better buildings, of brick this time, were constructed for it, and for ten years everything went smoothly at East Tennessee University.

However, after the resignation of President Estabrook in 1850, the University suffered a period of deterioration and decay. It closed its doors in 1861 when the Civil War began, but its buildings were used by Confederate and Union forces alternately throughout the war. During the siege of Knoxville, cannon were mounted on College Hill, and the hill was shelled repeatedly by the Confederates from the heights across the river. At the close of the war, the buildings were in such deplorable condition that a widespread rebuilding program was necessary before they could again be used for educational purposes.

With the readmission of Tennessee to the Union in 1866, East Tennessee University entered upon a period of good fortune. The United States Congress had, in 1862, passed another land-grant act. This act set aside certain public lands, principally in the west, to be sold for the ben-

efit of colleges and universities which would undertake to
establish departments of agriculture. Unfortunately for
Tennessee, the act stated that colleges must apply for these
benefits within two years, and 1866 was too late. However,
William G. Brownlow was Governor of Tennessee, and
Andrew Johnson was President of the United States, and
through their good offices the Congress was persuaded to
make an exception for the State of Tennessee. Accordingly,
in 1867 a special act of Congress entitled Tennessee to qualify for benefits under the Act of 1862, and the legislature
in 1869 gave the donation to East Tennessee University.
The trustees of the University purchased, as the law required, a large farm on the north bank of the river, just
west of Third Creek, and established a College of Agriculture there. The farm then purchased is still part of the University property, and is now the site of the handsome agriculture buildings.

Unlike the Land Grant Act of 1806, this one actually
paid considerable sums into the University's coffers; the
difficulty lay in persuading any students (but particularly
the sons of farmers) to avail themselves of the courses offered in the newly created College of Agriculture. When
the public at last understood that such courses were scien-
tifically helpful rather than backbreaking and laborious,
the agriculture courses became increasingly popular, and
their excellence added greatly to the prestige of the University.

This University that had reopened after the Civil War
was a very different type of institution from its predecessor. First of all, as a result of a requirement in the Land
Grant Act, it had become a military school. The students
were called cadets, and military discipline was rigid. Uni-

forms were worn, and drill was required of all students; a military commandant, second in authority only to the president, was added to the faculty. Secondly, the financial situation of the institution was greatly improved by the land-grant funds, which made possible the building of new dormitories and recitation halls. Old South College, still in use on the main campus of the University today, was one of the buildings constructed as part of this program of expansion in 1872. There was more money, too, for professors' salaries, and this made possible the securing of an excellent classical faculty, with resulting higher standards. These two things led to a development of even greater importance when in 1879, East Tennessee University became The University of Tennessee. However, it was not until twenty-five years later that the University received its first appropriation of funds from the State Legislature. The state was struggling under a great burden of debt during this postwar period. In addition, it was well-nigh impossible to collect state taxes from the impoverished citizens. As financial conditions in the South began to improve, money was forthcoming for educational purposes, and The University of Tennessee found itself for the first time relatively secure, financially.

The man selected to head the University when it was reorganized and reopened in 1865 was Dr. Thomas W. Humes. This was the same Thomas W. Humes who had been the editor of Perez Dickinson's newspaper, the *Knoxville Times* in the 1830's. He had meanwhile entered the Episcopal ministry and was for some years the rector of St. John's Episcopal Church in Knoxville. The congregation of St. John's Church was so divided in sentiment when the Civil War began that Dr. Humes resigned his pastorate and the church was closed. Dr. Humes himself was a strong and vocal advocate of the cause of the Union, and it was he who recited the Episcopal burial service by moonlight when General Sanders was buried in the churchyard of the Second Presbyterian Church on the first night of the siege of Knoxville. General Burnside himself, while the Union forces were occupying the city, requested Dr. Humes to reopen St. John's Church, and this was done, although the Sunday morning congregations were limited to those parishioners whose sentiments were with the Union.

It was therefore quite logical that the University which was to benefit by the good offices of William Brownlow and Andrew Johnson in securing the land-grant funds for it should have chosen Dr. Humes as its president. It was most fortunate that his qualifications were not limited to his political beliefs, but included a fine education and administrative talents, for the University had need of all three.

In 1875, the United Presbyterian Church had established in Knoxville a college for Negro students, with the primary purpose of preparing them for the Presbyterian ministry. This college, still flourishing today, has a distinguished history of service to the Negro race and boasts many successful graduates.

It is perhaps not generally known that Knoxville College was at one time a branch of The University of Tennessee. The State Constitution of 1870 provided that no school established or aided by the state "shall allow white and Negro children to be received as scholars in the same school." The earlier legislative act which endowed the University with the proceeds of the land grant said that: "no citizen of this state, otherwise qualified, shall be excluded from the privileges of the university by reason of his race or color; but the accommodation and instruction of persons of color shall be separate from the white." In the year 1880, four Negroes were elected to membership in the State Legislature. At this time, a certain number of college scholarships were offered by the state, and the holders of these scholarships were appointed by members of the legislature. Finding several colored students who were qualified for college entrance, the Negro legislators secured state scholarships for these members of their race. This meant that their tuition was paid by the state at either Fisk University in Nashville or Knoxville College in Knoxville. In 1884, the trustees required all of the Negro state students to attend Knoxville College, in order, so they said, that the poor colored boys could obtain employment on the University farm.

In 1890, the United States Congress passed the Second Morrill Act, which provided additional funds for land-grant colleges, and which also required that all participating institutions provide equal facilities for colored and white students. Of course, The University of Tennessee was anxious to take advantage of this opportunity to secure more funds, and the trustees felt that Knoxville College should be selected to serve as the University's colored branch, receiving a proportionate share of the land-grant funds. William Rule's *History of Knoxville*, which was published in 1900, explains:

> As soon, therefore, as the students then attending Fisk University could be graduated, steps were taken which led to the establishment of such a department at Knoxville. By contract with the trustees of Knoxville College, an excellent institution for the education of colored people, the buildings, grounds, and teaching staff of that in-

stitution were made available for the university as its
colored department.

The facilities there provided needed, however, to be
supplemented along the line of scientific and industrial
education. The president accordingly visited some of the
friends of this institution at the North, and secured the
funds for a new scientific and mechanical building. A
tract of land adjacent to the college was provided for
practical work in agriculture and horticulture. . . . The
new department is called the industrial department for
colored students, and is immediately under the supervision of the trustees and president of the university as any
other department of the institution, all of its teachers being elected by the trustees, and the entire expenses of the
department being paid by them. The several professors
of the university have supervision of the work there in
their respective departments.

This arrangement continued in force until 1909. In that
year, a legislative act established the Tennessee Agricultural and Industrial Institute and shifted the Negro's share
of the land-grant funds from Knoxville College to this new
institution near Nashville.

In 1887, Dr. Charles Dabney became president of the
University. In a program of sweeping reform, he promptly
fired all but two of the faculty. The new faculty he brought
in was so outstanding in scholarship and character that the
University began to grow by leaps and bounds. When Dr.
Dabney took office the total yearly income of the institution from all sources was only thirty-two thousand dollars
a year, and there were only one hundred and seventy-four
students. His task was not easy, for his liberal arts faculty
resented any attention paid to the College of Agriculture,
which they dubbed the "Cow College." Dr. Dabney was
firm in safeguarding the rights of the agricultural depart-

ment, because a large proportion of the University's income was derived from the land-grant funds. A new federal act, called the Hatch Act, gave further benefits to those colleges which would agree to establish agricultural experiment stations. These funds were secured to the University by the establishment of several stations, where a great deal was learned about best methods of farming for the region. Bulletins were written, published, and distributed to farmers, describing the results of the experiments. Unfortunately, however, the bulletins were couched in very erudite and scientific language, and were ignored by the farmers for whom they were intended.

This difficulty was overcome in 1914 when the Federal Extension Act (the Smith-Lever Act) created the offices of county agents, practical agriculturists who took the findings of the experiment stations directly to the farmers, discussed their problems with them face to face, and explained to them in language they could understand how to go about solving their difficulties. In 1917, the Smith-Hughes Act carried this personal contact teaching plan a step further with the establishment of home demonstration; the idea behind this act was to improve the whole farm by improving the farmer's home. As the county agents and home demonstration agents carried the University's practical agriculture into the very homes of the state's citizens, the University became a personal friend to people all over the state. This pleasant relationship with the residents of the farthest counties has helped the University to grow.

In the 1890's, Knoxvillians considered the University particularly their own and flocked to the events on the college calendar that were open to the public. Debates, moot courts, and graduation exercises were popular, but other occasions had even greater attractions to offer. There was an annual strawberry festival at the College of Agriculture on Kingston Pike where student-grown berries were served in as many delicious ways as visitors could manage to sample. There were also dress parades—glamorous affairs indeed. The uniform of the University's cadets was the same as that still worn by cadets at the United States Military Academy at West Point. There was a band to play stirring marches, and a tall drum major made even taller by his black bearskin shako. Well-polished brass buttons twinkled in the sun and swords flashed as cadet officers saluted the reviewing stand in passing. Knoxvillians felt that they had every reason to be proud of their University, and they were right. Something new was added in 1893, when the University opened its doors to women students for the second time. This was a step not lightly nor hastily taken by the administrative officers of the institution, for it presented many new problems. Of course, a large number of the young ladies who went to college in the nineties wanted the liberal arts course their brothers were electing, but there was a strong movement in educational circles to broaden the scope of college courses to include specialized training. It was a logical step for a University admitting young women to add to its curriculum courses in home economics, so the trustees acquired from the Knoxville Female Institute its large brick building on Main Street and established there a department of home economics. And the social life of the students of the University as a whole became immediately much more social.

In 1902, standards for teachers were uniform only in that they were uniformly low. Dr. Philander P. Claxton, one of Tennessee's foremost educational figures, had for

some time been advising that the state's public school system would best and quickest be improved by the improvement of the training of its teachers. In this year, with the
aid of President Dabney, Dr. Claxton launched a brilliant
idea which brought immediate fame to him and to the University. Dr. Claxton planned and established what he called
the Summer School of the South, for the purpose of teaching the South's teachers how to teach, combined with an
outstanding cultural program. Letters were written to the
various Southern states announcing the plan, and Dr. Claxton and his staff hopefully awaited registration day. They
felt that if three hundred teachers would only come, a good
start could be made toward raising Southern standards of
teaching. When the day dawned, they were swamped by
twelve hundred applications for admission to the Summer
School. Determined not to turn away a single teacher, plans
were hastily revised, and in all more than 2000 were somehow accommodated. A shed was speedily built atop the
campus of the University, and all available classroom space
was utilized. So many of the teachers had come from flat
country that they were alarmed and discouraged at the
thought of climbing the steep hill to the University buildings. Undaunted, Dr. Claxton had dry sawdust sprinkled
over the slippery walkways and hired hacks to transport
his wary students from the foot of The Hill to his classrooms at the top. In succeeding summers, there continued
to be more enrolled in the Summer School than there
were students in the regular University sessions. The result of the Summer School of the South was two-fold.
The University established a pioneer effort in summer-
time education and ultimately extended its school year to
include a regular summer quarter. Dr. Claxton, whose

fame as an educator had become nation-wide, was appointed United States Commissioner of Education, an office he held with distinction for many years.

In the succeeding administrations of Dr. Brown Ayres, Dr. H. A. Morgan, Dr. James D. Hoskins, and Dr. C. E. Brehm, changes for the University came thick and fast. It was the gentlemanly Dr. Ayres who made the difficult but just decision to locate the medical and dental departments of the University in Memphis, feeling as had Hugh Lawson White that it was not fair always to ask West Tennesseans to travel the longest distances. Tennessee became famous in educational circles over the years for the excellence of its College of Engineering and its College of Home Economics, which moved to a large new building in order to accommodate all the students who were electing its courses. An outstanding nursery school was opened where students could observe and work with children of preschool age. The College of Education was growing and growing, and the College of Agriculture was recognized as one of the nation's finest. The fine arts and the lively arts were given renewed emphasis. The expanded athletic program brought new renown to the University, as the Tennessee Vols continued year after year to play championship football to the delight of students, alumni, and Knoxvillians at large. Of course, as new departments and new courses were added at the University, the old established ones were retained and expanded, so there was a pressing need for new buildings and new dormitories. Obviously these could not all be fitted into the Main Campus, so a long-range building program was planned, a style of architecture selected (Ayres Hall was the first of this series of buildings), and the University began to spread over the streets adjacent to The Hill. New men's and women's dormitories (filled to capacity), new buildings for law, business administration, and education have gone up. A large armory and a larger field house have been built. A student center has been added. Plans for the future include many more buildings, and many more students, for the University continues to grow.

The University of Tennessee has come a long way from a handful of students instructed in a single frame building by a faculty of two, including the president. There are now more than seven thousand five hundred students regularly enrolled at Knoxville, and several thousand more attend the various branches of the University throughout the state. Still the University draws Knoxville citizens to its special events, though the events themselves are different—football, basketball, concerts, the theatre, Carnicus and the University All-Sing have replaced the strawberry festival and the dress parade.

Only two things really have remained unchanged about the University: Knoxville's pride in it, and Tennessee's affection for it.

CHAPTER ELEVEN

The Distaff Side

From the moment of its founding, Knoxville was a city of some cultural aspirations, and this is at least partly the result of the influence of its female citizens. East Tennessee has always been noted for its rugged individualists, and Knoxville has had its share of ladies with minds of their own who have sometimes had quite an effect on local history.

There was, for instance, Mrs. William Blount, who never wanted to be a "pioneer woman." Mary Grainger Blount was born in Wilmington, North Carolina, within sight and sound of the sea. The Graingers were people of means, and the Blount family into which she married enjoyed the same affluent circumstances. Mary's education was limited to household management and the social graces, but these lessons she learned well. Both the Blounts were sociable people, and from the first their home was open to a stream of visitors—family members, business associates, political allies. People of all walks of life found the Blounts hospitable and gracious. This, too, was a form of training that Mary Blount was to find very useful in her later life.

When William Blount was a member of the Continental Congress and the Constitutional Convention, Mary traveled with him to Philadelphia and New York, where she enjoyed every moment of the social life to which her husband's prominence entitled her. She was, of course, both pleased and proud when William Blount was appointed by President Washington to be governor of the newly created federal Territory South of the River Ohio, but when she realized that the Governor had every intention of moving his household to the Tennessee country, Mary Blount was horrified. She wept a great deal. She spoke at length of Indian perils in the new country. She deplored the dangerous mountain roads, the uncertain climate, and the distance from the healthful sea breezes. And she flatly refused to take the children to the dangerous frontier outposts.

If Mary Blount had been a trifle more determined, or William Blount a trifle less fond of his family and the comforts of his home, she might have stayed quietly in North Carolina and waited for letters from the Tennessee country. But William Blount agreed with his Mary that his position as governor of the territory called for a standard of living as near as possible like that of the eastern seaboard, no matter what the difficulty of obtaining and maintaining this standard on the frontier.

As soon as William Blount had settled upon Knoxville as the capital of the territory, he set about building a commodious log house which would serve as his residence during the construction of a really suitable mansion for his

Mary. The elaborate plans for the new house, and the necessity for being on the spot to supervise the details of its construction, lured Mary Blount to the frontier country. No sooner had she arrived than the wise William planned a little ceremony in her honor, of a type he knew would delight her.

The Governor had invested rather heavily in one of the most important business ventures of the frontier country, and his investment had made possible the enlargement of King's Ironworks at Kingsport and the installation of a new iron-smelting furnace. The opening of the new furnace was made the occasion for a two-day celebration which included games, wrestling, and various feats of strength, with prizes bestowed by the Governor himself. But the climax was for Mary Blount. The new furnace was charged with ore and charcoal, and a raised platform was built beside it. To this platform Mary Blount ascended, and, with a beribboned bottle of rum, gracefully christened the furnace "The Barbara" in honor of the Governor's mother!

Thus reassured that the amenities of life were to be preserved even in this far frontier, Mary Blount settled down in the temporary log house to watch the building of the Governor's mansion. Here was a good place to put to use her training in household management, for forethought and careful planning were absolutely essential. Each pane of glass, every kitchen utensil, all furnishings and bedding, hardware and nails—all these things must be brought by wagon from North Carolina, by way of Abingdon, Virginia. As the house took form, Mary Blount planned her garden—kitchen garden, herb plot, fruit tree plantings, and the beloved flower garden. Orders went off to North Carolina for seeds, plants, and cuttings. And in the amazingly short time, considering the difficulties, of one year, the mansion was finished, and the Blounts moved into it in 1792.

With seven children, the house was crowded; but crowded or not, there were usually guests. Mary Blount had thought she was busy with visitors in the early years of her marriage, but all that had merely been preparation for the years when as the Governor's Lady and mistress of his mansion she entertained a constant stream of callers. Some of the guests could be lodged at the nearby Chisholm's Tavern, and some (the Cherokee chieftains who came to consult the Governor) slept in the yard; but there were still ministers, government officials, missionaries, and family and friends who found it true that at the Blount Mansion there was "always room for one more." This was a sort of perpetual open house, but Mary Blount loved it.

At first she was not really happy on the frontier, but she was so busy that only once or twice was she able to make the long trip back to the North Carolina sea coast. To her surprise, she found that the Indians she had expected to fear were very friendly toward her. In fact, the chieftains who visited the Blounts admired her so much that Mary Blount was said to have had great influence upon them in preventing raids upon the territory's capital. Yet she was delighted when, in 1793, the federal government built a blockhouse in Knoxville for the defense of the city and sent a garrison of soldiers to man it. Here were officers whose uniforms lent glamour to her entertainments, and here were soldiers to drill and fire off salutes with the blockhouse cannon. Knoxville was beginning to feel like a city.

In 1793 there was a celebration in Knoxville that sounds as if Mary Blount had a hand in the planning. This was the first Fourth of July observance in the new city. At two o'clock in the afternoon, the federal troops under the command of Captain Rickard paraded through the streets and fired the federal salute. Very handsome they were in their uniforms, and the drill was impressive. At four o'clock in the afternoon, all the citizens of the town partook of an elegant banquet, which ended with the drinking of no less than fifteen toasts. In the evening, "Mr. Rickard's company was under arms; they were drawn up in a grove near the encampment, where they fired a 'feu de joie,' which, from the darkness of the evening and the judicious manner in which the company was disposed, produced a most pleasing effect; after which there was a display of fireworks, from an elegant colonnade in front of Mr. Rickard's marquee."

"Sweet Mary Grainger," as she was affectionately known in the Tennessee country, was greatly admired and appreciated in Knoxville. She kept her standards high, and they were copied by the other residents. Even the Territorial Legislature complimented her when it met in 1794, for the county seat of newly created Blount County was named Maryville in her honor, and a later legislature of the State of Tennessee named Grainger County for her.

When the Blounts went east to Philadelphia following his election to the Senate, they both enjoyed greatly this opportunity to engage in the wide social life of the national capital. There were dinner parties and receptions, plays and balls, and Mary Blount was positively radiant in such an atmosphere. So gracious, so attractive, so well-dressed, and so pleasant was she, that even her husband's political opponents had nothing but admiration for her. From the Senate gallery, she saw the inauguration of President Adams and Vice-President Jefferson, unaware that her husband would soon be expelled from the Senate under charges of conspiracy against the government. Yet, when the ex-Senator joined her in North Carolina, in 1797, it was Mary Blount who urged that they hurry home to Knoxville—her roots had gone deep into this new land, and she was surprised to find herself homesick for it.

Few Knoxvillians believed that William Blount was guilty of any offense against the interests of Tennesseans, and when the Blounts returned to Knoxville during his trial, the people of the city accorded Mary Blount the same affection and respect they had shown her before. Now she was busier than ever with her household of seven children. While the two eldest daughters were entertaining beaux in the withdrawing room of the mansion, the two eldest sons were enrolling in Blount College, and the three youngest children were noisily playing in the house and garden. His expulsion from the Senate had in no way impaired William Blount's popularity, and there were balls and dinners for Mary Blount to attend in Tennessee's capital, too.

Through many vicissitudes, Mary Blount had held her head high, but more was yet to be required of her. In 1800, usually healthy Knoxville suffered an epidemic of fever. Mary Blount's mother was the first member of the Blount household to be stricken, then the children fell ill, and Mary herself. The grief of her mother's death was followed by the shock of the death of William Blount, worn out with watching at the bedside of their eldest son. Too ill to attend her husband's funeral, it did not occur to Mary

Blount to attempt to return now to North Carolina. Knoxville was now her home. She roused herself to supervise
the education of her children, to receive the calls of her
many friends, but after a short two years she died of jaun-
dice and was buried with her husband in the First Presbyterian Churchyard.

It was a brief ten years that Mary Blount lived in
Knoxville, and the manner in which she lived here was
simply the one to which she was accustomed. Yet she
left her mark of gracious living and hospitality on the city,
and she proved equal to the problems of both popularity
and adversity. She never did become a "pioneer woman"
as we understand the phrase.

There was another lady important to Knoxville's early
history who, like Mary Blount, was the mother of seven
children; but this lady's children were all boys. In itself an
interesting fact, this is only the beginning of her story.
Margaret Russell was born near Dandridge, in what is now
Jefferson County, in 1777. Her father and her maternal
grandfather had both been officers in the Revolutionary
War. Pretty Margaret had many suitors, but she chose to
marry James Cowan, a young man of substance and high
principles. James Cowan's brothers, Samuel and Nathaniel,
had in 1792 opened Knoxville's first store at the corner of
State and Front streets, and they persuaded their young
brother James that Knoxville, an up-and-coming town in
1800, was a more profitable location for a merchant than
Dandridge.

So early in 1801, James and Margaret Cowan arrived
in the capital of Tennessee, and James set about renting a
building and acquiring a stock of merchandise. The fever

The University of Tennessee expands westward from "The Hill." Neyland Stadium is in the foreground, downtown Knoxville at right.

Above: Dominating the skyline of the expanded University campus is the Humanities and Social Sciences complex.

Below: Memorabilia of the late Senator Estes Kefauver are housed in this special wing of the University's James D. Hoskins Library.

that had caused the death of so many Knoxvillians (including William Blount) in 1800 had abated during the winter months. With the return of hot weather, there was a recurrence of the epidemic, not so widespread nor so severe as in the previous summer, but causing several deaths. One of those who died of fever in June of 1801 was James Cowan, who had but recently arrived in the city. The plight of his young widow was sad, for James Cowan had not managed to start his store, and a baby was expected. On December 23, 1801, James H. Cowan was born.

Remaining in Knoxville, where she was aided by her husband's brothers, Margaret Cowan announced her intention of taking good care of the estate left her by her husband, so that her son might be the fine and wealthy merchant his father had not lived long enough to become. The mother's ambitions were realized, for James H. Cowan became one of Knoxville's leading retail merchants and a pioneer wholesale "merchant prince." He was elected mayor of the city in 1856.

But this is only the first part of the story. In April of 1802, the attractive young widow of James Cowan married Thomas Humes, who was also a merchant. With the Humes on their wedding journey went the infant James H. Cowan, only five months' old, whose mother declined to leave him behind in the care of any relative, however devoted, or any slave, however faithful. Like James Cowan, Thomas Humes was a man of high principles, who took most seriously his responsibilities as an elder of the First Presbyterian Church. Four sons were born to Margaret and Thomas Humes—then suddenly, in 1816, Thomas Humes died. A few months after his death, their fifth son, Andrew, was born.

Left a widow with six young sons, Margaret Humes
determined that her boys would be brought up with great
regard for religious precept, and that they should have the
best possible education available at East Tennessee College.
East Tennessee was obviously a land of opportunity, and
there was a favorite local saying—"Only three generations
from the plow handle to the silk hat." But canny Margaret
Humes knew also that, without character, ambition and
education, it could be only three generations from the silk
hat to the plow handle. So well did she accomplish her intentions that one of her sons, Thomas W. Humes, became
in succession a newspaper editor (the *Knoxville Times*), an
Episcopal clergyman, president of East Tennessee University and its successor, the University of Tennessee, an author, and a librarian.

Having remained a widow for four years, Margaret
was married again in 1820 to Francis Ramsey, one of the
first men to settle in the Knoxville area, who had come
with James White to the Tennessee country in 1786. Mr.
Ramsey had been a surveyor and a prosperous farmer on
his Swan Pond estate, and he had held various positions
of distinction in the governments of the Territory South of
the River Ohio and the State of Tennessee. At the time of
his marriage to Margaret Humes in 1820, he had just been
named president of the State Bank of Knoxville. Francis
Ramsey's three surviving children by his first wife were
grown up in 1820—one of them was the celebrated Dr.
J. G. M. Ramsey, physician and historian. This third marriage for each of the Ramseys was short-lived, for in November of 1820, Francis Ramsey died of pneumonia. It
sounds impossible, but it was perfectly true. Three times
Margaret Ramsey had been widowed, and three times

she bore a son after her husband's death. Five months after the death of his father, Francis A. Ramsey was born.

Margaret's husband Francis Ramsey had been interested in education and was a great admirer of men skilled in the healing arts. His older son, Dr. J. G. M. Ramsey, talked much with his step-mother about medicine and about the early history of the Tennessee country. Francis Alexander Ramsey, growing up, followed his half-brother into the medical profession and was one of the organizers in 1845 of the East Tennessee Medical Society. He established the Confederate military hospitals in Knoxville during the War Between the States, while his half-brother, Thomas W. Humes, was the violently pro-Union rector of St. John's Episcopal Church. Later, it was Dr. Francis A. Ramsey who established Knoxville's first civilian hospital, in the Strong House on State Street.

Margaret Ramsey lived to be seventy-six years old, watching with interest the careers of her sons and her numerous grandchildren. She had other suitors, but firmly declined to take a fourth husband. When she died in 1854, her grave in the churchyard of the First Presbyterian Church was marked with a tombstone on which were inscribed the words: "Mother in Israel."

Even that is not quite all the story. One would think that this lady's life had been filled to overflowing with the concerns of her own family affairs. Certainly not much was expected of women in the early nineteenth century in the way of civic responsibilities. But Margaret Russell Cowan Humes Ramsey was active in the religious and cultural circles of her city, and she was a charter member (the only lady) of the Knoxville Library Company in 1817!

Education for girls was a matter of concern in nineteenth-century Knoxville, where the nation's first co-eds were enrolled at Blount College in 1804. Although the college discontinued the practice of admitting young ladies, the city saw to it that their education was not neglected. Nor was it limited to the three R's and the household arts; for Knoxville boasted a very superior school for girls, established in 1827, which was called the Knoxville Female Academy. In a fine building on Main Street, the young ladies of the period acquired culture under the tutelage of Professor Joseph Estabrook, a graduate of Dartmouth College. So successful was the Academy under the learned Professor Estabrook that he was offered the presidency of East Tennessee College, which he accepted. For a short time thereafter, the Academy was under the supervision of the Methodist Church and had as its principal a series of Methodist ministers.

Sweeping changes occurred in 1846. It was decided to sever the Academy's connection with the church, to change its name to the East Tennessee Female Institute, and to broaden the scope of the institution by conferring degrees upon students who completed the course of study. In 1850, the Institute created a new title for its graduates: Margaret H. White, Isabella M. White, Theodosia A. Findley, and Harriet A. Parker were awarded the degree of Mistress of Polite Literature.

From 1885 to 1890, the East Tennessee Female Institute was under the direction of a most remarkable woman, Mrs. Lizzie Crozier French. Daughter of a congressman and granddaughter of Knoxville's second postmaster, Lizzie Crozier was educated at the Convent of Visitation in Georgetown, District of Columbia, and at the Episcopal school at Columbia, Tennessee. She was married at twenty-one to William B. French, a grandson of Hugh Lawson White, but was widowed less than two years later. The intelligent Mrs. French, a gifted speaker, became an ardent champion of the cause of women's rights. She believed in all sorts of rights for women—educational, legal, civil, and social—rights that most women of her day were unaware they lacked. She used her time and her talents for the rest of her life to help secure these rights as benefits to her sex.

With her sisters (Miss Lucy and Miss Mary Crozier) to help her teach, she took over the management of the East Tennessee Female Institute in 1885; and her school was at once popular and successful. Mrs. French herself taught "elocution," considered at the time a very useful accomplishment, and published a book on the subject, entitled *A Manual of Elocution*, in 1887.

Believing that women should continue their education after leaving school by reading and discussion, Mrs. French organized Knoxville's first woman's club in 1885, naming it "Ossoli Circle" for Margaret Fuller Ossoli, another ardent feminist. She was founder and/or president of many other organizations that were new for women—the Penwomen, Parent-Teachers' Association, Tennessee Suffrage Association, Tennessee Federation of Women's Clubs, the League of Women Voters. She even ran, unsuccessfully, for the Knoxville City Council after women were granted the suffrage in 1920. She died in Washington, D. C., in 1926 while lobbying for the passage of a bill to benefit working women; but she had already seen her efforts bear fruit. Lizzie Crozier French was one of the first Tennessee ladies who advocated votes for women, and she had lived to vote!

In 1890, a "fine new building" was built on Main Street

for the East Tennessee Female Institute, which was then under the direction of Professor Charles C. Ross. This building was to have an interesting cycle of ownership. When The University of Tennessee once more admitted women as students, the building of the Female Institute was purchased to serve as a School of Home Economics for the co-eds. As more and more girls became interested in education on the college level, a new building for home economics became a necessity, and the old building on Main Street was given over to the College of Law. Then, to complete the cycle, it was sold by the University to the Church Street Methodist Church, for use as Sunday School classrooms. So the Female Institute passed out of existence, for the need for such a girls' school had ceased to exist. Still standing on the other side of Main Street is the large red brick house where lived the boarding students of the East Tennessee Female Institute as early as 1850.

The Blount Mansion, which had been for some years the home of the Boyd family, was a harmonious household in the years immediately preceding the War Between the States. Judge and Mrs. Samuel B. Boyd were the parents of fourteen children, and all the children were musical! Two of the Boyd daughters, Sue and Anna, sang so well together that guests always asked them to sing duets.

With the coming of war to Knoxville, Confederate military hospitals were established in the city by Dr. Francis A. Ramsey. These hospitals were a far cry from the well-staffed, antiseptic havens that bear the name today. They were housed in almost all the city's large buildings— the School for the Deaf, the First and Second Presbyterian Churches, the buildings of East Tennessee College. Sometimes there were shuck mattresses laid in rows upon the bare floors, sometimes there were only blankets spread upon the floor boards. There was a severe shortage of medicines. In a reprint from the *Galveston News*, the *Knoxville Register* reported a small item listed as "Worth Knowing," which stated:

> In the present scarcity of quinine, it is worth knowing that the berry of the common dogwood will break fevers as successfully as quinine. We know four plantations where they used it successfully last summer. One pill is a dose. The season is now at hand to collect and dry them for use. They will prove invaluable at home and in the hospitals of our soldiers.

The doctors of Knoxville, under Dr. Ramsey, were doing all they could for the sick and the wounded from the standpoint of the medical profession, but something more was necessary. The sick had to be fed, and they needed nursing care. It must be remembered that there was no such thing as a "trained nurse" in 1861. Even the names of Clara Barton and Florence Nightingale were unknown in Knoxville. Nursing the sick was something that women were thought to be born knowing how to do, just as they were expected to have an instinct for motherhood, cooking, and sewing. So the women of Knoxville prepared food in their home kitchens for the patients in the military hospitals; they made bandages and necessary articles of clothing; and they went themselves to the converted churches and schools to care for the sick and the wounded.

Some women *do* have a natural talent for nursing— such a one was Sue Boyd. At nineteen, she was lovely, graceful, kind, accomplished. She shrank from none of the harder tasks of nursing, but her mere presence was sometimes more soothing than even her deft ministrations, and she became known as Knoxville's "Angel of the Hospitals." It was written of her by Judge Thomas Speed: "At one time she speaks cheering words; at another time her voice is heard in marvelous song. With her own hands she bandages wounds; and she holds a cup of water to pallid lips."

During the war, the Blount Mansion housed a famous visitor, a cousin of Sue Boyd's father. The *Knoxville Register* one day printed a little article entitled "Belle Boyd," which read:

> This fair and fearless Virginia heroine, whose daring defense of her father's house when Charleston, Va., was first invaded by the Yankees, and whose invaluable services in conveying information to our lines in spite of the espionage of the craven foe, have won for her from the Northern press the title of the most courageous and dangerous of rebel female spies, is now sojourning in this city, at the residence of her cousin, Samuel B. Boyd, Esq. She was serenaded last night by the Florida Brass Band, and on being loudly called for by the crowd, appeared at the window, and made the following laconic and graceful response:
>
> "Gentlemen, like General Johnston, I can fight but cannot make speeches. You have my heartfelt thanks for your compliment."

So passed the busy war years, and Sue Boyd never stopped singing. She sang in the hospitals, she sang at home, she sang for friends at musicales, and she sang in the choir of the Church Street Methodist Church. At the close of the war, the Second Presbyterian Church had a new organist and choir director, young Alvin Barton, who was a merchant on weekdays. Mr. Barton greatly admired the voice of Miss Boyd and called often at the Blount Mansion to sing duets with her. He begged her to join his choir at the Second Presbyterian Church; but Judge Boyd declared that Miss Sue could not go alone to Presbyterian choir practice when all the Boyds were attending Methodist choir practice. This difficulty was easily overcome. Mr. Barton was only too happy to call for Miss Boyd and escort her to the church for singing sessions, lifting her gently across the great mudholes that scarred postwar Knoxville streets.

In 1867, Sue Boyd became Mrs. Alvin Barton, and now she sang more than ever—at musicales, in the Second Presbyterian Church choir, and now in public at the Philharmonic Society and at Staub's Opera House. "Knoxville's sweetest songstress," Mrs. Barton, was in demand in other cities, too. She journeyed to Atlanta and to Richmond, Virginia, to give concerts, and everywhere people loved her for her charm and for the thrilling beauty of her soprano voice.

Often Mrs. Barton sang duets with her sister, Mrs. Anna Boyd Fleming, and she was especially interested in the career of her musically talented niece, Mary Fleming. After attending Martha Washington College in Abingdon, Virginia, Mary Fleming studied voice in New York with the celebrated English tenor, William Courtney. Then she returned to Knoxville, where she joined her beautiful soprano voice with the equally beautiful voice of her aunt in the Second Presbyterian Church choir. From New York came flattering offers of opportunities in concert work and opera, but the Flemings were opposed to a professional musical career for Mary.

In 1896, Mary Fleming married young John Lamar Meek, and moved first to Chattanooga, then to Atlanta, then back to Knoxville in 1929. In each city she became a leader in musical circles, and everywhere she was honored as a singer. She represented the State of Tennessee at the Chicago World's Fair in 1893, sang at the St. Louis Exposition in 1904, sang at the Atlanta Exposition where she was accompanied by the famed composer, Victor Herbert, and sang on Knoxville Day at the Tennessee Centennial in Nashville in 1897. Mrs. Meek was one of the organizers of the Tuesday Morning Musical Club of Knoxville, was president of the Tennessee Federation of Music Clubs, president of Dixie District Music Clubs, and a member of many women's cultural organizations. Still she had time to be in charge of musical entertainment for the thousands of soldiers stationed near Chattanooga during World War I, and she led three hundred singing voices at the Confederate Reunion in 1921.

But Knoxvillians know something else about Mary Fleming Meek. The University of Tennessee's Alma Mater is considered one of the most beautiful college songs America possesses. Old grads and students alike, with a lump in their throats, remember Mary Fleming Meek with gratitude as they sing it, for it was she who wrote both the music and words that begin "On a hallowed hill in Tennessee."

It is doubtful whether many present-day Knoxvillians know for whom the handsome, recently erected Austin High School is named. Most of us would be surprised to learn that it honors a woman, and a native of Philadelphia at that!

At the close of the War Between the States, the emancipated slaves were the direct responsibility of a government agency called the Freedmen's Bureau. This bureau, which was cordially detested by the white residents of the Southern states, had as one of its objects the education of the Negro population. A school for colored children was established in the basement of the First Presbyterian Church, which was headquarters for the Freedmen's Bureau for several years after the war. One of the overwhelming obstacles in this laudable program of Negro education was the difficulty of obtaining teachers for the schools established by the bureau. Many ladies in the North were stirred by the stories of the plight of education in the South and in the true missionary spirit traveled into the Southern states to teach in colored schools.

In 1870, there arrived in Knoxville from Philadelphia Miss Emily Austin, a dedicated teacher past the first blush of youth who had decided to devote her life to Negro children. It was in this same year of 1870 that Knoxville's first free public schools were opened, in nine residences rented for the purpose throughout the city. Three of the nine schools were for Negro children, and in one of these Miss Emily Austin taught. As it became financially possible, the city began to replace the rented houses with buildings especially constructed for school purposes, and in 1879 a new building for colored children was going up on Central Avenue. Miss Austin informed the School Board that generous friends in Philadelphia and Boston had subscribed $6,500 to build a school for Negro children in Knoxville. The money was gratefully received, and the whole of it applied to completing and equipping the partially built school on Central Avenue, which was christened the Austin School.

Miss Austin felt that the Negro children had special needs that were not being met by the regular school curriculum, which was the same in white and colored schools, and it was largely through her efforts that a new type of school was established here in 1885. Known as the Slater Training School, it opened with two hundred colored pupils, $6,000 in funds (of which $5,000 was contributed by Northern friends), and a plan for practical industrial education. Three grades of the city schools were taught, and all pupils were required to take industrial training. Carpentry and printing were taught the boys, while the girls received instruction in sewing, cooking, and housekeeping.

In 1891, after seeing the Austin School and the Slater Training School well established, Miss Emily Austin returned to Philadelphia, where she died in 1897. Memorial services were held for her in Logan A.M.E. Temple here, and she was sincerely mourned by the colored people to whom she had been so real a friend. A tablet in her honor was placed in the Austin School (and transferred to succeeding schools that have borne her name). The inscription reads:

In Memory of
Miss Emily L. Austin
Born October 1, 1829; died May 4, 1897
Founder of the Austin School of Knoxville, Tennessee, and for thirty years a devoted friend of the freedmen, fearless of criticism, shrinking from no duty, unswerving in fidelity, coveting only Divine approval. She is gratefully remembered by those whose elevation she sought by educating mind and heart.

"She has done what she could."

Higher education for women was much talked about during the 1870's but Judge Oliver P. Temple of Knoxville was thought daring (if not downright foolhardy) when he sent his only daughter, Miss Mary Boyce Temple, all the way to Poughkeepsie, New York, to attend Vassar Female College. Miss Mary had inherited her father's brilliant mind, and at Vassar she received a type of education that was still unusual for women, because the curriculum and standards of the college were the same as those of Harvard and Yale. When she received her diploma with the Class of 1877, Miss Temple was Vassar's first Knoxville graduate, and she was one of the few college educated women in the South. She took her place at once in the vanguard of the movement for a change in the traditionally secondary position of women.

In 1885, a group of thirteen Knoxville ladies were called together by Mrs. Lizzie Crozier French to form a literary society. They organized themselves as "Ossoli Circle" (named in honor of feminist Margaret Fuller Ossoli) and thus became the first woman's club in the South. Miss Mary Boyce Temple was named Ossoli's first president, serving from 1885 to 1890. The stated purpose of the club was "to stimulate intellectual growth and moral development" and to be of "mutual benefit to women of literary taste and ability."

In 1890, a national organization of women's clubs was formed in New York City. The only representatives from the Southern states were Mrs. Samuel McKinney and Miss Mary Boyce Temple of Knoxville, representing Ossoli Circle. Nobody in Knoxville was surprised that Miss Mary Boyce Temple was elected the first recording secretary of the national organization.

The membership of Ossoli Circle grew by leaps and bounds. From thirteen in 1885, it had enlarged to seventy-

five by 1893. Women were delighted with the idea of themselves as intelligent, well-informed citizens and rushed to
ally themselves with such a group. Ossoli's example was
quickly followed in other Tennessee cities, and by 1896
there were sixteen women's clubs within the state who sent
delegates to Knoxville to organize the Tennessee Federation of Women's Clubs. In 1896 all this organization seemed
rather daring, and altogether delightful!

In 1893, Miss Mary Temple turned her attention to
genealogy. There was no chapter in Knoxville of the
Daughters of the American Revolution for her to join, but
that was a problem easily solved. She organized one herself, and named it Bonny Kate Chapter in honor of Bonny
Kate Sevier, wife of Tennessee's first governor. From this
time until her death in 1929, she was always regent, either
of the Bonny Kate Chapter or of the state chapter.

Having exerted her executive talents for her fellow
females, Mary Boyce Temple branched out into other
fields. She appointed herself Knoxville's official hostess and
entertained each and every celebrity who came to speak or
to make a state visit, from Frances E. Willard who came in
1883 to organize a chapter of the Women's Christian Temperance Union, to General Pershing who visited the city
after the First World War.

Her accomplishments were by no means unrecog-
nized, for in 1900 she was appointed by Governor Benton
McMillin as a commissioner to represent the State of Tennessee at the Paris Exposition. And how she loved it! But
the crowning accolade for her came in 1921, when she was
given an honorary doctorate of laws by Lincoln Memorial
University. It would have suited Miss Mary exactly if she
could have persuaded everyone to call her Doctor Temple,

and some people did. As the years passed, Miss Mary Temple was as much a part of Knoxville as The University of Tennessee or the Blount Mansion. She was interested in everything that went on, and, truth to tell, she usually had a finger in the pie.

For a great many years, the Blount Mansion had been the property of the Boyd family, who had lavished upon it the same care and attention as had the Blounts, and it had remained a center of hospitable entertaining and gracious living. The doctors Samuel and John Mason Boyd were among Knoxville's early physicians and were greatly respected and loved. The time came at last, however, when the Boyd family had moved away from the Blount Mansion, that the house fell into disrepair. The beautiful gardens were gone, and in their place had been built a number of small houses that had declined to slums. The mansion itself was finally a tenement housing several families, each of which lived in one of its stately rooms. Someone took the front door off, and the narrow winding stairs were visible from the street. In the early 1920's, automobile traffic was beginning to create a demand for filling stations and repair shops. It was announced in the newspapers that the owner of the Blount Mansion was planning to sell the property as a site for a garage. This announcement created very little stir among the citizens in general. Most Knoxvillians took a look at the dilapidated old house, shook their heads, and said: "Good riddance. Better tear the thing down. It's nothing but a fire trap!"

But *not* Miss Mary Boyce Temple. She and the other members of Bonny Kate Chapter of the Daughters of the American Revolution were outraged at the thought of the destruction of the mansion, the first two-story frame house

in the West. They decided to save the property. There
was no time to get an appropriation from the state (the
legislature also would have to be convinced of the importance of preserving this historic shrine), and Knoxville
businessmen were not very interested in the ladies' plans to
restore the mansion to its former appearance. So it was up
to the ladies themselves. They went to see the owner of the
property and took an option on it. No funds had yet been
raised for the purchase, so Miss Mary Temple gave her personal check for the amount of the option. It was a struggle
that lasted for years, but the ladies won out in the end. Public interest grew; support came from individuals, from historical societies, and finally from the state itself. Blount
Mansion was saved, restored, refurnished, and rededicated
to the people of Tennessee as an historic shrine. And, as
usual, Miss Mary had had a hand (or in this case a pen) in it.

Mary Boyce Temple was a pure individualist, and of
such are made the flavor of a city. She always did exactly as
she pleased, and therefore she was considered eccentric.
Many things that she did, perfectly logical to her way of
thinking, made amusing stories in the recounting. The apoc-
ryphal story about her concerns an invitation to one of her
dinner parties. She sent round by her faithful butler a note
inviting a learned professor at the University to dinner on
a certain evening. Surprised that his wife's name was not
also on the invitation, the good doctor paid a call upon Miss
Mary.

"I'm sorry, Miss Temple," he said, "but I will not be
able to attend your dinner. You see, I make it a practice
never to attend a social function to which my wife is not
invited."

"But my dear Doctor," cried the astonished Mary

Boyce Temple, "When one is having a party, one simply *has* to draw the line *somewhere!*"

There was another lady who greatly affected the social life of Knoxville, though in quite a different way, and this lady was written up in Ripley's "Believe It Or Not." In the 1880's, Mrs. Iva McMullen Boyd, the young widow of James Stephenson Boyd, found it necessary to earn a living for herself and her three children, John, Pattie, and Robert. Teaching was an obvious choice of occupation, for it was the only one really open to ladies at the time; but Mrs. Boyd did her teaching with a difference. She became a member of the faculty of the Tennessee School for the Deaf, and so proficient was she at teaching the use of the sign language to the deaf children that she became famous for it in a perfectly decorous and ladylike way. She lived on Summit Hill, the fashionable residential section conveniently located near the School for the Deaf, which then occupied its beautiful buildings that are now Knoxville's City Hall.

A teacher's salary was not large, and there was considerable expense. Daughter Pattie, growing up, was discovered to have a flair for writing. A family friend, Judge E. T. Sanford, the owner of *The Knoxville Journal*, suggested that perhaps Miss Pattie could write about the social events of the city for his newspaper. Of course, she need not go down to the newspaper office—that would never do! She could do her writing at home and send the stories down to the office by the butler. And so it was arranged.

Daily, Miss Pattie drove her mother to the school in a little basket phaeton behind a gentle mare. She returned home to manage the house, to do the marketing at the Market House (with the butler along to carry the basket of purchases, of course), and to write for the *Journal* the account of the city's social functions. Each noon, Miss Pattie called at the school for her mother, drove her home for dinner, supervised her rest period, and drove her back to school for the afternoon session. Each evening, she drove down once more to bring her mother home to supper, and to greet the callers. The Boyds had many callers. They attended many parties and knew everything that was going on. Miss Pattie wrote about it all for the *Journal*. Every Monday afternoon, the basket phaeton conveyed Mrs. Boyd and Miss Pattie to the meeting of Ossoli Circle. This routine continued for years. Editors came and went at the *Journal*, and the paper changed hands several times, but Miss Pattie stayed on. She was part and parcel of the paper, and at times it seemed that she was "Society" in Knoxville.

Times changed. Mrs. Boyd died, and Miss Pattie drove the little horse and the phaeton no more. She and Mr. Robert moved to their farm in the country, and Miss Pattie gathered her news items by telephone and did her writing in an office at the newspaper. She and Mr. Robert came into town each day to visit the Market House. But now there was no butler, and Mr. Robert carried the market basket. And for years, Miss Pattie was as much a part of Knoxville as the morning paper or the Blount Mansion, walking down Gay Street in her hat with its two jet butterflies attached by wires to its crown. Miss Pattie no longer attended the weddings and parties she described, but she wrote about them all. Sometimes she wrote what she thought should have happened instead of what actually did. She announced arbitrarily each autumn the names of the debutantes of the season. And somehow, she endowed parties and people with a vague, old-fashioned charm not found in more exact accounts of such affairs.

And so it was that Miss Pattie's picture appeared in "Believe It Or Not" in 1938, and the caption advised the nation at large that Miss Pattie Boyd, of Knoxville, Tennessee, had been Society Editor of the same paper, *The Knoxville Journal*, for more than fifty years!

CHAPTER TWELVE

The Great Smoky Mountains National Park

In the early days of Tennessee's history, it was a "fur piece," in terms both of travel and of mode of living, from the Great Smoky Mountains to Knoxville. The actual distance is only a matter of some thirty-five miles, but it was a two-day journey on horseback before roads shortened the trip. Until recently Knoxville, with its college and its cultural pretensions, its factories and its conveniences, was separated from its mountain neighbors by almost two hundred years of social and economic advancement. Yet Knoxville was the closest city of any size to the Great Smoky Mountains, and Knoxville's citizens had always taken a proprietary interest in the mountains, understanding and respecting the people who lived there.

The earliest settlers in the Great Smokies followed on

the heels of hunters who pushed their way across the mountain wilderness from North Carolina and Virginia to the Indian hunting grounds in Kentucky and Middle Tennessee. Their stories of the abundance of wild game, fine timber, and the richness of the virgin soil across the mountains tempted many men to move westward with their families. The most famous of these hunters was Daniel Boone. So many deeds of courage and feats of endurance have been attributed to Daniel Boone that he has acquired a sort of "Paul Bunyan" reputation. The fact remains, Daniel did exist; he did open a trail from the Carolinas to Tennessee and Kentucky; and he was personally responsible for the migration thither of several groups of settlers. Any present-day visitor to the Great Smokies who will pause to imagine what it would be like to cross these mountains alone, hacking out a trail through the dense underbrush, following the twisting, boulder-strewn beds of the mountain streams to reach the western lowlands, will readily understand why Daniel Boone should be regarded as a hero.

Those who came to settle in the western lands found Boone's trail well marked, but even with this for guidance it was no easy matter to cross the mountains. It was a trail barely wide enough for a packhorse to pick his way along —the easiest way to traverse it was on foot. Therefore, it is not surprising that sometimes settlers decided to go no farther than the upper western slopes of these mountains they had crossed with such difficulty. They found in the uplands plenty of wild game, plenty of timber to build houses for themselves, and an abundance of clear springs and sparkling streams to furnish that most pressing necessity of pioneer life, water. Obviously, they had brought with them across the Indian Gap only what they could carry themselves or what could be strapped on the backs of farm animals. This included little more than tools with which to make the things they urgently needed and seeds to ensure future crops. No one who was not confident of his own ability to produce with his own hands the necessities of life for his family would have attempted this journey in the first place. Only those whose confidence in their ability proved justified could survive under such circumstances. It was then small wonder that the descendants of these original settlers in the Smokies were proud of their heritage, and happy that they too were able to measure up to the rugged standard thus set for them. For in order to continue to live in the mountains, succeeding generations had to *remain* self-reliant. It has been said of the mountain people that "heredity and environment conspired to keep them pioneers."

Formal education was lacking in the mountains, but few people were entirely illiterate, and they were as far from unskilled as it is possible for people to be. Every man was his own carpenter and his own stone mason. He could shoe his own horse and could tan the leather from which he then made a harness for the horse and shoes for the family. He could fell the trees which he needed to build his house, and with simple hand tools he could make the necessary furniture for it. He was a dead shot with a primitive gun whose parts he was able to replace if they wore out. He could make the fish hooks with which he caught the wily mountain trout. Those animals he could not shoot he could catch in traps he constructed himself. And he had to be able to wrest a crop from his impossibly steep hillside acres in order to be able to subsist at all!

His wife was equally versatile, if not more so. She must know how to preserve and conserve the scant supply of food for winter. Not only did she sew the seams of the family's clothes, she also carded, spun, and wove the "linsey-woolsey" material from which the clothes were made. She found dyes for her homespun cloth in wild indigo, butternut, walnut hulls, and sourwood bark as well as in beet juice. She was the family doctor, too, and from her knowledge of herbs she made the medicines with which she treated the sick. Here is a partial list of the more common native plants and the uses to which she put them:

Mullein leaves—poultices for boils and "risins."
Pennyroyal—leaves rubbed on the skin to ward off insects.
Pennyroyal tea—tonic to improve the appetite.
Boneset tea—to aid in the setting of broken bones which had been placed in homemade splints.
Sassafras tea—for colds and as a blood conditioner.
Slippery elm bark—the inner bark was chewed for tuberculosis.
Wild cherry and honey—cough syrup.
Poke roots—for rheumatism.
Swamp root—spring tonic.
Plantain poultice—for bee stings.
Yellowroot—for dysentery.
Blackberry cordial—for stomach trouble.
Hot onion juice—for earache.
Elderberry wine—for weakness.
Corn whiskey—for snakebite.

It was also her practice to put copper coins in a damp place until they were covered with green mold. They were then applied to stubborn sores which refused to heal, and this primitive ancestor of penicillin is said to have worked remarkably well. Even the mountain children were able to find what they needed in the mountains and put it to its proper use—in the wax of the black gum tree they found the old original chewing gum!

The inhabitants of these homes considered only one book a necessity, and that book was the Bible. Enough schooling to be able to read the Bible, however laboriously, was enough schooling. Such widespread reverence for the King James Version with its beautiful phraseology and rhythmic cadence was one important influence upon the speech of the mountain people. In fact, the way of speaking peculiar to the mountains is not a dialect, but a case of arrested development. Most of the phrases which sound so unusual are perfectly good archaic English, which continued to be spoken in the mountains because the people heard no other way of speaking. Their literature was limited, their language outdated, their tastes in music equally old-fashioned. Many mountain people were very musical; most homes contained a "fiddle" or a "gittar" or a dulcimer, and everybody enjoyed singing. The real mountain music was not jug bands and hillbilly tunes, but old English ballads (such as "Reading Gaol" and "Barbary Allen") and similar songs about local events which were written and performed on the spot. The singing of hymns "by the notes" was an accomplishment learned in "singing schools" held occasionally by a singing master who traveled through the coves and valleys. One of the most popular entertainments was an "all day singin' and dinner on the ground."

Because they needed so little from the outside world, it was unnecessary for the mountain people to make the journey often to the closest settlements, and the lowlanders were not often inclined to attempt the steep mountain trails. Therefore, a way of life was preserved in the Great

Smokies that had long since vanished from the rest of the world.

The Cherokee who hid in the mountains after the Great Migration of 1838 did not molest the isolated homes of the white settlers. They were able to live amicably together in the mountains because the Indians had no use for the tiny cleared patches of land that constituted the settlers' farms, and there was plenty of wild game for everyone. Even during the War Between the States, there was no open conflict between the Indians and the mountain people, although they were on opposite sides.

To the people high in the mountains, the Revolutionary War seemed to have happened yesterday. They had fought that war for independence, and if there was one thing valued in the mountains above all others, it was independence. Slavery was unknown—even in the Bible, the King James Version used the word "servant." It was absolutely inconceivable to these people that anyone would wish to abandon the government which their forebears had managed to establish only after a bloody struggle for liberty. So the most determined Unionists in all East Tennessee were those who lived high in the Great Smoky Mountains. A few of these Unionists, like the Union sympathizers in Knoxville and Sevierville, left home to join the Union Army in Kentucky. Some of those who lived really high in the hills stayed where they were. They took Grandpap's long gun down from over the mantel and propped it behind the door primed and ready for any rebels foolish enough to venture into the mountains.

However far away from the settlements the mountain men lived, there were two things that always brought them

down to the nearest store. One was the necessity for buying salt (one of the few things they could neither make nor
find for themselves) and the other was an election. To these
people, the vote was a precious privilege, and they never
lost the opportunity to record their preference in any electoral contest. When in 1861 an election was held to decide
whether or not Tennessee should secede from the Federal
Union, nearly every voter in Sevier County (in which most
of the mountain homes were located) made his way to the
polls, and the vote was 1528 to 60 in favor of remaining
in the Union.

One of the votes for secession tells an interesting story.
Before the war, there was a little crossroads store at the
tiny settlement of White Oak Flats. The store was owned
by Radford Gatlin who, for some reason lost to history,
had chosen to come to the mountains from the farther South
to live. He had brought with him a Negro slave, an object
of great curiosity and pity to his neighbors in the Flats and
farther back in the hills. As the United States postal service
was expanding to reach even the most far-flung outposts,
word was received that White Oak Flats would have a post
office. Radford Gatlin volunteered to give the land on
which the post office might be built, on condition that the
name of the settlement it served be changed from White
Oak Flats to Gatlinburg. This was done, and for a few
years, Radford Gatlin was postmaster of the hamlet that
bore his name. Soon after casting his vote for secession,
it is said, he was sorely beaten by Union sympathizers and
in haste he left the mountains to join the Confederate
Army. At the war's end, he wisely decided not to come
back to Gatlinburg; for Sevier County, despite the mountain men who stayed in the upper coves, had sent more

volunteers to the Union Army than the county had registered voters!

A bargain, however, was a bargain; and the people saw no reason to change the name of the town, which has since become far more famous than Radford Gatlin could ever have foreseen. These were the same loyal people who traveled the many weary miles to Sevierville to listen to the Sunday morning speech of Parson Brownlow, and who scorned the reward offered for him by the Confederate authorities.

The Cherokee, who were still smarting from their treatment at the hands of the federal government, held very different views. Only twenty-five years had passed since they had been hunted through the hills by the United States Army under General Winfield Scott. They were still in hiding from the soldiers who had forced them to leave their homes and move to the hated Indian Territory in Oklahoma. After the failure of their appeal to President Jackson to permit them to keep their lands, they had been bitter enemies of the government they had once expected to protect them. Consequently, they were happy to hear of the Civil War, and immediately allied themselves with the forces of the Confederacy. For the first time, they and the mountain people were not on friendly terms.

A small detachment of Confederate troops was sent into the mountains to organize the Cherokee, with Colonel William H. Thomas in command. It was at this time, and almost by accident, that the first wagon road was built across the mountains at Indian Gap.

The Indians had been given arms by Colonel Thomas, and they formed a company known as Thomas' Indian Scouts. They made forays against the lower settlements, and no doubt enjoyed themselves very much. But this small Confederate force found itself well-nigh surrounded by the mountain men with their ancient rifles and their deadly accurate aim. The gunpowder brought with them by Colonel Thomas' men was almost gone, and there was no way, without powder, to force their way out of the mountains and back to the main body of Confederate troops. Colonel Thomas explained the gravity of the situation to his scouts, and they surprised him by having the answer to his problem. High up in the mountains, they told him, near the Indian Gap, there was a cave where there was plenty of black dust like the saltpeter Colonel Thomas' men were using for gunpowder. Soldiers who accompanied the Indian guides to the cave found they were right. There was all the saltpeter they needed, and more, too. But there was still the problem of how to get it out of the cave and down the mountain, for only a narrow Indian trail led to the spot. After careful investigation, Colonel Thomas decided it would be possible to build a rough type of road over which the powder could be transported on wagon beds without wheels which were called "sleds." These horse-drawn sleds were much used on the mountain sides where any vehicle with wheels was apt to tilt over and spill its contents.

The Cherokee, of course, lived on the North Carolina side of the Smokies, at the present site of the reservation, but the cave containing the saltpeter was beyond the Indian Gap on the Tennessee side. Under Colonel Thomas' direction, the Indians laboriously cleared a path wide enough to permit the passage of the sleds with their precious cargo of saltpeter, and Indians and Confederates together emerged from the trap in the mountains. Faint traces of this steep road across the summit of the Smokies may still be seen near Alum Cave Bluff, the very cave where the salt-peter was found.

In the 1890's, lumber had become big business in the Smokies, and with the lumber industry came many changes. Companies bought huge tracts of mountain lands and sent crews of men into the heart of the mountains to fell the wonderful trees that grew there, for the Great Smokies were filled with mighty chestnut, oak, maple, poplar, and wild cherry trees so tall and straight that they were extra valuable for the making of furniture. Sometimes it was possible to float the smaller logs down the mountain streams to a sawmill at a lower altitude; but mountain streams were not designed for this purpose. The shallow, swift-running water divides at great boulders and makes hairpin turns round the base of rocky cliffs. The logs would pile up in a jam that could be cleared only with long, dangerous hours of work. Some other way had to be found to get the logs out of the mountains, a way that would also bring supplies in for the lumbermen and their families.

The Little River Lumber Company solved this problem for its operations by building a narrow gauge railroad alongside the winding Little River from Maryville to Elkmont, high in the Smokies in the midst of the company's fine timberlands. This was no mean undertaking, for the little railroad clung precariously to the side of the steep cliffs that overhung the river, and the small engine labored mightily to pull the train of empty flatcars on the upward trip into the mountains. A caboose at the end of the train carried supplies for the lumbermen, who lived in frame cottages constructed for them at Elkmont.

Knoxvillians heard about the little railroad, with its wonderful scenic route along the clear mountain stream.

They heard, too, fabulous tales of the hunting and fishing to be found at Elkmont. The little train made a daily trip, up the mountains in the morning, and down again in the afternoon, and adventurous Knoxvillians found such an excursion great fun. Groups of sportsmen began to ride the caboose of the logging train to try their luck at trout fishing.

After a few years, the lumber company found the timber near Elkmont almost exhausted, and it was decided to move the lumbermen's camp to a new location. The fishermen were delighted to be able to purchase the abandoned logging camp, and they formed themselves into the Appalachian Club, and converted the lumbermen's houses into summer cottages. In 1912, nearby Wonderland Club was organized in the same way. The only way to reach the clubs was by means of the little train, which continued to make one round trip daily during the summer season. Whole families went to the mountains for the entire summer, taking with them trunks of clothes and crates of canned goods. Fathers of families took the train to Elkmont for the weekend, bringing with them fresh vegetables and replacements of staple foods. During the week, the vacationers depended upon the crew of the little train to bring up any needed supplies. This kind of summer recreation was rugged, but the devoted adherents of Elkmont and Wonderland claimed that nowhere in the world was the scenery so beautiful or the climate so wonderful as in the heart of the Great Smokies.

Shortly before World War I, a wagon road was built from Gatlinburg to Wonderland. This steep, recurving route was hardly more than two wheel ruts liberally sprinkled with boulders, but in 1918 two automobiles filled with pioneer motorists made the trip in less than a day. It was far more practical to go from the clubs to Gatlinburg by hack, and quicker too; still the only way to cross the Indian Gap from Gatlinburg was on horseback.

In 1923, a blacktop road was built from Maryville to Gatlinburg. This first highway in the Smokies was wide enough for only one car, but turnouts were provided at intervals where two cars could pass. Turns were steep and sharp, and automobiles often had to pull forward and back several times to get around them. Going up the steep grades, engines became overheated and had to be cooled with water from the mountain streams. Going down, there was always the possibility that the brake bands might wear through. This hazardous highway was, nevertheless, a remarkably beautiful drive for everyone except the driver, and automobiles filled with Knoxvillians frequently made the trip. Shortly after the completion of the highway, the daily train service to the mountains was discontinued. This caused consternation among the owners of the summer cottages. How would they get supplies all through the summer? It took much longer to reach Elkmont by car than by train, and the dusty automobile trip was far less comfortable than the ride in the familiar little caboose. Then, too, there were no bridges over the streams on the highway. Horse-drawn vehicles and automobiles forded the river several times between Maryville and Gatlinburg. Flash floods are not at all uncommon in the mountains, and sudden heavy rains are an almost daily occurrence. This made for an element of adventure in traveling the new highway by automobile, for if it rained, the stream rose and travelers were forced to wait in their cars until it went down in order to cross the fords. Members of Appalachian and Wonderland Clubs were loud in their longing for the good old days of the little narrow-gauge railroad, and many members sold their cottages because, they felt, automobile travel in the mountains would never be pleasant or practical.

As it became possible for more people to visit at least the foothills and the lower reaches of the Great Smoky Mountains, public interest in them was growing. This interest was not new, for there were many unusual things about the Smokies that had been discovered earlier and then more or less forgotten. The great French naturalist, André Michaux, visited the mountains first in 1793, and he was so impressed with the great variety of plants he found there that he came again in 1802. He described vividly the beauty of the rhododendron and the flame azalea, for these plants he considered the most unusual that he found. Henry Guyot, the famous mountain expert of the mid-nineteenth century, had established the fact that the highest peaks in the eastern United States were to be found in the Great Smokies. It was finally determined, with the aid of modern instruments for measuring mountains exactly, that North Carolina's Mt. Mitchell is tallest by forty-three feet, followed by Tennessee's Clingman's Dome and Mt. Le Conte.

In 1913, nearby Knoxville was host to the National Conservation Exposition. National forests had already been established in the Appalachian Mountain area, and the great national parks of the West had been carved out of the public lands and dedicated to the use and enjoyment of the American people. At the Knoxville meeting, the national association discussed the creation of a national park in the Great Smoky Mountains, an idea which had previously been suggested in various books and magazine articles about the area.

Mt. Le Conte dominates the valley of the Little Pigeon River in this view from Crockett Mountain, Gatlinburg.

A prominent citizen of the Great Smoky Mountains National Park.

Ten years went by before any real action was taken on the proposal. In 1923, Mrs. W. P. Davis of Knoxville revived the suggestion of a national park, and its creation became the aim of the Great Smoky Mountains Conservation Association. Knoxvillians who had traveled in the Smokies on the little narrow gauge railway, or fished for trout in the swift mountain streams, or made perilous automobile trips over rudimentary roads had fired the enthusiasm of their friends in the city for the mountains and their beauties. But as always, there were a few men whose tireless work actually accomplished what so many people wanted. Colonel David Chapman has been called, for his enthusiasm and his ceaseless efforts, the father of the Great Smoky Mountains National Park. He served for many years as chairman of the Park Commission and was ably seconded by such other Knoxvillians as Carlos C. Campbell and Frank Maloney. The times were right in the mid 1920's for the move to establish the park.

By 1925, a million dollars had been raised by subscription in Tennessee and North Carolina to purchase land in the Great Smokies. In that year it was learned that the Little River Lumber Company was willing to sell a tract of cutover land containing 76,500 acres. The Legislature of Tennessee agreed to appropriate funds for the purchase, provided the City of Knoxville would pay one-third the cost of the land. The City of Knoxville then voted to provide one-third the necessary money, and the legislature later passed an act giving the other two-thirds. Thus the first public money for the Great Smoky Mountains National Park came not from the federal government, nor from the State of Tennessee, but was a neighborly gift from the neighboring City of Knoxville.

President Coolidge signed the congressional enabling act for the Great Smoky Mountains National Park in 1926. The legislatures of Tennessee and North Carolina then appropriated state funds to buy more land to add to the original lumber company tract. North Carolina's share was $2,000,000, while Tennessee gave $1,500,000. These appropriations differed because the legislature of Tennessee and the City of Knoxville had already put up the funds for the original purchase. The total amount of money then available from the appropriations and from donations was $5,000,000, and that was not going to be enough. There were discouraging days when it seemed that the whole project had bogged down, and that the park would never become a reality.

It happened that Mr. John D. Rockefeller, Jr., was familiar with the Great Smokies. He had given generously to establish museums in the western national parks and had given public parks in Ohio and New York to the people of those states. In 1928, he gave through the Rockefeller Foundation a gift of $5,000,000 to match the funds already raised to establish the Great Smoky Mountains National Park. The gift was made in memory of his mother, Laura Spelman Rockefeller, and was added to the funds already set aside to purchase lands. It is fittingly symbolic that the Rockefeller Memorial within the park is built at New Found Gap, on the very crest of the mountains between the two states of North Carolina and Tennessee, for it was the generosity of Mr. Rockefeller that crowned the efforts of the states with success.

So it is that this park differed from the western national parks, which were simply set aside from public lands already owned by the government for the use of the people; for this was the first park whose land was purchased by the people and presented as a gift to their government.

Both Tennessee and North Carolina at once set up commissions to acquire the necessary land for the park, and this was to be no simple matter. North Carolina's commissioners had the easier task, since few people lived on the eastern slopes of the mountains, and most of the land was owned in large tracts by individuals or corporations. Things were different on the Tennessee side of the boundary line, for there were 6,400 owners of land on the Tennessee side of the park to be contacted and dealt with. Most of these parcels of land were small, but they were none the less valuable to their owners. It must be remembered that in many cases the land now to be taken for public purposes had been the property of a single family since before the Revolutionary War. Many of the people had known no other home than the one they were now required to leave. In most cases, there was not so much disagreement over the price to be paid for the land as disagreement over the right of anyone to force people to sell their homes when they most emphatically did not want to do so. But the mountain people had survived other types of hardship, and they were equal to this. When they found that the sale of their land was inevitable, they quietly agreed to it, and said remarkably little about it. Many of the people received the full purchase price for their land, but retained a life estate in it. This meant that so long as the head of the family was living, they could continue to occupy their homes. Others preferred, since they must leave eventually, to do so at once. These families moved down to the settlements at Gatlinburg or Sevierville, or moved to other mountain areas not included in the plan for the park. Few great social changes are accomplished without heartache for somebody, and the establishment of this newest national park was no exception.

When 150,000 acres had been secured, they were turned over to the government, and the park was in operation; but the acquisition of the fringe areas, with attendant lawsuits, continued for years. The first thing the park needed was roads, and good ones. The fine highway across the very crest of the mountain chain at New Found Gap is a marvel of modern engineering, but it follows closely the old East-West Indian Trail—nobody has yet beaten the Indians at finding the easiest and best way of getting around the mountains. With the new highways, there was a scenic loop from Knoxville through the mountains by way of Sevierville, Gatlinburg, and Maryville, returning to Knoxville. This pleasant afternoon's drive was a far cry from the first automobile roads in the area, and it was finished just in time, for Knoxvillians were joining the rest of the nation in discovering the Smokies.

Until the opening of the park, Gatlinburg was still a tiny town, unknown to all but a few lumbermen, engineers, and lovers of wilderness camping. The first of Gatlinburg's hotels, the Mountain View, was originally an old-fashioned farmhouse that served fried chicken and country ham dinners to the venturesome early tourists. As the roads improved, the town grew to meet the increasing demand for accommodations near the park, since no hotels or lodges were built within its borders. The population of Gatlinburg was increased too by the people from the park area who had been displaced in order that the mountains might return to their original uninhabited beauty. It is interesting to reflect that Gatlinburg's development was brought about not by outside capital, but from within, by the shrewd mountain people who knew a good thing when they saw it and who put aside farming to earn a fast dollar dispensing food, lodging and atmosphere to the tourists.

The tourists. First by the hundreds, then by the thousands, now by the millions each year they come, and the Great Smoky Mountains National Park tops all other national parks in number of visitors. Of course, there are reasons for this popularity. Perhaps the most important is the accessibility of this park to the great midsection of America. It is possible to drive to the Smokies in two or three days from almost all of the eastern half of the United States. But that does not mean that people do not come to it from greater distances. From the West Coast and from foreign countries come many interested visitors because they like what the park has to offer.

First of all, there are the mountains themselves. They were already old when the Rockies and the Alps were mere young upstarts. Untold centuries of rain and snow have softened their sharp outlines and have given them a rich topsoil that supports an amazing variety of plant life. The park's eight hundred square miles of territory is said to contain more different species of trees and flowers than any comparable area in the world. In driving one short mile from the lowlands to the highlands within the park, it is possible to see the same range of plants and trees as in the thousand-mile drive from Georgia to Massachusetts. Each season has its special beauties—the wild flowers and blossoming trees of spring, the glorious rhododendron and mountain laurel against the glowing green of summer, the hardwoods ablaze with color in the autumn, and the rich evergreen of balsam, fir, hemlock and pine shimmering with the hoar-frost of winter.

Then there are the animals, small and large, from the brilliant tiny salamanders to the great black bears—the clowns of the highways. The bear facts are these. The mountain people hunted bears in November, when they are fattest, for their meat; and in the very early spring, when their pelts are thickest, for their skins. Now, however, the bears enjoy year-long immunity from hunters. Since all national parks are wildlife sanctuaries, it is no longer permitted to shoot the bears, even when they come down, in dry seasons, to camps to steal food from cabins or forage in garbage cans. When a mischievous bear turns up near a campsite, the forest rangers bring a special bear cage on an automobile trailer. Into this cage the bear is enticed with some tidbit of food he especially likes, and he is then transported high up in the mountains and once more given his freedom. Tourists love the bears, but the bears do not necessarily love tourists. Traffic jams result when cars stop to watch a mother bear spank her cubs across a mountain highway or a clumsy he-bear lumbering along to the nearest picnic ground. In spite of repeated warnings on the roadside signs, several people each year are injured by the bears they thought so friendly; for the bears are numerous, and often humorous, but they are *not* tame.

Trout fishing in secluded streams lures many anglers, and there are many visitors who come to hike along the well-marked trails to Alum Cave, to the Chimneys, or to the top of Mt. Le Conte where the view includes two TVA lakes—Douglas and Cherokee—and the lights of several of East Tennessee's small towns. There is something for every-

one in the Great Smokies—sports for the outdoor en-
thusiasts, historical dramas and wild flower pilgrimages for
the seekers after knowledge. There are campsites set aside
for those who like to vacation in primitive style, and there
are plush hotels for those who crave their creature comforts.

A large majority of the visitors to the Great Smoky
Mountains National Park approach it by way of Knoxville,
and that too is appropriate. This is so true that Knoxville
is often now called the Gateway to the Great Smokies,
when once the trail across the Indian Gap was regarded as
a gateway to Knoxville. It might be more appropriate to
refer to Knoxville as the cornerstone of the Great Smoky
Mountains National Park, for without the interest and
generosity of Knoxville and her citizens, it is quite possible
that the park might not exist.

And if there were no park?

The birds, the animals and the wild flowers, and the
giant trees of the mountains would by now be disappearing
before the encroachments of "civilization." Millions of people would have been deprived of the opportunity to see at
first hand an area second to none in natural beauty.

CHAPTER THIRTEEN

The Tennessee Valley Authority

Ever since the formal history of Knoxville began with trading between the Cherokee and William Blount to make the Treaty of Holston, East Tennesseans have been noted for their ability as sharp traders. One of the *Knoxville Gazette's* first advertisements offered "goods for sale or trade," and life in the Tennessee country was for many years based on a system of barter. But it was not really economic necessity that made Knoxvillians so eager to swap everything from horses to stories—they enjoyed the trading for its own sake, and they were certainly thus trained to recognize a bargain when they saw one. Market Square in Knoxville was a busy place, despite its leisurely atmosphere; for a good trade must never be made in a hurry—there must always be time for a little joking and a little argument. Marketing was a daily adventure at the Market House, with small triumphs of shrewdness expected on both sides of each bargain.

Market Square had been given to the people of Knoxville in 1853 by William G. Swan and Joseph A. Mabry, on condition that the city should erect a market house on the property, and that it should always serve as a public market. From that time forward, farm wagons with the produce of the rich bottom land farms lined both sides of the square daily except Sunday, while meat and fish, eggs, butter, and country cottage cheese were sold in the relatively cool interior shade of the Market House. Nobody ever considered that the first price mentioned for an item was a final figure—everybody expected and enjoyed a little dickering. The standard conversation between buyer and seller went: "How much is your nice corn today?" "Ten cents a dozen, today. Real nice. Pulled fresh this morning." "Two for fifteen? I'll take two dozen." The west side of Market Square was the wholesale side, and to this row of wagons went those who wanted to purchase a bushel of peaches for preserves, or a coop of live hens to make chicken salad for a party. The story is still told of how one Knoxville matron made use of this side of the square. One morning, she approached a farmer on the wholesale side of the market to inquire the price of his chickens. "Thirty-five cents each, lady," he replied, "Corn fed. Nice and fat." "How much are they at wholesale?" the customer inquired. "Let you have 'em at wholesale for twenty-five cents apiece," the farmer stated. "All right, then," smiled the lady, "I'll take that big Dominecker hen there in the back of the coop— at wholesale!" People to whom a bargain is the breath of life know better than anyone else that, as the market people were wont to say, "Nobody never gets something for nothing."

In the 1920's, Knoxville was well satisfied with herself. The postwar boom following World War I had not greatly affected the city, for Knoxville enjoyed a peculiar economic stability. Because of the diversity of industry in the area, in which marble quarries, textile mills and the coal business provided fairly steady employment, the city was not entirely dependent upon agriculture for prosperity. However, agriculture entered the picture. Lands along the rivers and streams of the great Valley of East Tennessee were rich, and the staple crops of corn and tobacco were augmented by truck gardening and growing for the canneries to give the farmers a diversity of crops. Since the 1860's, the University, under the land-grant program, had been experimenting to find the best crops to grow in the area, and the best way to grow them; and since early in the twentieth century, the county agents and home demonstration agents had been at work in East Tennessee.

In nearby Blount County, the great Aluminum Company of America plant had been built and was utilizing the power generated at its own four man-made lakes high in the mountains to process the new metal that was revolutionizing the manufacture of many articles. The new town of Alcoa had sprung up around the plant, near the old East Tennessee town of Maryville, which had been named so long ago for Mary Blount.

Knoxville itself was growing rapidly. In the two decades that separated the census of 1910 from the census of 1930, the population of the city had nearly tripled, although the city limits had not been extended. A large sign on Gay

Street in the twenties called Knoxville the "City of Homes," and this was very descriptive of its way of life. Everyone who possibly could do so owned a home and lived in it quietly and contentedly. There was some suspicion that people who were content to be "renters" were not precisely trustworthy. Of course, there were hotels (the Andrew Johnson had just been built across Gay Street from the Court House, and the Farragut had stood for some time on the corner of Gay and Clinch streets). Knoxville had always had good accommodations for travelers, ever since John Chisholm opened his tavern in 1792. There were restaurants, too, in the downtown area, but these were patronized principally by businessmen at lunchtime (the old custom of going home for midday dinner was dying out as the city grew) and by visitors to the city. Knoxvillians ate at home and entertained at home, and that was the way they liked it.

Knoxville in the 1920's, then, was much the same sort of city it had always been—comfortable, friendly, reserved, and satisfied with a way of life that included no extremes. Knoxville had never boasted any really great wealth, and there had been little abject poverty. Like the mountain people, the residents of Knoxville were proud of the fact that they could take care of themselves and of their own.

The great depression was a little late in reaching Knoxville. The stock market crash of 1929 had small effect upon the great majority of East Tennesseans, and it was not until the markets for marble, textiles, and coal failed that the city began to feel a real pinch. In the early thirties, East Tennesseans had "tightened their belts" and "pulled in their horns," as they themselves said, and were sure that if the rest of the country could weather the economic crisis,

Knoxville could too. She always had. New graduates of The University of Tennessee found no high-salaried positions waiting for them—they were happy to find jobs in filling stations or grocery stores. There was no ready cash; but since nobody else had any money either, the lack of it was a mere inconvenience which was expected to be temporary.

Far down the winding Tennessee River lay Muscle Shoals, which over the years had caused Knoxvillians considerable trouble. It was because of the impassability of the river at that point that river trade and traffic from Knoxville to the Mississippi had been impractical. Speculation in lands in the Muscle Shoals area had caused William Blount to be face to face with bankruptcy and had cost John Sevier a bitter political struggle. Now Muscle Shoals was about to become vitally important.

During World War I, a huge government project had been undertaken at Muscle Shoals for the creation of needed water power. At war's end, there seemed no further need for such an installation, and Muscle Shoals became the greatest piece of war surplus in United States history. The government found the shoals a very large white elephant indeed. Various schemes for its use were suggested and discarded during the twenties. It was offered for sale, but there were no takers. Then Senator George Norris of Nebraska introduced a bill in the Senate that not only solved the problem of what to do with Muscle Shoals, but offered a broad framework within which could be tried out new ideas in national planning. This bill proposed the creation of a government agency which would be charged with the responsibility of planning and constructing a series of dams on the Tennessee River and its tributaries for the joint purposes of flood control and the production of hydroelectric power.

President Franklin D. Roosevelt saw a wider application for such an agency than Senator Norris at first intended. The President sent a special message to Congress urging the passage of the Norris Act, and in this message he set forth his own interpretation of its implications. "It is clear," he said, "that the Muscle Shoals development is but a small part of the potential public usefulness of the entire Tennessee River. Such use, if envisioned in its entirety, transcends mere power development; it enters the wide fields of flood control, soil erosion, afforestation, elimination from agricultural use of marginal lands, and distribution and diversification of industry. In short, this power development of war days leads logically to national planning for a complete river watershed involving many states and the future lives and welfare of millions. It touches and gives life to all forms of human concerns."

So many great social and economic upheavals begin when some one visionary person says: "Wouldn't it be nice if. . . ."

The Norris Act was passed by the Congress on May 18, 1933, and thus began the creation of what David Lilienthal was to call "the Great Lakes of the South." The agency established by the act was called the Tennessee Valley Authority, and it was destined to become something new under the sun. This single agency was to design and build the dams, buy the land, construct the transmission lines, and market the power the river produced.

The Tennessee River happened to be a splendid choice for such an experiment for two reasons. First, the western slope of the Unaka Mountains, where the rivers have their sources, enjoys the highest annual rainfall rate in the eastern United States. Second, the upper sections of the river and its tributaries flowed through hilly country where the newly created lakes could be relied upon to keep within boundaries known in advance; hence, there was no danger of inundating large areas if it were necessary for reasons of flood control to raise the level of these upper lakes.

So the Tennessee Valley Authority, with no historical precedents for guidance, embarked upon the tremendous program of building twenty new dams, and improving and modifying five dams that were already in existence. This was to be the largest job of engineering and construction ever undertaken by a single organization in our nation's history. It was to create a series of new lakes with a shoreline of more than ten thousand miles.

A preliminary survey by Army engineers had resulted in the decision to build the first dam of the series on the Clinch River, twenty miles from Knoxville. It was also decided to name this first dam after the author of the act which created TVA. So Norris Dam was begun in 1933, and it was completed three years later. Those three years were filled with turmoil for Knoxville and the Clinch River valley. The whole idea of public power was a new one, and other parts of the valley would later experience a like upheaval, but TVA was learning how while Norris Dam was being built. Knoxville, like the eldest child in a large family, bore the brunt of adjusting to the TVA.

Because it was the largest city in the area where the first dams would be built, and because excellent transportation facilities already existed, Knoxville was chosen as the headquarters of the Authority. Space was rented for offices in the downtown area, and as the scope of the agency increased, so did its office space. This was a boon to the city now in the full grip of the depression. The fact that TVA began its operations during the depression meant that there were available to it many experts in various fields who would in more prosperous times not have been lured away from industry. So TVA brought to Knoxville a splendid group of highly trained and educated persons to direct its wide operations; but most of the more than two hundred thousand persons who have since worked for the Authority have been residents of the Tennessee Valley.

TVA was lucky in the type of laborer available to work on its dams and in its plants. Perhaps not so large a number of "trained help" were to be found here as in other sections of the nation, but East Tennesseans had something better to offer than training alone. Here was a potential labor force of people taught to do a good day's work for a good day's pay, convinced for generations that there is dignity in labor and that "the laborer is worthy of his hire."

There is no doubt that these work opportunities in the midst of the depression were of the greatest aid to Knoxville and the whole region. The government found it expedient, so large was the number of laborers needed for Norris Dam, to build nearby the model town of Norris to house those workers who did not commute to the site from Knoxville and from the small nearby towns. Because Norris was the pioneer community in the field of public housing, many experimental ideas were tried out. There were, for instance, a few houses built of corrugated iron. The hot summer sun made uninhabitable sweatboxes of these dwellings, and corrugated iron was hastily crossed off the list of possible building materials. In the end, most of the houses then built at Norris were modifications of a pattern long found satisfactory in the area—one-story, farmhouse-type homes, with steeply pitched roofs for summer coolness and winter snow dispersion, and with shady porches to sit on in the long twilight of the hill country.

When the first wave of office employees of the TVA arrived in Knoxville, there was considerable surprise on both sides. The new residents who converged on Knoxville from all the compass points of the United States were firmly convinced, from what they had read in newspapers and magazines, that they were going to live in the most backward section of the nation. The country as a whole was having a little difficulty in swallowing the idea of spending public tax money for a project that would, they felt, be of benefit to only one area. In an attempt to make the dose more palatable, they were encouraged to feel that the people of the Tennessee Valley were more in need of the aid of a benevolent government than their more fortunate compatriots. So many stories were written of barefoot children, pellagra, and semi-starvation that the Tennessee Valley became in the eyes of those living at a distance a sort of gigantic Tobacco Road; for years, *Compton's Encyclopedia* describes the Tennessee Valley thus:

> Disastrous floods and poor farming methods have combined to impoverish the land. The hillsides and uplands have been cleared of their protecting forests, and fields have been planted year after year with corn and tobacco and cotton. These crops not only exhaust the soil, but they also fail to hold it in place as will forests or forage crops; hence the fields have become gullied and eroded by torrential rains that washed out the soil and swept it down the river. As a result, most of the farmers of the valley have found it hard to make a bare living. They have lived

in overcrowded, unsanitary houses or cabins, and they have lacked proper clothing and food.

In 1933 the United States government chose this "cross-section of America" for an elaborate experiment in social and economic planning, in the hope of making a new life for its inhabitants. . . . Other objectives sought in the T.V.A. plan were the prevention of soil erosion; reforestation; the balance of agriculture and industry by the promotion of small scale manufactures to use the cheap power and raw materials of the region; improved agriculture with dairying and diversified crops; education of the farmers in crop rotation and other sound farming practices; conservation of the basin's natural resources; the introduction of domestic industries to provide the farmers with free-time work and added income; and a general educational program including vocational training and education for health.

Since we usually see what we expect to see, many of the newcomers to Knoxville found evidences of the extreme backwardness they had been told they would find. Knoxvillians themselves, since they really *were* literate, read the same magazine articles and syndicated newspaper stories. They were often annoyed and sometimes downright angry at what they read; but, they said to themselves, the Tennessee Valley covers a large area. We know that this is not true right here in Knoxville, but for all we know, these might be the facts about some other part of the valley. Fortunately for everybody concerned, humor is as much a dominant trait of East Tennesseans as is pride. In the end, amusement won out, and Knoxvillians laughed among themselves at the "ridiculous" stories that were being told and printed about them. Like well-brought up children who have been taught not to brag of their own accomplishments, they said little, but waited confidently for their new neighbors to find out for themselves that the descriptions of the valley were for the most part, like the reports of Mark Twain's death, "grossly exaggerated."

The Tennessee Valley Authority took President Roosevelt's words to the Congress seriously and literally. Mr. Lilienthal, one of TVA's first directors, wrote that "the river was to be seen as part of the larger pattern of the region, one asset of the many that in nature are interwoven; the land, the minerals, the waters and the forests—and all of them as one—in their relation to the lives of the valley's people." This was a lofty and laudable plan, and many well-meaning people arrived in Knoxville with the avowed purpose of introducing to the city such unquestioned benefits as higher education, women's clubs, or social dancing. It was a shock to find that they were years too late in arriving on the scene in Knoxville; for in 1934, The University of Tennessee was celebrating the 140th anniversary of its chartering, Knoxville College for Negroes was in its 67th year, Ossoli Circle was making preparations for its 50th birthday party, and the Men's Cotillion Club was forty-five years old. There was also a local affiliate of the Junior Leagues of America, dating from 1918, and the Knoxville Garden Club had become a member of the Garden Club of America in 1932. These national organizations had long been in the forefront of advances in welfare and conservation. Men's civic clubs, such as Rotary and Kiwanis, were numerous and active, and the Knoxville Chamber of Commerce was right on hand to welcome the TVA.

Even the newcomers who had no wish to be reformers found much to criticize in the narrow streets laid out by Charles McClung in 1791 and the complete lack of planned entertainment. It was all too often said in those days that

Knoxville was the kind of town where they rolled up the sidewalks at nine o'clock at night.

As a result of this critical attitude, so frequently expressed, Knoxvillians were rather slow to make friendly advances toward their new neighbors. Friends in East Tennessee had always been made slowly and carefully, but for all time. Knoxvillians were hiding their hurt feelings behind a front of reserve that created hurt feelings in return. It was not long, however, before some of the new citizens also began to find amusing some of the things they had formerly believed about their new home. They began to find that the leisurely and quiet way of life was restful, and that the countryside was beautiful. They came to love the mountains and the rivers and the hilly fields of East Tennessee; and they came to love the city, too, for its obvious faults as well as for its sometimes hidden virtues. The old residents could feel the atmosphere changing, and finally both they and the new citizens of Knoxville were able to laugh at the situation together. Everybody continued to criticize Knoxville, but kindly and humorously, as a parent deprecates the charm of a well-beloved child.

Meanwhile, the building of Norris Dam was going on apace. If the building of the dam had been the whole of the problem, there would have been no difficulties; for TVA had the benefit of the best engineering minds in the country on how such technical problems should be solved. The point was that once the dam was finished, it was going to hold water. And when that happened, farms and houses and roads and towns were going to be hundreds of feet down at the bottom of a lake. This was an idea that was very difficult for the people to comprehend. When the Great Smoky Mountains National Park came into being,

people had had to move away from their homes and had
seen their houses torn down and their fences removed so
that the land might look as it had before they came. But the
land itself, the beloved land, had remained. There was
something frightening, and to some people almost sacrile-
gious, in so changing the face of the valley that the very
hills and streams that the Lord had seen fit to put there
would disappear. The cool springs and the age-old shade
trees were going to be drowned, and it was enough to
make the people sad.

The Land Acquisition Division of TVA began to
negotiate for the purchase of the land fated to be covered
by Norris Lake, but found itself confronted by East
Tennessee's famous traders. The TVA was in a hurry to
complete the purchases, for the river could not be allowed to cover the territory until all the land had been
bought and all the people had been moved. But the people were in no hurry at all. This was too big a bargain to be
entered into hastily. They expected to do considerable dickering before they signed on the dotted line. As time grew
short, condemnation proceedings were instituted in the
courts against many of the landowners who had not yet
signed agreements. Now the residents of East Tennessee
had never been averse to going to court to protect what
they believed to be their rights, but they were not at all
pleased with the idea that "the law" could force them to
sell their land, and then tell them what price they had to
take for it. But "the law" could, and it did.

There was one question on which "the law" found itself to be up the creek. Many country churches with their
fenced-in graveyards, and many family burying grounds
on the valley's farms, were in the area to be flooded. The

TVA offered at once to move the thousands of graves in the hundreds of cemeteries to new locations on high ground selected by the families or churches involved. One of the cemeteries to be moved in this way was that of the Shields family in Grainger County, which contained the last resting place of John K. Shields, former judge and United States senator, who had once made a decision famous in Tennessee law. The Judge had had to decide a case which involved the moving of a cemetery against the wishes of the family that owned it and whose ancestors were there buried. The Judge's decision, unquestioned in the courts of Tennessee for many years, was that "the wheels of progress must stop at the grave." Neither Judge Shields nor his decision could halt the removal of the cemeteries in the Clinch River valley. The TVA patiently pointed out that, if the cemeteries were not moved, they would simply have to be covered by the waters of the lake; and so it was to be.

There was a brisk real estate market in farms that would not be covered by the lake, for although some of the families displaced by the TVA moved into Knoxville or to the smaller towns out of the way of the water, most of the people liked life on the farm. They took the money paid them for their land by TVA and set out to find new homes for themselves; but here a new difficulty arose. Norris was not the only dam that was to be built in the area, and a glance at the map of East Tennessee as it was destined to be when all the lakes were filled showed plainly that there would be almost no river bottom land left in the whole of the Tennessee Valley. Where, then, would the displaced farmers find land like that they had been forced to leave? They were mad all over again. Some of them had portions of their farms left to them because those portions were hilly

land, so high that the lake water would not reach them.
This was land the farmers had not previously used, prefer-
ring, as the University had advocated for so long, to leave
it in timber or use it for grazing. To farms like these many
of the newly homeless valley people went, to build themselves new homes, and to talk to the county agent about
what to do with this "pore land." The houses on the floor
of the Clinch valley were torn down, the trees felled, the
cemeteries moved. And then the water came.

Gradually the water built up behind the great white
height of the completed Norris Dam. Knoxvillians drove
out often to watch the familiar contours of the hills disappearing one by one. In a very short time, there was the
lake, looking as if it had always been there, with its fingers
of clear water reaching back into the hills that surrounded
it. For awhile people would say: "Right over there where
the water's the deepest used to be the town of Loyston," or
"Back from the dam apiece was the house my great-grand-
pappy built when he come from North Carolina way back
in 1795." But the coming of this lake and the others that
followed it had changed more than the appearance of the
Tennessee Valley, and people had to become reconciled to
the changes.

While Norris Dam was being completed, others were
in the planning stages. Soon there was Douglas Dam on the
French Broad River, Cherokee Dam on the Holston River,
and Fort Loudoun Dam on the Tennessee River itself. All
four of these dams are within twenty-five miles of Knoxville, where the Tennessee River as it flowed through the
city was beginning to be called Fort Loudoun Lake. And
Knoxville became, as well as the Gateway to the Great
Smokies, the Gateway to the Great Lakes of the South.

What did this mean? It meant that East Tennessee was suddenly possessed of recreational facilities unequalled in the nation, with tourists to match.

State parks were created on the shores of the lakes to provide camping areas and rental cottages for vacationers. Small speedboats began to trouble the placid waters that covered Loyston. Sailboats spread their white wings and sped past the surprised town of Concord and the birthplace of Admiral David Farragut on Fort Loudoun Lake. Tourists who came to catch fish on Douglas Lake went home to talk of how a great dike had been built to save the charming old town of Dandridge.

And then there was river transportation. Muscle Shoals would no longer, as André Michaux had described, block Knoxville's boats from reaching the broad Mississippi. Each of the dams below the city on the Tennessee River was equipped with locks, the locks at Fort Loudoun Dam being the highest in America, and thus inland Knoxville acquired access to the sea. No longer were there docks at the foot of Market Street for flatboats and rafts to unload their cargoes, but now there were storage facilities and loading cranes along the shore of Fort Loudoun Lake. Barges that brought sulphur and oil and chemicals up the river to Knoxville could be loaded with marble, or coal, or manufactured products for the return trip to points along the historic route to New Orleans.

After World War II, the government even built a naval reserve training station at Knoxville, and one morning the citizens were startled to see moored beside it on Fort Loudoun Lake an L.S.T. looking rather out of place, ringed as it was with the green hills of East Tennessee. Excursion boats and palatial river steamboats could come to

Knoxville and give Knoxvillians the thrill of seeing the river front of their city from the deck of something larger than an outboard motor boat. Seagulls followed the boats that came up the river, but they did not always follow them back; now there are gulls to wheel about the bridges and the sailboats at Concord. They, too, look just a little out of place.

Knoxville, which has been called upon to adjust to many changes in her history, has grown accustomed to the lakes. We find it difficult now to remember what it was like before the coming of the TVA. In 1956, when the water of Norris Lake was at an unprecedentedly low level, the site of the town of Loyston suddenly reappeared—houses and trees gone, to be sure, and much silt deposited on streets and foundations in the twenty years, but Loyston as sure as ever was. People who had lived there hurried out to look, and held an impromptu reunion where their town had once stood. But no one was sorry when the lake began to rise again, and Loyston disappeared once more. It was better to remember it as it had been before it was flooded, and anyway, people had gotten used to the lake.

Every year, when Congress is fighting the annual battle of the budget, articles appear in the press that lead one to believe that a large part of the country has the feeling that residents of the Tennessee Valley are furnished electric power free by TVA at their expense. It is perfectly true that Knoxville enjoys low rates on electric power. Proof of this is the fact that ninety per cent of the new small homes constructed in the Knoxville area in the 1950's are electrically heated. It is also true that the rural electrification program of the TVA has been of immeasurable benefit to the farms of East Tennessee. City dwellers in the valley are grateful for the cheaper power rates they enjoy, but women on the farms, whose every home comfort is dependent upon TVA's rural power lines, are devoutly thankful for this modern miracle.

The federal funds allotted to TVA to build these dams and power plants were not an outright gift from the government. They were made available in the form of a sort of long-term loan on which no interest is paid, but upon which the Tennessee Valley Authority makes yearly payments on the principal. In each state and in every county in which it operates, TVA pays local and state taxes. It does not, however, pay any federal taxes; thus its rates may be less than those of private power companies and still show a profit on its operations.

Abundant hydroelectric power plus an available labor force lured many industries to the Tennessee Valley. The TVA now, with its dozens of completed dams, produces ten per cent of all the hydroelectric power available in the United States, yet this is not enough. The great Aluminum Company of America, whose own four dams are operated in cooperation with the TVA system, must buy additional power from TVA because of its tremendous wartime expansion. Oak Ridge, undreamed of when plans were made for TVA in 1933, is one of the largest customers. Steam plants have been built in several areas to boost the power output, and these plants use the coal no longer needed for furnaces in the electrically heated homes.

The State of Tennessee, the University, and the TVA have cooperated on many things—reforestation, conservation, highway planning, etc. The Agriculture Department of the University and the county agents and home demonstration agents have had whole new fields of endeavor opened up for them. Farmers have learned that dairying and sheep raising are more practical for their hillside acres than the former truck gardening and are planting upland orchards of fruit and nut trees as the University and the TVA advise. They are also making plantings of seedling pines as future raw material for the region's new paper industry, and are thinning and replanting hardwood trees for sale to lumber companies. There are no trucks nowadays on Market Square, and the produce offered is found in the Mall's small marketing facility. Beans are sold by the pound rather than by the peck, corn by the ear instead of by the bushel. Many Knoxvillians frequently come to purchase plants and flowers—the beautiful perennials and annuals that grow as well on the slopes as on the level land; and, the climate being generous, there are flowers or berried shrubs or evergreens for sale each month of the year.

One thing that the TVA accomplishes has the unqualified approval of Knoxville's residents and visitors alike. The pestiferous mosquitoes that would otherwise breed in the shallow backwaters of the TVA lakes are literally drowned by raising the water a matter of a few inches, then dropping it back suddenly. This method of control is a great advance over the fly swatter and the mosquito net.

So Knoxville is in the center of the TVA lake district, where the lakes are extra beautiful because their shores are lovely wooded hills. Knoxvillians like the cheap electric power they enjoy and the lakeside recreation areas, the year-round fishing and the year-round tourist trade. They have gradually assimilated their new neighbors, and Knoxville is the better for the changes that have come, for with-

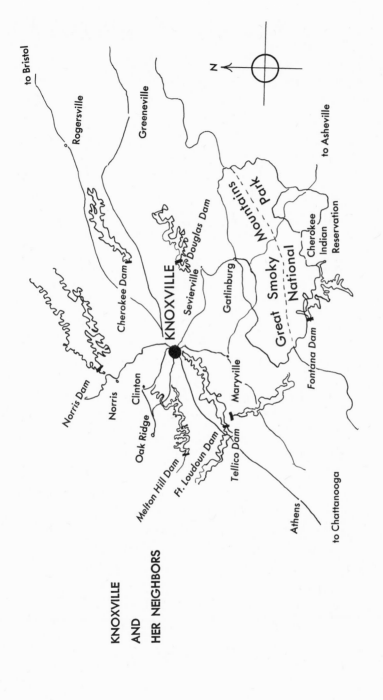

KNOXVILLE
AND
HER NEIGHBORS

N

to Bristol

Rogersville

Greeneville

to Asheville

Cherokee Dam

Douglas Dam

KNOXVILLE

Sevierville

Gatlinburg

Great Smoky Mountains National Park

Cherokee Indian Reservation

Fontana Dam

Norris Dam

Norris

Clinton

Oak Ridge

Melton Hill Dam

Ft. Loudoun Dam

Tellico Dam

Maryville

Athens

to Chattanooga

out change there is always stagnation. There is one thing, though, that the sharp traders of East Tennessee know about TVA of which the rest of the nation is unaware— nobody never gets something for nothing! They are convinced too, even as once proclaimed on advertising matches, that the Tennessee Valley is still "the best dam place in the country."

CHAPTER FOURTEEN

Oak Ridge

With the outbreak of World War II, Knoxville had a reputation to uphold. East Tennesseans had always been more than ready to fight for their rights or to protect their way of life, and in this respect the global conflict was no different from any of the wars preceding it. Many Knoxville graduates of The University of Tennessee held commissions in the Reserve Officers' Training Corps; many doctors and lawyers from Knoxville were directly commissioned because the Armed Forces had need of their specialized training; but there were thousands of others who volunteered for military service with the same promptness that had come to be expected of East Tennesseans. Over and over was repeated the story of how Tennessee had earned the title of the Volunteer State—how at the outbreak of the Mexican War the Governor's call for 2400 men was answered by 30,000 volunteers. Tennessee was determined to continue to deserve the title.

In Knoxville, however, another phase of Tennessee's history was repeating itself. John Sevier had been forced to draft men to stay at home from the Battle of King's Mountain; now Knoxvillians by the thousands found themselves drafted to stay home from World War II. Employees of the Aluminum Company of America, the Fulton-Sylphon plant, and Rohm and Haas Company were told that their work was just as vital to the winning of the war as that of the soldiers. Many other Knoxville industries were classified as essential to the war effort because they were engaged in supplying necessities for the Armed Forces. There was none of the glamour of war apparent in Knoxville early in World War II. No large military installations were nearby, so there was little of the parading and band playing that so arouses the patriotic fervor of Americans; but nothing was needed to arouse the citizens of East Tennessee to patriotism. "Service stars" appeared in the windows of Knoxville's homes; stores and churches and clubs proudly displayed rows of such stars with the names of their employees and members who were in the service. Plants displayed just as proudly the blue "achievement banners" awarded for meritorious service to the war effort. The University, whose masculine enrollment dropped almost to the level of fifty years before, welcomed an Air Force training squadron. The squadron drilled on Temple Avenue and on the football field, and marched to classes on The Hill as had the cadets in the old days of the University in the 1880's and 1890's.

Events were taking place in Washington in 1942 which would literally have world-shaking effects—Knoxville was destined once more to be in the midst of things. On August 13, 1942, President Roosevelt created a special segment of the Corps of Army Engineers to be called the Manhattan District. Actually, it was intended from the first that the name should be misleading, for this group was never meant to have anything to do with Manhattan Island or the City of New York. In accordance with previously made plans, the engineers at once began a secret survey in the counties of Anderson and Roane in East Tennessee. By September 9, they were ready to make their report to Washington, stating that they considered the tentatively selected site ideal for their purpose. Immediately the Army set about acquiring ninety-two square miles of land along the Clinch River, eighteen miles north of Knoxville.

The acquisition of this land was made easier because its owners had seen the TVA at the same work in the valley of the same river, and they knew that there was no use fighting against the government to save their land. There was the added factor of their love of country, for the patriotic East Tennesseans were told that their land was urgently needed for the war effort and these citizens of the Volunteer State responded readily. Of course, those who left their homes did so with heavy hearts; but at least the land itself would still be there, they thought—not covered with water like the farms of those who had had to sell to TVA. Perhaps, they thought, when the government had finished using their farms, they could buy them back. Some of the families who were forced to give up their homes in 1943 were the same families who had moved before the encroaching waters of Norris Dam; and there was at least one family that was displaced three times—by the Great Smoky Mountains National Park, by the Tennessee Valley Authority, and finally by "the war." These veterans of previous encounters with the government in condemnation proceedings advised their neighbors to try to get the best possible price for their land by negotiation with the purchasing agents, but not to go to court about the forced sale of it. So the purchase of the tract in Anderson and Roane counties was quicker and easier than had been the case for the park or for the TVA.

Naturally, the farmers wanted to know what the government was going to do with their land, and they were not the only ones who were asking the question. In Washington, Congressman Albert Gore of Tennessee made an official announcement that the government was purchasing the land for use as a demolition range. This statement was to prove closer to the actual truth than anyone at the time realized.

Early in 1943 the land acquisition was complete, and building could begin. Two plants were scheduled to be built on the spot the government had decided to call "Oak Ridge." One plant was to attempt to obtain U-235 by gaseous diffusion, the other by an electromagnetic process —but this information was top-secret. Nobody except the very highest echelon of engineers and a few trusted advisers of the President were to know for more than two years what the purpose of the installation at Oak Ridge really was.

Bulldozers moved into the placid Clinch River valley to rearrange its contours overnight. Trees were ruthlessly uprooted, roads built, underground plants constructed. The whole area was surrounded by an impregnable fence and was heavily guarded by the Army, which was in charge of the entire undertaking. The area could be entered by four gates from existing main highways, but only authorized per-

Norris Dam, built by TVA in 1936, created Norris Lake, the first of the man-made Great Lakes of the South.

Portions of Oak Ridge, Tennessee's newest city and the birthplace of the Atomic Age, are still restricted.

sonnel could pass the guards who manned the gates. Forty-seven thousand men worked to build the plants in which forty thousand persons would later be employed. Of course all of these employees were carefully screened and selected —only one was hired out of every three interviewed for jobs. The peak of employment was reached in May of 1945, when eighty-two thousand persons were employed on construction, maintenance, and manufacturing in the Oak Ridge area at the same time.

Where did all these people come from? The largest number was recruited from the Knoxville area and from the surrounding small towns; but Knoxville already had "defense plants" that were employing more people than they did in ordinary times, and there were simply not enough workers to go around. Many Knoxvillians left their peace-time jobs in the city for employment at Oak Ridge. They liked the larger pay checks, and they liked also the feeling that they were doing something vital to help win the war; for about the whole enterprise at Oak Ridge there was an air of controlled haste and of important pressures, even though nobody knew what those pressures were. Thousands of people arrived in Knoxville who were going to work at Oak Ridge. By heavily-loaded car, by crowded bus, by jam-packed train they came, and at first there was no place to put them. The hotels were full. The tourist courts were renting their cottages by the month to families of defense workers. Private homes with rooms to rent were besieged with calls. Families were doubling up and renting the house or apartment thus left vacant. And there were the trailers. Overnight, trailer parks sprung up along the highways and even in vacant lots and back yards within the city. They were crowded and uncomfortable, these people who came, but they were hardly more crowded or more uncomfortable than the people who were already here.

Amazing shortages developed. Not only the people who had poured into Knoxville to live, but all the others housed at Oak Ridge and the surrounding towns had to be fed by means of Knoxville's wholesale markets. For reasons of security, the number of workers at Oak Ridge could not be told, or even hinted; so Knoxville's wholesale allotments were not measurably increased and no other adequate provision was made to secure extra supplies. Some of the shortages were trivial to be sure—candy bars, cigarettes, and nylon stockings had gone to war all over the country—but there were many things really needed that were in very short supply. Meat, poultry, eggs, fats, coffee, and canned goods were very hard to find, and (which was even more alarming) canned baby foods and canned milk disappeared from the stores for weeks at a time. There were very few fresh vegetables, for since the disappearance of the river bottom farms beneath the TVA lakes, Knoxville had come to rely on fresh produce brought in from a distance. The press of the nation insisted that rationing would insure a reasonable supply of needed items to all parts of the country, and Knoxville housewives duly presented themselves and their ration books at the grocery stores only to be told that there was no bacon, no shortening, no coffee, *no soap.* Something was wrong somewhere. Prices zoomed. Knoxville was number one on the nation's list of cities showing a tremendous increase in the cost of living. Sometimes harassed Knoxvillians, confronted with the latest wave of new arrivals, felt like shouting at them the words seen everywhere on posters in railway stations and bus terminals: "Is your trip really necessary?"

Suddenly housing, which had seemed to be in a hopeless muddle, began to get better. Not only was the government building plants at Oak Ridge, but there was being built a complete city, which by 1945 had 75,000 inhabitants and was the fifth largest city in the State of Tennessee. The feat of providing living quarters for all these people could never have been accomplished without the newly developed prefabricated houses—plywood and cemesto—and the use of trailers. Whatever the type of housing the newcomers found assigned to them at Oak Ridge, it was surrounded by a sea of thick red clay mud, which for several years was to be the trademark of Oak Ridge. The town constructed in such frantic haste was at first terribly unattractive, yet there were remarkably few complaints from the residents. They had not, after all, come to Oak Ridge simply to live and work—they had come to win a war. To live with shortages and with mud was far less of a sacrifice than America's young men in the services were being called upon to make.

In addition to all those who could be housed on the spot, thousands more continued to commute daily from Knoxville and the surrounding towns to work there. Each workman knew the name of the company for which he worked (there were originally three: Eastman Corporation, Monsanto Chemical Company, and American Carbide and Carbon), and each knew what his own job was. But of the total plan, absolutely no explanations were made. The right hand *never* knew what the left hand was doing. Rumor was rife: there could be no harm in guessing what was going on, and people surmised that Oak Ridge was making everything from poison gas to synthetic rubber.

In 1943, the United States government had asked permission from the legislature of the State of Tennessee to make Oak Ridge a federal reservation. Had this been done, the area would have been under the direct control of the War Department, even as the Indian affairs of the Territory South of the River Ohio had been in the long ago before Tennessee's admission to statehood. But it would also have meant that the laws of Tennessee would not apply to Oak Ridge, and the legislators did not like the idea that a portion of the state would be exempt from her laws. The government could buy up land if it liked, and bring in people to build whatever it was they were building over there at Oak Ridge, but it was *not* going to take most of Anderson County and part of Roane County out of the State of Tennessee!

The race between the two great plants at Oak Ridge for first place in the atom-splitting contest was won on November 4, 1943, when the first atomic chain reactor was placed in operation. It had been built in the incredibly short time of eight and one-half months by the E. I. duPont de Nemours Company. On January 27, 1944, occurred the first run of U-235 by the electromagnetic method in Plant Y-12 of the Tennessee Eastman Corporation. No public announcement was made of either event, and a veil of secrecy continued to overlie the entire operation.

There was a feeling of mounting tension in Oak Ridge and in Knoxville. Sooner or later, it was felt, the lid would have to blow off.

August 6, 1945, was the fateful day of the bombing of Hiroshima. With the news of the bombing came the announcement that it was at Oak Ridge, Tennessee, that the radioactive heart of the atom bomb had first begun to beat. Knoxville and Oak Ridge were stunned to hear it. It was a strange, frightening day. Knoxville radio stations and newspapers received the formal announcement from the information headquarters at Oak Ridge; the people living and working at Oak Ridge received the news first through the newspapers and radio stations of Knoxville. Oak Ridge was the most famous town in America that day, and the stories carried about it all over the nation were emanating from Knoxville, where from the city's founding, it had been considered important to report the news. As the days passed, and more and more stories appeared about the enormity of the possibilities opened by the splitting of the atom, Knoxvillians began to have an uneasy feeling that they (in the center of a triangle that had Oak Ridge, Norris Dam, and the great Alcoa aluminum plants as its points) would be entirely too attractive a target if the United States should suffer an invasion by air.

The use of the atomic bomb at Hiroshima and Nagasaki was the beginning of the end of World War II, as the breaking of the Hindenburg Line had hastened the surrender of Germany in the previous World War. "And now what will they do with Oak Ridge?" people asked. "All that money spent and all those men working so long just to make two bombs no bigger than a gallon jug!" If that had been the sole use of Oak Ridge, the time and money would still have been well spent to bring about the termination of a global conflict, but the war's end was not to be the end of Oak Ridge. The end of the war was in fact the beginning of the Atomic Age. Scientists had said all along, from the very day the news of the atomic bomb was first released to the public, that atomic energy would serve humanity better in peaceful pursuits than as an agent of destruction, but this facet of the discovery was almost overlooked in the terrible excitement of the moment.

It was widely felt that, although it had been necessary for the Army to have the manufacture of radioactive material under strictest controls during wartime, the best interest of the public would be served if control were now removed from the military and vested in civilian authorities. It seemed only fair that men of science who could comprehend the theory of atomic energy should be the ones to direct its future destiny. So, on August 1, 1946, President Truman signed a bill establishing the Atomic Energy Commission, a civilian agency to take over the entire atomic project from the War Department. Oak Ridge immediately began the manufacture of "atoms for peace." When the peaceful uses for this great new force were first discussed, they seemed to be centered upon heating and upon fuel for all types of transportation, but these announced possibilities have been slow of realization. There are other uses for atomic energy that proved immediately practical and easy of accomplishment. The broad fields of medicine, industry and agriculture have found themselves advancing by giant strides because of the discoveries made in this new medium. Radioactive isotopes, or tracer atoms, are already helping Americans toward better health, bigger crops, and higher industrial production.

Of course, not all this experimentation could be carried on at Oak Ridge and the other atomic laboratories. The best place to conduct agricultural experiments is naturally on a farm, and a factory is too large to be reproduced in toto for experimental purposes only. Doctors alone are capable of using the atom in the field of medicine, and it is far more practical to take the atom to the farm, to the patient, or to the factory than to try to produce artificial laboratory experiments along these lines at Oak Ridge. This presents the problem of the transportation of radioactive material. Like the bears in the Great Smokies, the atoms are not harmful to man if they are properly treated, *but* they are not tame. Those who know most about radioactive material are the most careful in handling it. If such a material, potentially very dangerous, was to be sent elsewhere for research purposes, the public must be protected while it was in transit. Different types of protection are required for different types of radioactive material, for certain of the rays may be deflected by a single sheet of white paper, while others must be buried deep in many feet of lead. A particle of this latter type of radioactive cobalt no larger than a dime must be shipped in a huge lead container weighing several tons. The problem of transportation is further complicated by the fact that some radioactivity lessens markedly in a very short time. It is easy to see why the proximity of Knoxville's enlarged McGhee Tyson Airport, with its excellent facilities, has been of the utmost importance in getting the tracer atoms to their destinations in time to be of value.

It was not until 1949 that the town of Oak Ridge became an open city. The guards were removed from the four gates in the surrounding fence, and the American public was invited to come and see for themselves the Atomic City. Of course, there is still a restricted area where no one may go who is not specially qualified and identified, but the residential and business area of the town may be freely visited. The greatest attraction is the world's only Museum of

Atomic Energy, especially created to explain to interested visitors just what the atom is, how it was split, and what that fission means. This highly technical knowledge is so simply and vividly presented that at least the younger generation of Americans who visit the museum seem to understand it all. There is an apparatus which conclusively demonstrates the effect of static electricity by causing the investigator's hair to stand on end. It is fascinating to watch the huge mechanical hands that perform their delicate tasks with such dexterity. There are the miniature models of the great reactors themselves to be carefully examined. Then there is the favorite souvenir of Oak Ridge to be procured by dropping a dime into a machine that returns the same dime, made harmlessly radioactive. The museum presents to the public a vital chapter in American history, which at Oak Ridge is still being written every day.

In 1956, the houses in the town of Oak Ridge were offered for sale to private owners for the first time, and the town began to lose its "housing project" look as the new owners made all sorts of improvements. Many of the unsightly flat-tops had already been sold when the urgent need for them had passed, and they had been moved away to farms and towns in the surrounding counties, and to the shores of TVA lakes to serve as summer cottages. Many of the trailers that had seen service at Oak Ridge had moved to Knoxville. A trailer village was even located for a time on the Main Campus of The University of Tennessee to help ease the housing shortage made newly acute by the wave of students attending the University on the "G.I. Bill." The houses remaining at Oak Ridge were permanent structures, and essentially comfortable, but there was a depressing similarity about them. It was soon found that their appearance could be altered in many ways, and every way has been tried. The hated mud has disappeared under green grass and bright flowers, and trees offer grateful shade now along the residential streets. The casual visitor to Oak Ridge would never guess if he were not told that the town had mushroomed almost overnight out of the red clay hills of Anderson County.

As early as 1945, scientists at Oak Ridge were suggesting that there should be a new hospital near the Atomic City, especially equipped and staffed to take full advantage of the use of the "tracer atoms" in medicine. In 1956, this suggestion was finally realized with the completion by the State of Tennessee, Knox County, and the City of Knoxville of a very special new isotopic research hospital in Knoxville. The cost of the hospital had been equally divided between the state and the city and county, but it was not so easy to divide its supervision. It was feared that what was everybody's business might be nobody's business, so it was necessary to find an agency capable of assuming its administration. That is how the new hospital came to be The University of Tennessee Memorial Research Center and Hospital, for the University amply fulfilled all the requirements for the supervisory body. This University already had a long record of successful cooperation with the City of Knoxville; it was the head of the public education system of the state, and it was also a land-grant college, having faithfully performed its required duties in order to qualify for funds under the various federal land-grant acts. The new hospital is obligated to care for the charity patients of Knoxville and Knox County, but it does more than that. It offers the opportunity of very special internships in the finest of research hospitals to some fortunate young doctors each year—many of them graduates of the University's College of Medicine. Its location is close enough to the national laboratories at Oak Ridge to make it promptly available for medical research. It demonstrates within itself that many things are possible when there is cooperation.

The entire history of Oak Ridge has been filled with such examples of cooperation with other governments and governmental agencies. There has also been wonderful cooperation between industry and labor—if they had not been united, the atom would never have been divided. Oak Ridge stands out, too, as a remarkable example of America's scientific progress and leadership.

However, the most remarkable thing of all about this atomic energy project is the fact that it existed as a secret for almost three years. Certainly every possible security precaution was taken, but where thousands of people are involved there is always a possible margin of error in the human element. It speaks volumes for the integrity of the more than forty thousand East Tennesseans employed at Oak Ridge that there were no leaks of vital information. One Knoxvillian, when asked how the secret could have been so well kept, put the answer in a nutshell when he replied: "Well, if they wanted to keep it a secret, they just came to the right place!"

CHAPTER FIFTEEN

Here and Now

It has sometimes occurred to Tennesseans that other people start wars for them to finish. For instance, it was John Sevier and his mountain men who turned the tide of the Revolutionary War in the South at the Battle of King's Mountain. Fresh from decisive victories in the Creek War, Andrew Jackson and his volunteer troops marched on to New Orleans, and won the final battle of the War of 1812. In the Mexican War, Tennessee retained the undisputed title of Volunteer State by sending more than thirty thousand men in response to the Governor's call for a mere twenty-four hundred. The loyal Unionists of East Tennessee made this state the last to secede from the Union to join the Confederacy, and the first to be readmitted to statehood after the Civil War. World War I ended quickly once the supposedly impregnable Hindenburg Line was broken; Tennessee's General Lawrence Tyson directed the battle to breach it. Oak Ridge's first atomic bombs brought

World War II to a speedy close and at the same time marked the opening of a new atomic era.

Whenever a war ends, a period of readjustment must follow; in 1945, it was up to Knoxville to gather up the jigsaw puzzle pieces of peaceful existence and fit them together once more. Then, exhausted by the anguish and the effort of the war years, weary residents sank back with a sigh of relief into comfortable apathy.

Sometimes the shock of criticism is required to galvanize a complacent community into action. In 1949, John Gunther's *Inside U.S.A.* was published; therein Knoxville was designated "America's ugliest city." The insult rankled. Startled and horrified Knoxvillians took a sharp look around to see what had prompted so harsh an evaluation; slowly (for such things take time) they began to eliminate or ameliorate the more obvious eyesores.

All over the country, the postwar population explosion had set off a chain reaction of suburban subdivisions. Urbanites, anxious to escape from overcrowded living conditions and rising municipal tax rates, joined in a mass exodus from older residential areas. Outlying shopping centers drained dollar volume from center-city stores. Use of public transportation declined—in a nation of two-car families, nobody rode the bus. America's cities were suffering from chronic heart disease, complicated by traffic arteriosclerosis.

A further complication arose under the name of aid from the federal government. In a laudable effort to better housing conditions by removing real and potential slums, urban renewal programs cleared huge tracts of substandard dwellings in the hearts of cities. The displaced residents fled to peripheral areas.

Knoxville was no exception. From the high central plateau of the business district, the city's growth spread out like spokes from the hub of a wheel—north, east, south, and west. But Knoxville's prosperity was predicated upon the fact that this was the center of a vast trade area, and "center" was the definitive word. Downtown Knoxville, covering only 2 percent of the land within the city limits, was paying 26 percent of all city taxes; while the tax rate was going up, rental income was going down. "Somebody," businessmen told each other sadly, "ought to do something."

What one man cannot do alone, many men working together may accomplish. In 1957, an association of downtown property owners was formed, and the Downtown Knoxville Association began to take steps, one at a time. Completion of the Promenade in 1960 gave handsome new rear entrances to a block of Gay Street stores; shoppers found it fun to travel from parking lot to Promenade on the South's first moving sidewalk. Each and every owner of the property involved had participated in planning the project, and each had paid a proportionate share of the total cost. This was to be the formula for mid-town rejuvenation: constructive thinking plus local financial support equals progress.

But when the Downtown Knoxville Association announced plans to replace Knoxville's antiquated market house with a pedestrian mall, a storm of protest greeted the suggestion. Knoxvillians never *welcome* innovations. Knowing well from past experience that what is changed can never be the same again, they clutch at the coattails of each vanishing era and cry aloud against any alteration until it is complete; then they invariably settle down to

make the best of it. Traditionalists raised their voices in
lamentation. They contended that the Market Square, established in 1854, was the city's most symbolic spot—a
daily reminder of past and present "good providing."
Where else could you buy country ham, shuck beans,
homemade cottage cheese, or sulphured apples? The controversy might have raged for years, but it was suddenly
and dramatically resolved when the obsolete Market House
was irreparably damaged by fire.

In 1961, Market Square Mall was complete. Since the
Market House had been city property, the City of
Knoxville paid for the improvements that supplanted it;
owners of the buildings on both sides of the Mall shared the
expense of sidewalk canopies. "A patch of giant toad-
stools," diehards dubbed the umbrella-shaped sections of
these canopies and the marketing facility; but not even the
most ardent antiquarians were permanently immune to the
charm of trees and fountains. Meanwhile, the DKA was
hard at work on a third project, Gay/Way, which
was a preventive rather than a curative measure. Along
two of Gay Street's prime business blocks, sidewalks
were widened and given sheltering, sky-lighted canopies. New street lighting of quadrupled intensity was
installed.

The 1960 census figures made depressing reading.
Comparable cities had recorded phenomenal population
gains. Knox County's numerical increase was encouraging,
but Knoxville, whose city limits had not been extended in
more than forty years, was barely holding her own. The
solution seemed obvious: annex the heavily populated surrounding districts, give city services, and levy city taxes.
Despite violent opposition from the affected suburbs,

Knoxville increased her area and her population in one fell swoop. Then residents of the "old city" also objected; they were called upon to help pay the cost of sewer lines and street lights for the annexed areas.

"Enough's enough," reactionaries wailed. "Leave us alone!" And Knoxville's deeply entrenched bootleggers echoed these sentiments.

But enthusiasm proved more contagious than sleeping sickness. Roused to responsible action by a militant Committee of One Thousand, citizens marched to the polls and voted *for* the legal control of alcoholic beverages. Thus Knoxville relinquished the dubious distinction of being the nation's largest "dry" community.

In the meantime, a fine five-million-dollar coliseum complex was going up, and sidewalk superintendents were calling it "the world's largest caterpillar." The James White Memorial Auditorium-Coliseum opened in 1961. Here at last was an outstanding concert hall and theatre, an indoor sports arena, and exhibition space; now the city could, and did, compete for major conventions. Coming attractions included "Holiday on Ice," Broadway plays, the Metropolitan National Opera, the circus—citizens lined up for tickets and asked each other: "How did we ever get along without it?" Enumerating the benefits of the Coliseum became a popular pastime; quite suddenly, people found it pleasanter to count blessings than to catalogue complaints.

An amazing variety of spectator sports events was taking place at the Coliseum and elsewhere: football, basketball, baseball, ice hockey, wrestling, boat races, horse shows—the list went on and on. The athletically inclined could participate in swimming, tennis, bowling, horseback riding, ice-skating, year-round golf, and year-round fishing.

On the map, Knoxville was pin-pointed at the center of a star composed of five TVA lakes. Norris, Cherokee, Douglas, and Melton Hill lakes were all within twenty-five miles. Fort Loudoun Lake's headwaters actually bordered downtown Knoxville. The total surface area of these lakes was 115,320 acres. Such an expanse of water could inundate the enlarged city of Knoxville, plus the District of Columbia, Manhattan Island, the Principality of Monaco, and the Vatican City—and still have ten square miles of lake left over! The five lakes' combined shoreline added up to 2,322 miles—a measurement greater than the distance from Key West, Florida, to the Canadian border. To tourists and to industries alike, Knoxville invited: "Come on in! The water's fine!"

There was year-round culture, too. The Knoxville Symphony Orchestra and its composer-conductor, David Van Vactor, enjoyed international acclaim. As well as regularly scheduled concerts featuring renowned guest artists, the Symphony was offering a series of children's programs for the pupils of area schools. University Concerts, the Lyceum Series of Knoxville College, the Knoxville Choral Society, and even a local chapter of the Society for the Preservation and Encouragement of Barbershop Quartettes gave the public a balanced musical diet.

In addition to dramatic productions booked for the Auditorium, Carousel was providing community theatre at its best. This pioneer theatre-in-the-round, under the direction of The University of Tennessee, had a building no less interesting than the plays presented with professional brilliance by actors recruited from University students and

Above: The Mall, which replaced the old Market House, is still a market place.

Below: Mall greenery, set in the midst of an active business district, continues down Market Street to the Court House.

Bridges over Fort Loudoun Lake welcome visitors to Knoxville.

Above: The auditorium facade is featured in this view of the multi-purpose James White Memorial Coliseum.

Below: Shoppers along the Promenade, reached by a moving sidewalk, use the handsome rear entrances of stores that front on Gay/Way, another Downtown Knoxville Association project.

from the community at large. What's more, Junior Carousel was bringing school children into the act with suitable plays well-costumed and well-directed.

The University's new McClung Museum and the city's new Dulin Gallery were complementing each other in giving re-emphasis to art. The Museum was bringing exhibitions of contemporary paintings, providing a showcase for the works of local artists, and graphically displaying Tennessee's natural history and sciences. The Dulin Gallery of Art had a three-fold appeal: changing loan exhibits, a growing permanent collection, and a rental gallery.

On the home front, too, there was cause for civic pride. Many early homes had been carefully situated to take advantage of a view of river, bluffs, and distant mountains. As new houses proliferated, not every building site could command a sweeping panorama, but a pleasant outlook over gentle slopes and majestic trees was almost always available. Driving through residential sections offered a delightful element of surprise—just over this hill, just around the next curve, there would be something different, something beautiful. Sequoyah Hills, Holston Hills, Fountain City—Knoxville was blessed with charming homes, and scenic drives led out in all directions through verdant countryside.

East Tennesseans had always known, since André Michaux first described the rare and wonderful plants he found on the western slopes of the Great Smokies, that their homeland was a garden spot. These mountains, spared the ravages of a destructive glacier, harbor varieties of trees, shrubs, and flowers that elsewhere vanished during the last Ice Age; "Botany's antique shop," horticulturists have christened the area. Something about the soil or the climate in the foothills of the Smokies made the dogwood different here: the trees are tall and the blossoms giant size. On shady slopes this spectacular wild dogwood is profuse; each April a lacy mantle of white bloom envelopes Knoxville in evanescent beauty.

As early as 1949 it was suggested that Sequoyah Hills' most outstanding streets be designated a dogwood trail. Route markers would be necessary, even for native Knoxvillians, since residential roads meander up hill and down dale and intersect at will. In 1955 the first annual Dogwood Trail was a community effort. Knox Beautiful Commission had established a committee to formulate and implement plans; the Chamber of Commerce furnished materials for artistic signs made in the woodworking shops of city schools. The Knox County Council of Garden Clubs stressed the planting of new dogwood trees on lawns and highways, and suggested routes for additional trails. City crews mowed grass and pruned shrubbery on city property. The University's Department of Horticulture gave the heartening opinion that it would be fairly safe to set the dates for the trail well in advance, since the third week in April had almost always found the trees in bloom.

The first trail was a modest success, but many people missed it because they had no time during daylight hours to drive around in search of beauty; so in 1956 a short section of one street, overarched and canopied with dogwood, was lighted for night viewing. The effect was startling. The trunks and twigs of the trees became invisible against the surrounding darkness while the blossoms, snowy white or glowing pink, seemed to float unsupported in mid-air.

Like the population, dogwood trails spread north, east, south, and west to surround the city. Residents along each route strove to bring their grounds to a peak of perfection; at their own expense they floodlighted or spotlighted their trees to create a cumulative spectacle.

But perennial pessimists were unimpressed. "You can't," they were fond of saying, "make a silk purse out of a sow's ear."

Knoxvillians, who were just getting around to self-congratulation, were brought up short by this defeatist attitude, and they resented it. Hadn't they worked hard in community improvement campaigns? Hadn't they switched from soft-coal furnaces to electric heat? Hadn't whole neighborhoods been sacrificed in the name of progress to expressways and to the University's expansion program? Hadn't they earned the title of Dogwood Capital of the World with more than forty miles of winding trails?

Step up their efforts? Yes. But find some way to point up their achievements, too.

In 1960, under the joint sponsorship of the Chamber of Commerce and the Junior League of Knoxville, the annual Dogwood Arts Festival began. Since then, dozens of participating groups have concentrated their efforts to bring together the fine arts and the lively arts in happy juxtaposition. Special musical programs are arranged. Outstanding exhibitions of art are assembled. The Coliseum becomes the busiest building in town, sheltering every type of indoor event from classical concerts to sports spectaculars. On the Mall, ablaze with the color of cut flowers and blooming plants, art classes, craft exhibits, pop concerts, and square dances succeed each other. The Promenade, masquerading as an instant garden, devotes its windows to informative displays. Regional history is emphasized at an increasing number of house museums. Sports events pro-

vide a change of pace, and boating exhibitions on Fort
Loudoun Lake within the city limits draw attention to the
recreational facilities of TVA's encircling lakes. Garden
club groups and interested individuals flock to private gardens opened to the public. High school bands from several
states, here to take part in a mammoth competition, open
the festivities with a colorful and tuneful parade. But nature's own parade of flowers tops all other Festival events in
popularity; daily, by car and by bus, thousands of persons
travel the six Dogwood Trails, each accessible from a major
highway.

It's a fine thing, Appalachia's native sons and daughters
readily admit, to cultivate culture in an affluent society, but
it's also comforting to know that *some* of the best things in
life still are free!

The hard work of many groups endeavoring to make
Knoxville more prosperous and more attractive did not go
unremarked. The Downtown Knoxville Association was
accomplishing a gradual rejuvenation of the business district; civic groups across the nation wrote for step-by-step
instruction in private enterprise; and delegations from other
cities came to see for themselves. Knoxville had natural
beauty and a crowded calendar of cultural events; when
these attributes were combined and concentrated into the
Dogwood Arts Festival, they made news. People from
neighboring towns drove over. Tourists came. TVA's
official visitors from around the world carried home the
story. Everybody agreed that capsule culture was very easy
to swallow.

Then, in 1963, *Look* magazine named Knoxville an
All-American City! "John Gunther, please take note," one
exuberant newspaper article began. Running like a leit-

motif through Knoxville's composite accomplishment has been the harmonious theme of cooperative effort. "Do-it-yourself" became a famous advertising slogan in the 1950's, but it had been a way of life in East Tennessee for more than a hundred and fifty years.

What Knoxville was continues to influence what Knoxville is. Certain natural endowments have favored the city through the years: geography made her an early and continuing center for transportation and trade; climate has been propitious, too. Summers are long, and lush, and seldom *too* hot. Breezes mitigate the sultriest day; nights are comparatively cool. Winters are chilly, with an occasional sharp freeze or heavy snow, but even in mid-winter come week-long stretches of invigorating sunny days. Autumn is one long Indian Summer, when the hills' brilliant color carpet fades and blurs to the muted hues of an ancient tapestry. Spring, beginning timidly with January's jasmine and culminating in April's burst of glory, is a recurrent miracle. At any season, a sudden rain may turn the red clay soil to gummy glue, but without so much precipitation there would not be profuse flowers, towering trees, and sparkling lakes. All in all, James White chose well for his family, and for those who have followed.

From the beginning this has been a Christian community: the first cleared land in the Knoxville area was set aside for church purposes at the time the town was surveyed. Today, three of four major hospitals are the specific concern of religious denominations: one Catholic (St. Mary's), one Baptist (East Tennessee Baptist Hospital), and one Presbyterian (Fort Sanders Presbyterian Hospital on the site of the Civil War fortification whose name it bears).

Education has long been Knoxville's business, in more ways than one. In 1794, America's first Territorial Legislature made this a center of learning by establishing here Blount College, which for years was housed in a single building on Gay Street. By the 1960's, the lineal descendant of that self-contained and self-supported school was a publicly financed educational institution with a Knoxville campus covering hundreds of acres. The University of Tennessee, adding new professors to teach new courses in brand new buildings to an ever-escalating number of resident students, is the city's largest single enterprise.

Charles McClung's plan for the capital of the Territory South of the River Ohio set aside the land contiguous to the town on the north as a park, or commons. That area (between Church and Clinch streets in downtown Knoxville) did not long remain public property, but other open spaces have been acquired by the city as opportunity has arisen. Small parks and playgrounds are scattered through populous areas; city recreation centers and programs serve old and young. Under the federal Open Spaces Act, new parklands are being acquired for the suburbs annexed in the early 1960's. The first, Ijams Park, is near the Tennessee School for the Deaf on the south side of the river. This city park, purchased with matching federal funds, is nevertheless in a very real sense the property of the people; it was suggested by the Knoxville Garden Club, sponsored by the Knox County Council of Garden Clubs, and supported in its restoration by private contributors.

Convinced that beauty is good business, the Downtown Knoxville Association adopted as its fourth project a rejuvenation of Market Street from the Mall to the Courthouse corner; trees, fountains, and flowers were an integral part of the proposal. This was exactly the sort of center-city redevelopment that the Urban Beautification Act of 1965 was intended to promote, and Knoxville became the first city in the southeast to qualify for the federal funds it made available.

In the same amount of time required for a New Yorker to travel, say, from Staten Island to Central Park, or for a resident of South Chicago to reach the Lincoln Park Zoo, fortunate Knoxvillians may drive over scenic highways to Big Ridge State Park on Norris Lake or to the largest national park east of the Mississippi, in the Great Smoky Mountains. Gradually (and economically) Knox County has transformed long stretches of the Fort Loudoun lakefront into a splendid series of public recreation areas.

In 1966, Knox County embarked upon a different type of park development with the creation of the extensive Forks of the River Industrial Park. Lying between the Holston and French Broad rivers, it occupies much of the land first selected for settlement by James White and his friends in 1785; Francis Ramsey's venerable home, Swan Pond, has new neighbors.

This, then, is Knoxville—rock-ribbed and remarkable—the heart of a metropolitan area whose residents number a third of a million, the center of an industrial and trade area that embraces most of eastern Tennessee and parts of three adjacent states, the focal point of the entire region's educational and cultural development. Yet Knoxville manages to clasp the past with one hand while reaching out with the other for the future—meanwhile keeping both feet firmly on the ground!

CHAPTER SIXTEEN

Seeing is Believing

Where else in America could a family share so wide a variety of exciting adventures, yet *never spend a night away from home?* Here it's possible to

Hunt Indian arrowheads within the city limits (Fort Loudoun Lake shores)

Visit an Indian Reservation (Qualla Reservation at Cherokee, North Carolina)

Wander through underground caverns beside a buried stream, or sail a lake hidden deep inside the earth (Tuckaleechee Caverns, near Townsend; Lost Sea, near Madisonville and Cleveland)

See the first British fort in the Southwest (Fort Loudoun, two hundred years old in 1957)

Visit America's first Territorial Capitol (Blount Mansion) and "the cradle of Tennessee History" (William Blount's office)

Be a guest at a pioneer farm home that served as a governor's mansion (John Sevier's plantation)

Explore a Civil War fort (Fort Dickerson)

Step back a century into a house that was General Longstreet's headquarters during the siege of Knoxville
(Confederate Memorial Hall)

Take a motorboat cruise to see two great rivers merge
to form a third (Holston River plus French Broad
River equals Tennessee River)

Travel by boat through the highest river locks in America (Fort Loudoun Dam)

Hike in the highest mountains east of the Rockies (Great
Smoky Mountains National Park)

Ski in winter (Gatlinburg Ski Lodge) and in summer
(on TVA lakes)

Ice skate all year round (James White Memorial Coliseum)

Study pioneer life in a living museum and see cornmeal
ground at an ancient gristmill (Cades Cove)

See a marble quarry at work, and hear the chant of a
tobacco auctioneer

Tour a hydroelectric plant contained within a towering
dam (Norris Dam) or discover how electricity is
made from coal (Bull Run Steam Plant)

Learn the workings of an agricultural experiment station
and the Tennessee Valley's largest arboretum (University of Tennessee), or a wild bird farm (Buffalo
Springs State Quail Farm, Grainger County)

Stroll through a zoo, and see the largest African elephant
in captivity (Chilhowee Park)

Watch the jets streak by (McGhee Tyson Airport)

Tour a naval training station (Alcoa Highway)

Enjoy the world's only Museum of Atomic Energy
(Oak Ridge)

Knoxvillians can, and they do!

Begin if you like at the corner of Hill and State streets
with Blount Mansion, built in 1792, the first two-story
frame house in what was then "the West." This was actu-

ally America's first Territorial Capitol, for it was the seat of government of the Territory South of the River Ohio until 1796, when Tennessee became the sixteenth state of the Union. The office of William Blount in the Mansion's side yard is called "the cradle of Tennessee history"—here the "Tennessee plan" for statehood was formulated, and here the constitution probably was written. The office contains the desk of David Henley (whose larger office was rented for the meetings of the constitutional convention) upon which the document was signed.

Step inside Blount Mansion and step back to the eighteenth century. The mansion is beautifully furnished with authentic family and period pieces, all in use before 1800. Walk out into Mary Blount's garden and visit the office, the cooling cellar, and the kitchen. Prepare to be surprised by ancient counterparts of so-called "modern conveniences": wall ovens, heated serving dishes, and an automatic barbecue spit!

Across State Street is Craighead-Jackson House, built in 1818, an excellent example of the comfortable town residences of the period. The well-proportioned rooms of its carefully restored interior are now enhanced by woodwork carved by Knoxville's pioneer architect, Thomas Hope. Rare and exciting are the furnishings here, for Craighead-Jackson House displays the fine furniture and elegant English silver collection of the late W. P. Toms and brings the city something new and different in house museums. The back porch overlooks the spot where First Creek flows into the Tennessee River; here William Blount met with the Cherokee chieftains to sign the Treaty of Holston. Because of the success of this meeting, Blount chose White's Fort as the capital of the territory he governed, and renamed it Knoxville in honor of Major General Henry Knox who was Secretary of War and in charge of Indian affairs.

Two blocks north, on State Street at Cumberland, the Volunteers of America occupy one of Knoxville's first brick residences, designed and built about 1804 by Thomas Hope for Dr. Joseph C. Strong. In the 1890's, this house served as the city's first civilian hospital.

At the opposite end of the Hill Avenue viaduct from Craighead-Jackson House is the site of the restoration of James White's home (the first built in the Knoxville area) and the reconstruction of White's Fort. Early in this century, Knoxville's oldest house was moved from its original location on Central Avenue near First Creek to Woodlawn Pike on the south side of the river. Half a century later, the City Association of Women's Clubs raised funds to purchase the house and move it to property overlooking the James White Memorial Auditorium-Coliseum, newly named for the city's founder.

The Auditorium-Coliseum, completed in 1961, commands a striking view of the downtown skyline from its hillside site between East Main and East Church avenues. This is a multipurpose building. The Auditorium at the north end of the structure comfortably seats an audience of twenty-four hundred for concerts and theatrical performances. Up to seven thousand persons may attend events in the Coliseum at the building's south end, and every seat has an unobstructed view. The huge floor of the Coliseum triples with ease as an ice-rink, a sawdust-covered three-ring circus, or a ballroom floor. Large exhibition halls and quiet meeting rooms add to the value of the building as a convention center.

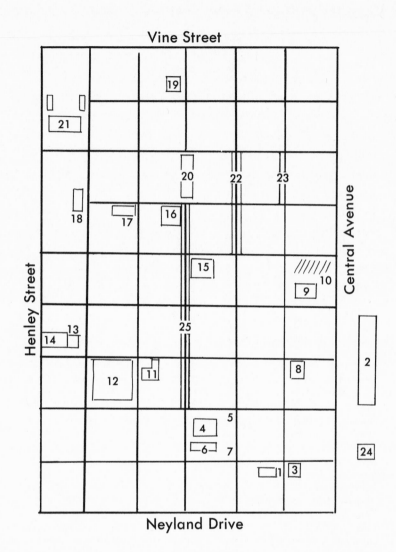

Across First Creek from the Auditorium, at the west end of the Church Street viaduct, is the First Presbyterian Church. It occupies the plot of ground cleared first by James White and planted to his first turnip crop; at the time the town was surveyed, Knoxville's original settler gave this lot to the city for church purposes. An earlier church building on this site served as headquarters for the Freedmen's Bureau after the War Between the States, and in its basement Knoxville's pioneer Negro church (Shiloh Presbyterian) was organized. In the cemetery here sleep Knoxville's founders, among them James White, William Blount, Hugh Lawson White, and Samuel Carrick (the church's first minister and the first president of Blount College).

DOWNTOWN KNOXVILLE TODAY

1—Blount Mansion. 2—James White Memorial Auditorium–Coliseum. 3—Craighead–Jackson House (one of oldest brick houses in city). 4—Knox County Court House. 5—Grave and monument of John Sevier. 6—Knox County Criminal Court Building. 7—Marker designating Knoxville as the first capital of Tennessee. 8—Strong House (one of city's oldest brick residences, and the first civilian hospital in Knoxville). 9—First Presbyterian Church. 10—Cemetery (burial place of James White, William Blount, Mary Grainger Blount, Hugh Lawson White, and Samuel Carrick). 11—Sevier–Park House (now contains the museum of the Academy of Medicine). 12—Post Office and Federal Court Building, built of Tennessee pink marble. 13—Tennessee Supreme Court Building. 14—State Office Building. 15—Old Post Office, built in 1867 of Tennessee white marble (now contains branch post office and offices of the Tennessee Valley Authority). 16—TVA offices. 17—TVA offices. 18—Old Masonic Temple (originally the residence of Colonel Charles McGhee). 19—Lawson McGhee Library, containing McClung Historical Collection. 20—Market Square Mall. 21—Knoxville City Hall (buildings built in 1848 for the Tennessee School for the Deaf). 22—Gay/Way. 23—Promenade. 24—White's Fort. 25—Redeveloped Market Street.

One block north of this quiet God's acre is the busy Promenade, where a moving sidewalk rises from the State Street parking level to the rear entrances of a block of Gay Street stores. These same stores have front entrances on the covered Gay/Way, another comfort-and-convenience project of the Downtown Knoxville Association.

On Market Square Mall, one block west of Gay/ Way, trees, shrubs, and fountains mark the spot where an antiquated but beloved Market House stood; yet the square has retained its inherent function as a market place. Home-grown vegetables and fruits, and the profusion of bright flowers for which the old market was famous, are now sold from the small marketing facility at the north end of the Mall.

One block north of the Mall on Summit Hill (the former fashionable residential section where batteries were mounted by the Confederate and Union armies in turn during the Civil War) is Lawson McGhee Library. This main city library occupies, with some additions, the marble building constructed for it in 1916 through the generosity of Colonel Charles McGhee. It bears the name "Lawson McGhee" in honor of the Colonel's beloved daughter and contains the renowned McClung Collection. The original gift of historical and genealogical material compiled by Calvin M. McClung has been augmented by many other valuable donations of family papers and memorabilia to become one of the finest historical collections in the United States, a veritable mecca for scholars and historians in search of source material.

Summit Hill was also the site of Knoxville's first Roman Catholic church, miniature in size but quite large enough to seat its few parishioners. Near the end of the War Between the States the famed Poet-Priest of the Confederacy, Father Abram Joseph Ryan, was in charge of this mission. When word reached Knoxville of the surrender of General Robert E. Lee at Appomattox, Father Ryan composed his most famous poem, "The Conquered Banner." Unable to find even one sheet of paper for sale in the shortage-beset city, he penned on a brown peanut-bag the often quoted lines:

> Furl that Banner, softly, slowly!
> Treat it gently—it is holy—
> For it droops above the dead.

At the corner of Market and Clinch streets is the Old Post Office Building, built in 1867 of Tennessee white marble. The uptown branch post office occupies its first floor, while the upper stories serve as offices for the Tennessee Valley Authority. Another beautiful marble structure, the Tennessee Supreme Court Building, graces the corner of Cumberland and Locust streets.

Four blocks south of the Mall, where rejuvenated Market Street meets Main Street, stands the Knox County Court House, built in 1884 upon the site of the blockhouse erected in 1793 to protect the capital of the Territory South of the River Ohio from Indian attack. Look in the northeast corner of this tree-shaded lawn for the monument to John Sevier, first governor of the State of Tennessee, whose body was brought to Knoxville in 1889 from a desolate resting place in Alabama. Flanking the tall shaft are markers to his wives, Sarah Hawkins Sevier and Catherine Sherrill Sevier who was affectionately known as "Bonny

Kate." On the nearby front lawn of the Criminal Courts
Building a stone marker commemorates Knoxville's years as
first capital of Tennessee.

On Main Street, one block west of the Court House,
the main Post Office occupies a classically beautiful building of Tennessee marble that changes color from white to
pink on rainy days. Just east of the Post Office, at the
corner of Cumberland and Walnut streets, stands the Sevier-Park House, which was begun by John Sevier while he
was Tennessee's first governor but was never occupied by
him. Instead the house was the home of the Park family for
more than a century. Now the property of the Knox
County Academy of Medicine, it houses the Academy's
medical museum, which includes a room arranged as a
replica of a typical doctor's office of the 1850's. Here Walnut Street makes the distinct jog that earned for it the early
name of Crooked Street. Tradition insists that the foundations of Sevier's house were in place before the street was
cut; because of his prestige, the street was set over several
feet to give him house-room.

Just seven blocks away, the columned City Hall (built
in 1848 on land donated by a public-spirited merchant,
Calvin Morgan) crowns a low hill at the corner of Henley
Street and Western Avenue. This has been called the most
beautiful municipal building in the South. Constructed to
house the Tennessee School for the Deaf, it was comman-
deered for a Confederate military hospital early in the Civil
War and later was taken over by Union Army surgeons.
Returned to its former owners at the close of hostilities, it
once again served children handicapped by lack of hearing.
Early in the present century it became Boyd Junior High
School, and is now the seat of city government. This has

East Tennessee's native dogwood, famous for the size and beauty of trees and blossoms, has earned for Knoxville the title of the Dogwood Capital of the World.

During the annual Dogwood Trail in April, the trees are night-lighted for spectacular beauty.

been Knoxville's way of preserving things—by putting them to a new use as the old use became impractical. Long before World War II made famous the slogan "Use it up, wear it out, make it do," East Tennesseans had understood the principle very well.

Just west of the downtown business district, on Cumberland Avenue, buildings of The University of Tennessee crowd the steep hill to which Blount College moved from Gay Street in 1828. This University was the first non-denominational college in America, and it admitted the nation's first co-eds in 1804. During the Civil War a gun battery was mounted on College Hill; Union soldiers and their horses were quartered in the quadrangle of brick buildings. After the Battle of Fort Sanders the main recitation hall saw service as a hospital. When the buildings were returned to the trustees of East Tennessee University at the close of the war, they were in such deplorable condition that they had to be renovated or replaced. The oldest structure now standing on The Hill, South College, is the sole survivor of this rebuilding program. Completed in 1872, South College was for many years a dormitory; students hauled coal in scuttles for the small stoves that heated the large rooms, and carried buckets of water from a rainwater cistern to the washstands.

For a century The Hill was the entire campus; in the 1920's, the University began to spread along neighboring tree-lined streets. Many fine large residences built in the days of Knoxville's prominence as a wholesale center became fraternity houses. Tyson House, the home of General (and Senator) Lawrence D. Tyson, served as administrative offices for the Division of University Extension. A plan for gradual expansion was formulated and a style of archi-

tecture selected—Ayres Hall atop The Hill was its proto-
type.

Across the street from the entrance to the hill campus
the James D. Hoskins library was located. It has acquired
an outstanding collection of rare books and manuscripts,
including the correspondence of Parson Brownlow, Oliver
P. Temple, and Governor Ben Hooper, and houses in a
special wing the private papers and mementoes of the late
Senator Estes Kefauver.

East of the library was built the College of Home
Economics—an early and continuing leader in the teaching
fields of textiles and dietetics. Behind the college, on White
Avenue, is the Nursery School used by the Department of
Child Study.

West of the library rose the College of Law, like other
buildings in architectural style but combining colorful
crab-orchard stone with the customary red brick. Later,
this block also became the site of the Panhellenic Building,
where each campus sorority has spacious quarters. Across
Cumberland Avenue the University Center (with its cafe-
terias, bookstores, lounges, bowling alleys, ballrooms, banquet halls, and meeting rooms) teemed with activity.

On Temple Avenue, new self-contained Colleges of
Business Administration and Education were built. A
Hearing and Speech Center nestled in the shadow of
high-rising Neyland Stadium. On Circle Park, the first of
five sections of the McClung Museum provided at least
some display space for the University's collection of Indian
relics and artifacts, the nation's largest. On Yale Avenue the
Armory-Field House harbored indoor sports and centered
the military training program required of the University as
a Land-Grant College.

New men's and women's dormitories were constructed; before they were completed, more were needed.

When President Andrew Holt's administration began, enrollment was enlarging at so rapid a rate that this step-by-step expansion simply would not suffice—a giant stride would be required. In a mammoth urban renewal program, the University acquired a hundred and thirty-five acres of land between The Hill and the campus of the College of Agriculture. As hundreds of homes were razed to make way for new dormitories and academic buildings, the quiet residential area took on the appearance of a bombed city. Fires smouldered in cellars open to the sky; concrete steps led up to nothing. Students spoke of "Hiroshima West."

Then bulldozers levelled the hills and hollows of the new Main Campus. Circle Park would be its pivot point, where new Administration and Communications buildings would neighbor a greatly enlarged McClung Museum. Temple Avenue, Yale Avenue, and 23rd Street would merge to form a crescent boulevard. The historic Hill would be shared by the exact sciences and the renowned, expanded College of Engineering. An area between Temple Avenue and 17th Street was chosen for the high-towered complex of the College of Liberal Arts. The Music Building and proscenium theatre would be close to the Museum and to Carousel Theatre. Fraternities would be grouped together beyond the Armory-Field House, across the boulevard from the new locale of field sports and the Natatorium. A new undergraduate library would pre-empt the site of the Faculty Club. And still more dormitories would dot the scene!

The growth of the University could not be restricted by an obsolete expansion plan, nor could its style of architecture be kept static. Innovations in building techniques, rising construction costs, and changing patterns of use made necessary a new look for the buildings on the extended campus. But along the broad curving boulevard, trees and lawns blend old and new in green continuity; in a short few years the scars of rapid expansion will have disappeared, and the enlarged University will have become a homogeneous whole.

On College Street, about two miles north and west of The University of Tennessee, Knoxville College also occupies a campus that is called The Hill. This hill was the scene of encampment for a portion of General Longstreet's army during the siege of Knoxville in 1863, and faint traces of the trenches then dug may still be seen on the front campus. Established in 1875 by the United Presbyterian Church, this outstanding member of the American Association of Negro Colleges also is enjoying a period of expansion; from its hill, too, buildings are spreading out as its enrollment rapidly grows.

Just west of the extended University campus, West Cumberland Avenue underpasses the L&N Railroad tracks and the Alcoa Expressway Interchange to become the Kingston Pike. Between the railroad and the interchange, on the right, is the entrance to Tyson Park, presented to Knoxville by Senator and Mrs. L. D. Tyson as a memorial to their son, the first flying officer killed in World War I. The park was originally larger. Much of its shady, sloping picnic area was commandeered for the superhighway; however, there are still outdoor fireplaces and picnic tables along a winding creek, as well as tennis courts and a wading pool. A few hundred feet beyond the park entrance is Ossoli Circle's Clubhouse, the home of the South's oldest women's club, which was founded in 1885. Nearby is Tyson Junior High School, named for Knoxville's celebrated general and senator.

On the left, the handsome buildings of the University's College of Agriculture form a background for the horticultural experiment station beside the Pike. Across Neyland Drive, the Faculty Club's impressive new home overlooks the lake. Nearby, at 2728 Kingston Pike, is the city's oldest house that has been continuously occupied as a residence. Originally known as "Crescent Bend," this gray stucco home was built by Drury P. Armstrong in 1823.

At the next curve, on the left, dark green magnolia trees frame the Dulin Gallery of Art. The gallery occupies a beautiful V-shaped building designed in 1915 by John Russell Pope, who also was the architect for the Jefferson Memorial in Washington, D. C. This home of the late Mr. and Mrs. H. L. Dulin is now a memorial to them presented to Knoxville's citizens by their daughter, Mrs. Clifford Folger. Here selected exhibitions from the collections of large museums, business firms, and individuals succeed each other; the gallery's permanent collection features a fascinating group of the famous Thorne miniature rooms.

A few hundred feet west, at the apex of the curve, is Confederate Memorial Hall. Built in the early 1850's, the house was a wedding gift from Drury Armstrong to his son, Robert H. Armstrong. It was constructed by the "trained servants" of the bride's father, Colonel Franklin of Jefferson County; they had learned to make brick and mix plaster under the supervision of a New Orleans architect. This is the very house that served as General Longstreet's headquarters during the siege of Knoxville in 1863.

After more than a century as a residence it has become

the property and the pride of Chapter 89 of the United Daughters of the Confederacy. Beautiful furnishings grace its stately rooms; their intricately garlanded plaster ceilings are unique in the upper South. A cannon ball remains imbedded in the *inside* wall of the drawing room; the square tower, reached by steep and narrow stairs, bears upon its plaster three portrait sketches made by a sharp-shooter stationed there in 1863. Period costumes, a small museum, and an inclusive library are on display.

The extensive gardens, terraced to the river, have been cleared and bloom anew. A special point of interest in the garden is an enormous anchor with a length of heavy iron rods and rings; it was recently recovered during channel-dredging operations near the south bank of the river, above the Gay Street Bridge. This is part of the "great chain" stretched across the stream by Union Army engineers to protect from ramming the pontoon bridge that connected the city with the forts on the south shore.

Near this house General William P. Sanders fought to delay the Confederates' attack on the city until Union defenses were complete. In the favorite account of the incident, the general, a conspicuous figure on his white horse, rode forward to rally his troops, and was wounded by a sharpshooter's bullet fired from the Hall's tower. While the skirmish was still going on, General Sanders was carried into the city; he died that evening, and was buried by moonlight in the churchyard of the Second Presbyterian Church. A marker was later placed on the north side of Kingston Pike, at the spot where he fell.

After all, it is coincidence that makes truth stranger than fiction. At the time of General Sanders' burial, Second Presbyterian Church occupied with its cemetery a city block on Market Street, adjacent to the Market Square—this location was chosen when the congregation was formed in 1818. The church moved in 1906 to the corner of Church and Walnut streets; in 1957 it moved again, to a new edifice on a hill overlooking Kingston Pike. By a strange coincidence, the marker to General William P. Sanders is on the new lawn of this old church!

Cherokee Boulevard, the main thoroughfare of Sequoyah Hills, is bordered by a lakeshore city park and boasts an Indian mound in its centerstrip. Each April thousands of cars, their wheels straddling the white guidemarkers painted on the street, travel the Sequoyah Hills Dogwood Trail. Lighting of the trees began here in 1956, and this was the first trail completely illuminated for night viewing.

Veering left off Kingston Pike onto Lyons View Pike, another dogwood trail leads to Westmoreland past a magnificent panoramic view—the horseshoe bend of Fort Loudoun Lake with four tiers of mountains in the distance. Cherokee Country Club, established in 1907, takes full advantage of the view from the mid-point of the bend. Eastern State Hospital for the mentally ill has an unsurpassed situation—in fact, the location has given its name to the hospital, which has always been known locally as "Lyons View." In the beginning the hospital was housed in one large turreted and crenelated structure, constructed in 1883; now its many functional buildings face the lake. Internationally famous is The Village (a complex of church, library, shops, and houses), where patients may spend several weeks readjusting to the world outside before being discharged.

Ten miles west of Knoxville, near the Kingston Pike

which he surveyed and built, Charles McClung's "States-view" still stands. Planned by Knoxville's first trained architect, Thomas Hope, this is a house so simply designed and so well kept that it belies its age. Not only did Charles McClung build the first good road leading out of Knoxville to Campbell's Station, he was also Knoxville's original town planner. It was he who surveyed and laid out the city in 1791 for his father-in-law James White at the behest of William Blount. His wife Margaret was a daughter of the city's first settler and a sister of Hugh Lawson White the Just. The McClungs' daughter, Polly, was one of the University of Tennessee's famous first five co-eds, entering the then Blount College in 1804.

Not far from Statesview, on Northshore Drive near Concord Park, is the birthplace and childhood home of Admiral David Glasgow Farragut, hero of the Battle of Mobile Bay and the first full admiral in the U. S. Navy. The waters of Fort Loudoun Lake have made a peninsula of the Farragut homesite. It would surely astound the admiral to know that nowadays his own flagship could move majestically up the Tennessee River and drop anchor beside the inland farmhouse where as a boy he dreamed of ships and the sea. Farragut community, a few miles toward the west, was named in the admiral's honor.

At the Ten Mile Creek, a dignified red brick house is the former home of Abner Baker, Knoxville's unreconstructed rebel who was hanged on Hill Street in the stormy Reconstruction Era. His father, Dr. Harvey Baker, was killed by Union soldiers in this yard during the Civil War, and a stone marker near the road relates the facts.

When James White and his friends crossed the Smokies in 1785 to settle in the Tennessee country, the land they first selected was that surrounding the "confluence of the waters"—the spot where the Holston and French Broad Rivers join to form the Tennessee, five miles east of downtown Knoxville. Many points of interest are found in this easterly direction. From the Blount Mansion, the way leads across the Hill Avenue viaduct, skirting the Mountain View Urban Renewal Area onto Riverside Drive, which is graced by several handsome nineteenth-century houses. A small marker on the land side of the drive a mile beyond the viaduct marks the spot where James White built the first shelter for his family while he was deciding on the site for his permanent home.

Turning left on Dandridge Avenue finds a branch of the Tennessee School for the Deaf which served as its Colored Division from 1885 to 1965. No cold and institutional-looking building this, but a magnificently preserved home, one of the city's oldest and most interesting. James White, who owned the land east of the city as well as the site of the city itself by virtue of land grants from the State of North Carolina, gave this portion of his property to his daughter Melinda, who was the wife of a soldier and statesman. John Williams fought in the War of 1812 and the Creek War, and was Minister to Guatemala under President John Quincy Adams as well as United States Senator from Tennessee. Tradition says that while her husband was serving in the Creek War, Melinda White Williams took her servants to this site and personally supervised the burning of the brick and the construction of the house as a surprise for John Williams upon his return. The splendid condition of this property proves that a building can be put to other use than the one for which it originally was intended without losing its dignity or its beauty.

Signs for Ramsey House are posted at intervals along Riverside Drive. Follow them to "Swan Pond," the home of Francis Ramsey who accompanied James White to the Tennessee country in 1785 and who was one of three men who remained in the area first chosen for settlement. Near the Forks of the River Industrial Park stands his sturdy stone house, now the property of the Association for the Preservation of Tennessee Antiquities and open to the public. This was the first house built in the Tennessee country by Thomas Hope; it reflects his English homeland in its stone construction and Gothic style. Guided by an inventory of Francis Ramsey's household furnishings made shortly after his death in 1820, the A.P.T.A. has recreated a livable "gentleman's house" of Tennessee's period of settlement.

Riverside Drive itself leads on to Boyd's Bridge, which spans the Holston River; one and a half miles downstream, the Holston joins the French Broad River to form the Tennessee. The farms bordering these rivers were the salvation of Knoxville during the siege of 1863, for from them produce was floated on rafts to feed the Union soldiers and the civilians in the beleaguered city.

The actual spot where the rivers meet is now the property of Eastern State Hospital, and from the hospital buildings the wide view of the merging streams narrows to a glimpse of Knoxville in the distance. This section of the mental hospital is a farm, where patients are benefitted by outdoor exercise and the varied interests of farming as well as by the therapeutic beauty of the situation.

In the very forks of the rivers where the two, one cloudy and one clear, flow side by side for several hundred yards before their waters gradually combine, is the oldest church in the entire area—Lebanon in the Forks. Like First Presbyterian Church in Knoxville, it was founded by the Reverend Doctor Samuel Carrick, but Lebanon is the older by a few years. Dr. Carrick lived nearby when first he came to the Tennessee country, and in the churchyard of Lebanon in the Forks is the tomb of his wife; he himself is buried in the First Presbyterian Church cemetery in Knoxville.

Elizabeth Carrick's gravestone bears the date 1793. In that year the Cherokee, with their fierce Creek allies, determined to destroy the newly completed blockhouse in Knoxville. Warned of the impending attack, settlers from the surrounding countryside gathered to defend the capital of the Territory. Samuel Carrick was a minister of the gospel, but he was first and foremost a pioneer; he went at once to join the other settlers in defending Knoxville, leaving his family unprotected in their home on the Holston River. During his absence his young wife died. Under cover of darkness, the women of the household moved Elizabeth Carrick's body downstream by dugout canoe to Lebanon in the Forks, where they buried her in haste and in stealth. Such caution was necessary; had Indian scouts spotted a group of women undertaking such a task, an attack would immediately have been made on this and other unprotected homes.

Also buried at Lebanon in the Forks are Francis Ramsey and his son, Dr. J. G. M. Ramsey, the author of the *Annals of Tennessee* which details so vividly the early history of the region. Next to the church itself is a marble quarry, first in the area to be discovered and worked, and the support of the church for more than a century. This quarry contains some of the famous Tennessee pink marble whose color deepens to rose when dampened by rain.

Going east from downtown Knoxville on Magnolia Avenue one drives over a small section of spreading Chilhowee Park. There is a large skating rink here and an amusement area that features a miniature train and an antique fire engine along with standard "rides." Near the small lake is the Municipal Zoo; its inhabitants include animals and birds native to the Southern Appalachian region as well as wild beasts and birds of brilliant plumage from around the world, and its star boarder, Diamond, is the largest elephant in captivity. Barns adjoin the riding ring where horse shows are held. Each September Chilhowee Park is host to the Tennessee Valley Agricultural and Industrial Fair— exhibits of livestock and of the household arts (nostalgic reminders of the region's not-so-distant past) vie for attention with industrial, commercial, and conservation displays and a large midway.

Passing the Burlington Interchange and proceeding on the Asheville Highway, one arrives at Holston Hills, where wild dogwood is especially profuse and where an outstanding dogwood trail draws appreciative visitors each spring. Holston Hills Country Club shares with surrounding homes a superb view of the Holston River winding like a silver ribbon between the bright green golf course and the hazy blue foothills of the Great Smokies.

The Asheville Highway crosses the Holston River; here the new Governor John Sevier Highway, on the right, leads past the Forks of the River Industrial Park and Ramsey House to the Chapman Highway. Further on, U. S. 11E veers left from the Asheville Highway and continues on to Morristown, Greeneville, and Bristol. This has long been a major highway, and it follows closely the route of the great North-South Indian Warpath, used by the Cherokee and other Indian tribes long before the white settlers came.

For a short southerly drive, one may cross Fort Loudoun Lake by the Gay Street Bridge, remembering that this was the location of the Civil War pontoon bridge that linked the city with the forts that crowned the rugged hills ahead. Turn left and follow the river upstream to Island Home Boulevard; the double row of trees in the center-strip arched first over the carriage drive to Colonel Perez Dickinson's Island Home, and later over streetcar tracks. Stone pillars at the end of the boulevard mark the entrance to the main campus of the Tennessee School for the Deaf, and at the top of the hill is the square white house famous for entertainment during Colonel Dickinson's lifetime. Now the home of the superintendent, it is almost surrounded by the red brick buildings of the school. Spreading trees and ancient shrubs still beautify the lawn, where Perez Dickinson erected a tablet bearing these words of his own composition:

> Welcome to view the beauties of this place
> Raised by the gardener's skill on nature's face,
> But no rude hand should fruit or flower pull;
> For pulling fruit without the Gardener's leave
> Mankind was ruined by our Mother Eve.

A road skirts the riverbank just below the school property and leads to Downtown Airport (for private planes) which is reached by a small bridge. The airport is on Dickinson's Island, once Colonel Dickinson's model farm.

At the end of Island Home Boulevard a street climbs the steep hill toward the right; this is the way to Ijams Park, with its forest of virgin timber and its slopes carpeted with wild flowers.

To reach Chapman Highway, which is the most direct route to the Great Smokies, cross the Henley Street Bridge. This bridge (along with the older Gay Street span) was built before Knoxville's stretch of the Tennessee River was rechristened Fort Loudoun Lake. The stream is no wider at this point than it ever was, but there is one mighty difference in it: inland Knoxville, at the headwaters of the TVA's system of lakes and locks, now has egress to the sea by means of a nine-foot channel winding more than nine hundred miles to the mouth of the Mississippi.

Turn right, where Woodlawn Pike joins Chapman Highway, to enter Fort Dickerson, said to be the best preserved of all earthworks forts dating from Civil War days. The fort was not accessible by public road until 1956; hence it remained undisturbed. The outlines of breast-works, rifle-pits, cannon embrasures, and central powder magazine remain clear and sharp. The entire hill is a city park, with picnic tables shaded by stately trees and a look-out point that commands a magnificent view of Knoxville and its environs. Fort Dickerson (named for its first com-mander, who was killed in a skirmish before the battle for Knoxville began) was one of a series of hill fortifications, on the south side of the river, built by U. S. Army engi-neers as part of the defense plan for Knoxville. The Con-federates, realizing the very strategic location of the site, ferried a force of a thousand men across the river and attacked. They planned to capture the fort and train its guns on the city it was meant to protect. Fort Dickerson withstood the assault. Nevertheless, the Confederates were successful in occupying Cherokee Heights on the south side of the river, and from that point they were able to shell College Hill and a portion of the city. In 1963, Fort Dickerson was once again the scene of battle. Here the assault on Fort Sanders was reenacted with startling realism, under the auspices of the Tennessee Civil War Centennial Commission—the original battle site could not be used, since Fort Sanders' hilltop is now occupied by the hospital that bears its name.

On the Neubert Springs Road, also reached from Chapman Highway, stands the log plantation home built and occupied by John Sevier when he became Tennessee's first governor in 1796. Once the restoration of the main house was complete, a gradual reconstruction of the outbuildings and dependencies was begun; much of the work has been accomplished by interested residents of the Sevier Home community. Although it was built in the same year as was Ramsey House, John Sevier's home looks much older. It is of primitive style and construction—far more typical of the homestead "stations" that were the nuclei of settlement in the area.

The Chapman Highway Dogwood Trail, in an area where native redbud trees abound, is noteworthy for the profusion of rare wild flowers along its route. The trail's climax is a sweeping view of the majestic expanse of four mountain ranges.

Chapman Highway (named for Colonel David Chapman who was instrumental in establishing the Great Smoky Mountains National Park) leads on to Sevierville and Gatlinburg. Sevierville is the town where Parson Brownlow, with a price of two thousand dollars on his head, addressed thousands of his fellow Union sympathizers one Sunday morning during the Civil War. He remained hidden for weeks in nearby Tuckaleechee Cove while Confederate military authorities searched for him in vain.

Bustling Gatlinburg, on the edge of the Great Smoky Mountains National Park, was a mere hamlet when the first automobile road through the mountains opened in 1923. The specific purpose of the town has been to provide shelter, food, and recreation for visitors to the Park. At first, tourists came only during the mid-summer months; then, braver souls began to arrive early to see the green glory of spring in the mountains, or to linger late while the highlands wore a Joseph's-coat of many colors. With the building of the ski lodge, where artificial snow augments the natural variety to extend the winter sports season, Gatlinburg became a year-round resort. Abundant hotel and motel accommodations and a fine Civic Auditorium make it a favorite convention center.

Within the Park a road winds upward to Newfound Gap, where the Rockefeller Memorial spans the line that divides Tennessee and North Carolina. It was the Rockefeller Foundation's gift of five million dollars that finally made possible the establishment of the Park, for this gift matched the amounts donated by the states of Tennessee and North Carolina, the City of Knoxville, and private individuals. From the crest, the road descends on the North Carolina side in the direction of Asheville, passing at the foot of the mountains the Qualla Indian Reservation. This is the home of the descendants of those Cherokee who resisted the United States Army in order to avoid the Great Migration to Indian Territory in 1838. Each summer sees the reenactment in an outdoor amphitheatre of *Unto*

These Hills, the moving story of Tsali and his sons.

Between Gatlinburg and Newfound Gap is the hiking trail to Alum Cave, which furnished gunpowder for Confederate troops during the War Between the States. Faint traces of the first wagon road across the mountains still exist near this cave.

A second route to the Smokies from Knoxville may be reached by driving west on Neyland Drive, past Neyland Stadium and the University's oldest agricultural experiment station, in continuous operation on this site since 1867. As another reminder of the past, a large Indian mound rises from the flat bottomland near the buildings of the College of Agriculture.

Turn right, uphill, to cross the bridge onto Alcoa Highway. Another experimental farm extends on both sides of the highway to the entrance of the University of Tennessee Memorial Research Center and Hospital, where atoms for peace are studied and used in the field of medicine. Beyond the Naval Training Station, the entrance to Loudoun Lake Dogwood Trail appears; here lakes and mountains meet in a series of unsurpassed views.

Alcoa Highway then passes the gigantic plants of the Aluminum Company of America, as well as McGhee Tyson Airport—although the airport is in Blount County, it is the property of the City of Knoxville. McGhee Tyson, named for Knoxville's first officer-pilot killed in World War I, serves Knoxville, Alcoa, Oak Ridge, and the surrounding area.

The route to the Smokies continues through Maryville and up the Little River Gorge. Sam Houston, the pride of Texas, spent his childhood near Maryville; like many another prominent Tennessean, he began his adult life as a teacher. The one-room log building where he taught is still standing a short distance off the Old Maryville Highway, near Rockford; highway signs direct visitors to the spot. Several years ago the State of Texas requested permission to purchase the schoolhouse and move it to the state where its erstwhile schoolmaster had (they said) attained fame as governor. The offer was politely declined, and the schoolhouse remains a memento of Governor Houston in Blount County. After all, Sam Houston was governor of Tennessee before he moved to Texas!

A few miles south and west of Maryville (not far from the highway to Atlanta) is Fort Loudoun. This first British fortification in the "Southwest" celebrated the two-hundredth anniversary of its completion in 1957 and is now undergoing final stages of a painstaking reconstruction. Fort Loudoun played an important part during the French and Indian War in protecting the Cherokee towns on the Little Tennessee River. Near here Sequoyah was born. He was the greatest of the Cherokee, and the only man in modern times to accomplish the feat of inventing an entire alphabet, or syllabary.

The road from Maryville up the Little River Gorge follows the route of the narrow-gauge railroad that served the mountains in the days of extensive logging operations. Between Maryville and Townsend a stretch of the Foothills Parkway leaves the highway and crests a high ridge; this scenic drive parallels the Smokies and affords, across the broad valley of East Tennessee, a view of the Cumberland Mountains toward the west. Winding downward through a narrow gap, the Parkway emerges at the very shore of Chilhowee Lake, set like a jewel between prongs of green encircling hills.

Inside the Great Smoky Mountains National Park, signs point the way to Cades Cove, one of the most interesting things-to-see in the entire area. Visitors often wonder what life was like in the mountains before the Park came into being, and Cades Cove provides answers to their questions. Here descendants of the people who occupied property now within the Park live in the kind of houses their ancestors built, farm by primitive methods, and demonstrate their innate skills with simple tools. Deep inside the Cove, travellers should stop for a visit to the ancient gristmill powered by a moss-covered waterwheel.

Off the Maryville-Gatlinburg loop near Fightin' Creek Gap is a three-mile drive past a modern ranger station and archaic Wonderland Club (the only hotel within the Park) to Elkmont in the heart of the Smokies. Cottages have disappeared one by one as their life-estate owners have died; eventually Park officials plan to leave no trace of this secluded and beloved resort. Elkmont Campground already spreads along the rushing mountain stream nearby.

Just below Fightin' Creek Gap, where the hiking trail to spectacular Laurel Falls begins, is an overlook that commands a breathtaking view of Mount Le Conte and of the valley where Gatlinburg nestles like a toy town. Down winds the road—through Gatlinburg, Pigeon Forge, Sevierville—back to Knoxville, midway between the Great Smokies and the Great Lakes of the South.

Twenty miles northwest of Knoxville is Norris Dam, first of the series of dams built by the Tennessee Valley Authority along the Tennessee River and its tributaries. To reach Norris, one drives north on Broadway from the center of town. On the left side of the street, between Fifth Avenue and Central Avenue, is the entrance to Old Gray

Cemetery where William G. Brownlow, Perez Dickinson, and Lawrence D. Tyson are buried. Joining Old Gray on the west is the National Cemetery, the resting place of thousands of United States soldiers. The oldest headstones mark the graves of veterans of the Mexican War, which established for all time Tennessee's title of Volunteer State.

Broadway leads on, past Sharp's Ridge with its large scenic picnic park, to Fountain City which was once a summer resort. Spring comes a little later to these high ridges than to Knoxville's other residential areas, and this means that the dogwood blossoms often are just opening here when elsewhere they have reached their peak of beauty. Each year, the Fountain City Dogwood Trail furnishes fortunate Knoxvillians with a second look at spring.

The power plant at Norris Dam is open to visitors. A highway crosses the dam itself and affords a look across spreading, tree-rimmed Norris Lake. A few miles from the dam, the cottages of Big Ridge State Park rim the lake shore.

Douglas and Cherokee dams are twenty-five miles from Knoxville toward the north and the northeast. At Douglas Lake a massive dike protects Dandridge, the county seat of Jefferson County, from inundation. This very old and charming town honors Martha Washington by bearing her maiden name. In this part of the "greenest state in the land of the free," Davy Crockett spent his youth. The Jefferson County Court House has two romantic mementoes of him on display. One is a marriage license issued to David Crockett and Margaret Elder, which was returned unused. The other is the actual marriage-bond for

David Crockett and Polly Finley. Not far away, on U. S. Highway 11E in Morristown, the restored Crockett Tavern welcomes visitors. This ancient inn, of log construction, was operated for many years by Davy's father, John Crockett; exhibited here are various types and patterns of cloth hand-carded, spun and woven long ago of wool and "linsey-woolsey."

Twenty-five miles west of Knoxville, Melton Hill Dam's locks and lake bring water transportation to the Atomic City. Oak Ridge itself, eighteen miles west of Knoxville, is the birthplace of atoms for war and peace; here, in the Museum of Atomic Energy, the creation of this most potent force is understandably demonstrated and explained. Exhibits are constantly changing, as new uses for peaceful atoms are developed in nearby laboratories. Nearby, the University of Tennessee is developing the Tennessee Valley's largest and most inclusive arboretum.

The circle is completed twenty-five miles south and west of Knoxville by Fort Loudoun Dam. Viewed from below, the gigantic doors of the lock and the towering bulk of the dam itself have the appearance of an impregnable fortress; the original Fort Loudoun, first British fortification in the wilderness west of the Appalachian Mountains, is only a few miles southeast of its twentieth-century namesake. By 1975, Fort Loudoun's rocky eminence will have become a peninsula; its bastions will no longer overlook, across a fertile plain, the site of Chota, sacred city of the Cherokee. TVA's Tellico Dam will inundate the lower Little Tennessee and Tellico valleys, and this sixth lake in the Knoxville area will have a unique feature: it will be linked to nearby Fort Loudoun Lake by a navigable canal.

Fort Loudoun Lake sometimes stretches wide in a shimmering expanse of placid water; at other times it narrows between the constricting cliffs that marked the boundaries of the Tennessee River. On these scenic shores, Knox County continues the development of a series of peerless parks; hundreds of homes overlook the lake and its encompassing hills. The city spreads along the waterside, and downtown Knoxville's skyline rises from the high plateau along the northern bank.

Here, then, is Knoxville—bridging the gap between the aborigine and the atom. From prehistoric times disparate peoples in succession have loved this rich red clay, these wide rivers laving steep stone bluffs, this foreground of serried green hills against the close horizon of blue mountains. Generations have found it a good place to live, a hard place to leave.

In fact, a Knoxvillian might truthfully say with the Psalmist: "The lines are fallen unto me in pleasant places; yea, I have a goodly heritage."

Acknowledgments

The author wishes to express sincerest thanks to:

Dr. James D. Hoskins, President Emeritus of The University of Tennessee, from whose personal library and whose storehouse of memory came much of the information for this book;

Dr. Stanley J. Folmsbee, Professor of History of The University of Tennessee, who with courteous patience pointed out many instances of historical error;

Professor T. M. N. Lewis and Professor Madeline Kneberg of The University of Tennessee Department of Anthropology, for interesting information on the culture and history of the Cherokee;

Mrs. J. Earnest Briscoe (Isabelle White) for assistance with the chapter on Hugh Lawson White;

Mrs. John Hudson (Lucie Dickinson Givin) for much new information in the chapter on Perez Dickinson;

Mr. J. F. Brownlow for interesting anecdotes of Parson Brownlow, and for assistance with the chapter on the War Between the States;

Mr. E. E. Patton for suggestions for the chapter on the War Between the States;

Mr. Charles Wayland for the facts about Fort Dickerson;

Mrs. Victor Holloway (a descendant of Robert H. Armstrong) for the details of Bleak House;

Mrs. W. C. Ross (Lida McClung) for many incidents in the chapter on Lawrence D. Tyson;

Mr. James M. Meek for the story of his uncle, Abner Baker, and an incident in Chapter Nine.

Mr. S. W. Duggan for facts for the chapter on Lawrence Tyson;

Mrs. W. P. O'Neil (Lelia Boyd) for information for the chapter on the Distaff Side;

Mr. Joseph P. Murphy for facts on the lumber industry in the Great Smoky Mountains;

Mrs. H. H. McCampbell, Sr., for facts for the chapter on the Great Smoky Mountains National Park;

Mr. Robert A. Russell for his kindness in lending the daybook of the Campbell's Station store;

Mr. J. P. Hess for checking the chapter on The University of Tennessee, and for specific information on its Memorial Research Center and Hospital;

Miss Pollyanna Creekmore of Lawson McGhee Library for information on the home of John Williams (Colored School for the Deaf);

Mr. Aubrey Couch for an incident in the history of the Market House;

Mrs. U. D. Beeler (Bessie Hoskins) for aid in tracking down elusive facts;

Mr. Julian Harriss, for news of the new in the University area.

Bibliography

Timberlake, Henry. *Memoirs, 1756–1765.* Watauga Press, 1927.

Ramsey, J. G. M. *The Annals of Tennessee to the End of the Eighteenth Century.* Charleston: Walker & James, 1853.

History of Tennessee. (East Tennessee Edition.) Nashville: Goodspeed Publishing Co., 1887.

Phelan, James. *History of Tennessee.* Boston: Houghton Mifflin & Co., 1889.

McGee, Gentry R. *History of Tennessee From 1663–1930.* New York: American Book Co., 1899.

Rothrock, Mary U. *Discovering Tennessee.* Chapel Hill: University of North Carolina Press, 1936.

Scott, Nancy N. *A Memoir of Hugh Lawson White.* Philadelphia: J. B. Lippincott & Co., 1856.

Memoirs of General W. T. Sherman. New York: Charles L. Webster & Co., 1891.

Personal Memoirs of P. H. Sheridan. New York: Charles L. Webster & Co., 1888.

Rule, William. *Standard History of Knoxville, Tennessee.*
Chicago: Lewis Publishing Co., 1900.

Folmsbee, Stanley J. and Deaderick, Lucile. *The Founding
of Knoxville.* Knoxville: East Tennessee Historical Society's Publications, 1941.

Masterson, William H. *William Blount.* Baton Rouge:
Louisiana State University Press, 1954.

Rothrock, Mary U. (ed.). *The French Broad–Holston
Country.* Knoxville: East Tennessee Historical Society,
1946.

Lilienthal, David E. *TVA: Democracy on the March.* New
York: Harper & Bros., 1944.

Duffus, Robert L. *The Valley and Its People.* New York:
Alfred A. Knopf, 1944.

Thornborough, Laura. *The Great Smoky Mountains.*
Knoxville: The University of Tennessee Press, 1956.

Robinson, George O., Jr. *The Oak Ridge Story.* Kingsport:
Southern Publishers, 1950.

History of Homes and Gardens of Tennessee. Nashville:
Parthenon Press, 1936.

Moore, John Trotwood. *Hearts of Hickory.* Nashville:
Cokesbury Press, 1926.

Compton's Pictured Encyclopedia. Chicago: F. H. Compton
& Co., 1947.

The Heritage of Every American: The Conservation Activities of John D. Rockefeller, Jr. New York: Alfred A.
Knopf, 1957.

Kelley, Paul. *Historic Fort Loudoun.* Fort Loudoun Association, 1858.

Daybook of the Campbell's Station Store for 1855, used as a
scrapbook during the Civil War years, and containing
articles from *Harper's Weekly* and the *Knoxville Register.* (Property of Robert A. Russell.)

Records of the Knox County Registrar of Deeds.

Fort Loudoun Association Newsletters, 1956–57.

Brownlow's Knoxville Whig.   *The Knoxville Times.*

The Knoxville Journal.   *The Knoxville News-Sentinel.*

Index

050763